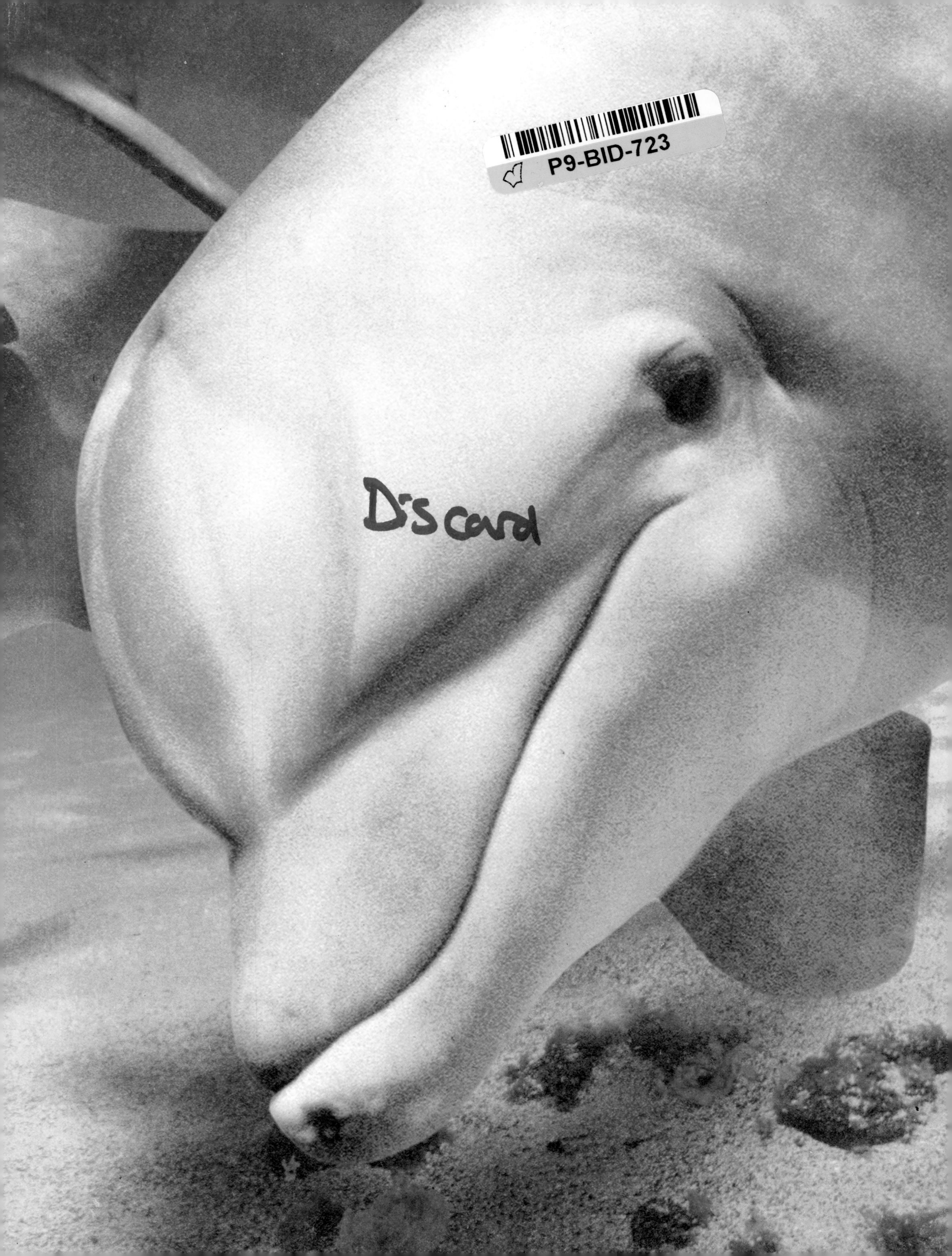

Scott Foresman
Science

The Diamond Edition

PEARSON

Glenview, Illinois • Boston, Massachusetts • Chandler, Arizona • Upper Saddle River, New Jersey

Series Authors

Dr. Timothy Cooney
Professor of Earth Science and Science Education
University of Northern Iowa (UNI)
Cedar Falls, Iowa

Dr. Jim Cummins
Professor
Department of Curriculum, Teaching, and Learning
The University of Toronto
Toronto, Canada

Dr. James Flood
Distinguished Professor of Literacy and Language
School of Teacher Education
San Diego State University
San Diego, California

Barbara Kay Foots, M. Ed
Science Education Consultant
Houston, Texas

Dr. Shirley Gholston Key
Associate Professor of Science Education
Instruction and Curriculum Leadership Department
College of Education
University of Memphis
Memphis, Tennessee

Dr. M. Jenice Goldston
Associate Professor of Science Education
Department of Elementary Education Programs
University of Alabama
Tuscaloosa, Alabama

Dr. Diane Lapp
Distinguished Professor of Reading and Language Arts in Teacher Education
San Diego State University
San Diego, California

Sheryl A. Mercier
Classroom Teacher
Dunlap Elementary School
Dunlap, California

Karen L. Ostlund, Ph.D.
UTeach Specialist
College of Natural Sciences
The University of Texas at Austin
Austin, Texas

Dr. Nancy Romance
Professor of Science Education & Principal Investigator
NSF/IERI Science IDEAS Project
Charles E. Schmidt College of Science
Florida Atlantic University
Boca Raton, Florida

Dr. William Tate
Chair and Professor of Education and Applied Statistics
Department of Education
Washington University
St. Louis, Missouri

Dr. Kathryn C. Thornton
Former NASA Astronaut Professor
School of Engineering and Applied Science
University of Virginia
Charlottesville, Virginia

Dr. Leon Ukens
Professor Emeritus
Department of Physics, Astronomy, and Geosciences
Towson University
Towson, Maryland

Steve Weinberg
Consultant
Connecticut Center for Advanced Technology
East Hartford, Connecticut

Acknowledgments appear on pages EM 41–43, which constitute an extension of this copyright page.

ISBN-13: 978-0-328-45581-2
ISBN-10:   0-328-45581-4
1 2 3 4 5 6 7 8 9 10   V063   13 12 11 10 09

Consulting Author

Dr. Michael P. Klentschy

Superintendent
El Centro Elementary School District
El Centro, California

Science Content Consultants

Dr. Frederick W. Taylor

Senior Research Scientist
Institute for Geophysics
Jackson School of Geosciences
The University of Texas at Austin
Austin, Texas

Dr. Ruth E. Buskirk

Senior Lecturer
School of Biological Sciences
The University of Texas at Austin
Austin, Texas

Dr. Cliff Frohlich

Senior Research Scientist
Institute for Geophysics
Jackson School of Geosciences
The University of Texas at Austin
Austin, Texas

Brad Armosky

McDonald Observatory
The University of Texas at Austin
Austin, Texas

Content Consultants

Adena Williams Loston, Ph.D.

Chief Education Officer
Office of the Chief Education Officer

Clifford W. Houston, Ph.D.

Deputy Chief Education Officer for Education Programs
Office of the Chief Education Officer

Frank C. Owens

Senior Policy Advisor
Office of the Chief Education Officer

Deborah Brown Biggs

Manager, Education Flight Projects Office
Space Operations Mission Directorate
Education Lead

Erika G. Vick

NASA Liaison to Pearson Scott Foresman
Education Flight Projects Office

William E. Anderson

Partnership Manager for Education
Aeronautics Research Mission
Directorate

Anita Krishnamurthi

Program Planning Specialist
Space Science Education and
Outreach Program

Bonnie J. McClain

Chief of Education
Exploration Systems Mission
Directorate

Diane Clayton Ph.D.

Program Scientist
Earth Science Education

Deborah Rivera

Strategic Alliances Manager
Office of Public Affairs
NASA Headquarters

Douglas D. Peterson

Public Affairs Officer, Astronaut Office
Office of Public Affairs
NASA Johnson Space Center

Nicole Cloutier

Public Affairs Officer, Astronaut Office
Office of Public Affairs
NASA Johnson Space Center

Reviewers

Dr. Maria Aida Alanis
Administrator
Austin ISD
Austin Texas

Melissa Barba
Teacher
Wesley Mathews Elementary
Miami, Florida

Dr. Marcelline Barron
Supervisor/K-12 Math
and Science
Fairfield Public Schools
Fairfield, Connecticut

Jane Bates
Teacher
Hickory Flat Elementary
Canton, Georgia

Denise Bizjack
Teacher
Dr. N. H. Jones Elementary
Ocala, Florida

Latanya D. Bragg
Teacher
Davis Magnet School
Jackson, Mississippi

Richard Burton
Teacher
George Buck Elementary
School 94
Indianapolis, Indiana

Dawn Cabrera
Teacher
E.W.F. Stirrup School
Miami, Florida

Barbara Calabro
Teacher
Compass Rose Foundation
Ft. Myers, Florida

Lucille Calvin
Teacher
Weddington Math &
Science School
Greenville, Mississippi

Patricia Carmichael
Teacher
Teasley Middle School
Canton, Georgia

Martha Cohn
Teacher
An Wang Middle School
Lowell, Massachusetts

Stu Danzinger
Supervisor
Community Consolidated
School District 59
Arlington Heights, Illinois

Esther Draper
Supervisor/Science Specialist
Belair Math Science
Magnet School
Pine Bluff, Arkansas

Sue Esser
Teacher
Loretto Elementary
Jacksonville, Florida

Dr. Richard Fairman
Teacher
Antioch University
Yellow Springs, Ohio

Joan Goldfarb
Teacher
Indialantic Elementary
Indialantic, Florida

Deborah Gomes
Teacher
A J Gomes Elementary
New Bedford, Massachusetts

Sandy Hobart
Teacher
Mims Elementary
Mims, Florida

Tom Hocker
Teacher/Science Coach
Boston Latin Academy
Dorchester, Massachusetts

Shelley Jaques
Science Supervisor
Moore Public Schools
Moore, Oklahoma

Marguerite W. Jones
Teacher
Spearman Elementary
Piedmont, South Carolina

Kelly Kenney
Teacher
Kansas City Missouri
School District
Kansas City, Missouri

Carol Kilbane
Teacher
Riverside Elementary School
Wichita, Kansas

Robert Kolenda
Teacher
Neshaminy School District
Langhorne, Pennsylvania

Karen Lynn Kruse
Teacher
St. Paul the Apostle
Yonkers, New York

Elizabeth Loures
Teacher
Point Fermin
Elementary School
San Pedro, California

Susan MacDougall
Teacher
Brick Community Primary
Learning Center
Brick, New Jersey

Jack Marine
Teacher
Raising Horizons Quest
Charter School
Philadelphia, Pennsylvania

Nicola Micozzi Jr.
Science Coordinator
Plymouth Public Schools
Plymouth, Massachusetts

Paula Monteiro
Teacher
A J Gomes Elementary
New Bedford, Massachusetts

Tracy Newallis
Teacher
Taper Avenue Elementary
San Pedro, California

Dr. Eugene Nicolo
Supervisor, Science K-12
Moorestown School District
Moorestown, New Jersey

Jeffrey Pastrak
School District of Philadelphia
Philadelphia, Pennsylvania

Helen Pedigo
Teacher
Mt. Carmel Elementary
Huntsville Alabama

Becky Peltonen
Teacher
Patterson Elementary School
Panama City, Florida

Sherri Pensler
Teacher/ESOL
Claude Pepper Elementary
Miami, Florida

Virginia Rogliano
Teacher
Bridgeview Elementary
South Charleston, West
Virginia

Debbie Sanders
Teacher
Thunderbolt Elementary
Orange Park, Florida

Grethel Santamarina
Teacher
E.W.F. Stirrup School
Miami, Florida

Migdalia Schneider
Teacher/Bilingual
Lindell School
Long Beach, New York

Susan Shelly
Teacher
Bonita Springs Elementary
Bonita Springs, Florida

Peggy Terry
Teacher
Madison District 151
South Holland, Illinois

Jane M. Thompson
Teacher
Emma Ward Elementary
Lawrenceburg, Kentucky

Martha Todd
Teacher
W. H. Rhodes Elementary
Milton, Florida

Renee Williams
Teacher
Central Elementary
Bloomfield, New Mexico

Myra Wood
Teacher
Madison Street Academy
Ocala, Florida

Marion Zampa
Teacher
Shawnee Mission
School District
Overland Park, Kansas

Science

See learning in a whole new light

Unit A Life Science

How do the different parts of a plant help it live and grow?

Chapter 1 • Plants and How They Grow

Chapter 2 • How Animals Live

How do different animals live, grow, and change?

Unit A Life Science

How are ecosystems different from each other?

Chapter 3 • Where Plants and Animals Live

Chapter 4 • Plants and Animals Living Together

How do plants and animals interact?

Unit B Earth Science

How does water change form?

How does weather follow patterns?

Chapter 7 • Rocks and Soil

Why are rocks and soil important resources?

Unit B Earth Science

How do forces cause changes on Earth's surface?

Chapter 8 • Changes on Earth

Chapter 9 • Natural Resources

How can people use natural resources responsibly?

Unit C   Physical Science

Chapter 12 • Forces and Motion

How do forces cause motion and get work done?

Unit C Physical Science

How does energy change form?

Chapter 13 • Energy

Chapter 14 • Sound

How does energy produce the sounds we hear?

Unit D Space and Technology

What patterns do the Earth, Sun, Moon, and stars show?

How are the planets in the solar system alike and different?

Chapter 15 • Patterns in the Sky

Chapter 16 • The Solar System

Chapter 17 • Science in Our Lives

How does technology affect our lives?

How to Read Science

A page like the one below is found near the beginning of each chapter. It shows you how to use a reading skill that will help you understand what you read.

Before Reading

Before you read the chapter, read the Build Background page and think about how to answer the question. Recall what you already know as you answer the question. Work with a partner to make a list of what you already know. Then read the How to Read Science page.

Target Reading Skill
Each page has one target reading skill. The reading skill corresponds with a process skill in the Directed Inquiry activity on the facing page. The reading skill will be useful as you read science.

Real-World Connection
Each page has an example of something you might read. It also connects with the Directed Inquiry activity.

Graphic Organizer
A useful strategy for understanding anything you read is to make a graphic organizer. A graphic organizer can help you think about the information and how parts of it relate to each other. Each reading skill has a graphic organizer.

How to Read Science

Reading Skills

Compare and Contrast
When you **compare** things, you tell how they are alike. When you **contrast** things, you tell how they are different.
- Words and phrases such as *similar, like, all, both,* or *in the same way* are clues that things are being compared.
- Words and phrases such as *different, unlike,* or *in a different way* are clues that things are being contrasted.

Magazine Article

Rock Collectors
Ben and Misha both collect rocks. Ben prefers brightly colored rocks. He is a member of a rock hunters club that goes on collecting trips. Misha has a different way of collecting his favorite kinds of rocks—fossil rocks. His uncle sends Misha fossil rocks from all around the world. Unlike Ben, Misha just has to make a trip to his mailbox to add to his collection.

Apply It!
You can use a graphic organizer as a **model** to show how things compare and contrast.

Different · Alike · Different

Ben · Misha

Use a graphic organizer to show ways that Ben and Misha are alike and different in the way they collect rocks.

197

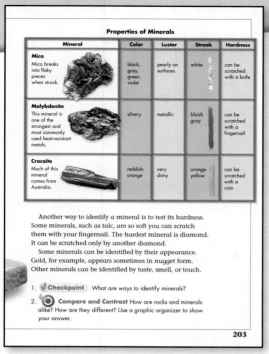

Properties of Minerals

Mineral	Color	Luster	Streak	Hardness
Mica Mica breaks into flaky pieces when struck.	black, gray, green, violet	pearly on surfaces	white	can be scratched with a knife
Molybdenite This mineral is one of the strongest and most commonly used heat-resistant metals.	silvery	metallic	bluish gray	can be scratched with a fingernail
Crocoite Much of this mineral comes from Australia.	reddish-orange	very shiny	orange-yellow	can be scratched with a coin

Another way to identify a mineral is to test its hardness. Some minerals, such as talc, are so soft you can scratch them with your fingernail. The hardest mineral is diamond. It can be scratched only by another diamond.

Some minerals can be identified by their appearance. Gold, for example, appears sometimes in nugget form. Other minerals can be identified by taste, smell, or touch.

1.  **Checkpoint** What are ways to identify minerals?

2. **Compare and Contrast** How are rocks and minerals alike? How are they different? Use a graphic organizer to show your answer.

203

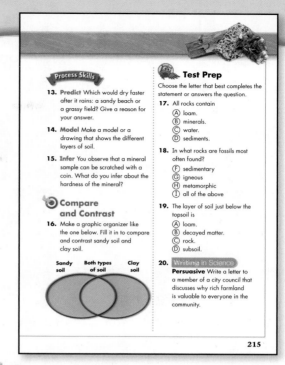

Process Skills

13. **Predict** Which would dry faster after it rains: a sandy beach or a grassy field? Give a reason for your answer.

14. **Model** Make a model or a drawing that shows the different layers of soil.

15. **Infer** You observe that a mineral sample can be scratched with a coin. What do you infer about the hardness of the mineral?

Compare and Contrast

16. Make a graphic organizer like the one below. Fill it in to compare and contrast sandy soil and clay soil.

Sandy soil — Both types of soil — Clay soil

Test Prep

Choose the letter that best completes the statement or answers the question.

17. All rocks contain
   Ⓐ loam.
   Ⓑ minerals.
   Ⓒ water.
   Ⓓ sediments.

18. In what rocks are fossils most often found?
   Ⓕ sedimentary
   Ⓖ igneous
   Ⓗ metamorphic
   Ⓘ all of the above

19. The layer of soil just below the topsoil is
   Ⓐ loam.
   Ⓑ decayed matter.
   Ⓒ rock.
   Ⓓ subsoil.

20. **Writing in Science**
   Persuasive Write a letter to a member of a city council that discusses why rich farmland is valuable to everyone in the community.

215

During Reading

As you read the lesson, use the Checkpoint to check your understanding. Some checkpoints ask you to use the target reading skill.

After Reading

After you have read the chapter, think about what you found out. Exchange ideas with a partner. Compare the list you made before you read the chapter with what you learned by reading it. Answer the questions in the Chapter Review. One question uses the target reading skill.

Graphic Organizers

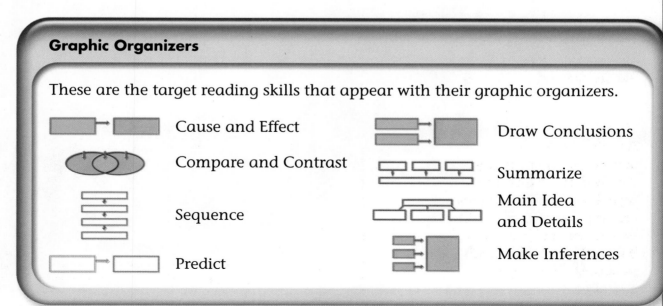

These are the target reading skills that appear with their graphic organizers.

Cause and Effect

Compare and Contrast

Sequence

Predict

Draw Conclusions

Summarize

Main Idea and Details

Make Inferences

Science Process Skills

Investigating Weather

Scientists use process skills when they investigate places or events. You will use these skills when you do the activities in this book. Which process skills might scientists use when they investigate weather?

Observe

A scientist who studies weather observes many things. You use your senses too to find out about other objects, events, or living things.

Classify

Scientists classify clouds according to their properties. When you classify, you arrange or sort objects, events, or living things.

Estimate and Measure

Scientists estimate how much rain will fall. Then they use tools to measure how much rain fell.

Infer

Scientists infer what they think is happening during a storm, based on what they already know.

Predict

Scientists predict how weather will change. Then people know how to get ready for the change.

Make and Use Models

Scientists make and use models such as pictures and maps. Models are like real events in some ways, but are different in other ways.

Make Operational Definitions

Scientists can use what they know to make operational definitions about what they observe during a storm.

Science Process Skills

Form Questions and Hypotheses
Think of a statement that you can test to solve a problem or answer a question about storms or other kinds of weather.

Investigate and Experiment
As scientists observe storms, they investigate and experiment to test a hypothesis.

Identify and Control Variables
As scientists perform an experiment, they identify and control the variables so that they test only one thing at a time.

If you were a scientist, you might want to learn more about storms. What questions might you have about storms? How would you use process skills in your investigation?

Collect Data
Scientists collect data from their observations of weather. They put the data into charts or tables.

Interpret Data
Scientists use the information they collected to solve problems or answer questions.

Communicate
Scientists use words, pictures, charts, and graphs to share information about their investigation.

Using Scientific Methods for Science Inquiry

Scientists use scientific methods as they work. Scientific methods are organized ways to answer questions and solve problems. Scientific methods include the steps shown here. Scientists might not use all the steps. They might not use the steps in this order. You will use scientific methods when you do the **Full Inquiry** activity at the end of each unit. You also will use scientific methods when you do Science Fair Projects.

Ask a question.

You might have a question about something you observe.

What material is best for keeping heat in water?

State your hypothesis.

A hypothesis is a possible answer to your question.

If I wrap the jar in fake fur, then the water will stay warm the longest.

Identify and control variables.

Variables are things that can change. For a fair test, you choose just one variable to change. Keep all other variables the same.

Test other materials. Put the same amount of warm water in other jars that are the same size and shape.

Test your hypothesis.

Make a plan to test your hypothesis. Collect materials and tools. Then follow your plan.

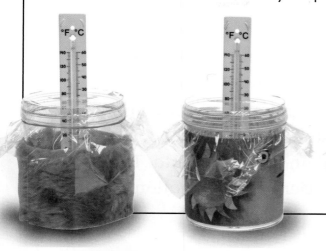

Collect and record your data.

Keep good records of what you do and find out. Use tables and pictures to help.

Interpret your data.

Organize your notes and records to make them clear. Make diagrams, charts, or graphs to help.

State your conclusion.

Your conclusion is a decision you make based on your data. Communicate what you found out. Tell whether or not your data supported your hypothesis.

Fake fur kept the water warm longest. My data supported my hypothesis.

Go further.

Use what you learn. Think of new questions to test or better ways to do a test.

Ask a Question

State Your Hypothesis

Identify and Control Variables

Test Your Hypothesis

Collect and Record Your Data

Interpret Your Data

State Your Conclusion

Go Further

Science Tools

Scientists use many different kinds of tools. Tools can make objects appear larger. They can help you measure volume, temperature, length, distance, and mass. Tools can help you figure out amounts and analyze your data. Tools can also help you find the latest scientific information.

You should use **safety goggles** to protect your eyes.

You use a **thermometer** to measure temperature. Many thermometers have both Fahrenheit and Celsius scales. Scientists usually use only the Celsius scale.

You can use a **telescope** to help you see things that are very far away, such as stars and planets.

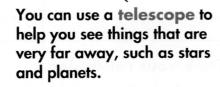

Binoculars make far-away objects appear larger, so you can see more of their details.

A **hand lens** doesn't enlarge things as much as a microscope does, but it is easier to carry.

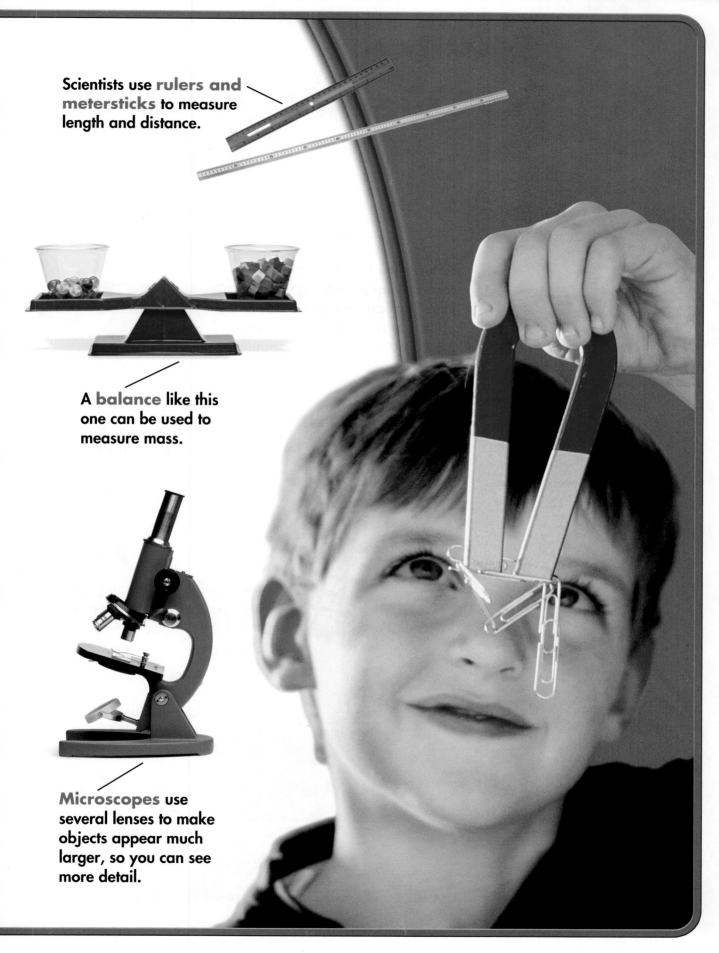

Scientists use **rulers and metersticks** to measure length and distance.

A **balance** like this one can be used to measure mass.

Microscopes use several lenses to make objects appear much larger, so you can see more detail.

Science Tools

Magnets can be used to test if an object is made of certain metals such as iron.

Pictures taken with a **camera** record what something looks like. You can compare pictures of the same object to show how the object might have changed.

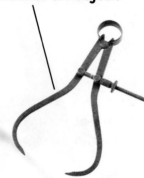

A **graduated cylinder** can be used to measure volume, or the amount of space an object takes up.

Calipers can be used to measure the width of an object.

You can figure amounts using a **calculator**.

Scientists use **computers** in many ways, such as collecting, recording, and analyzing data.

You can talk into a **sound recorder** to record information you want to remember.

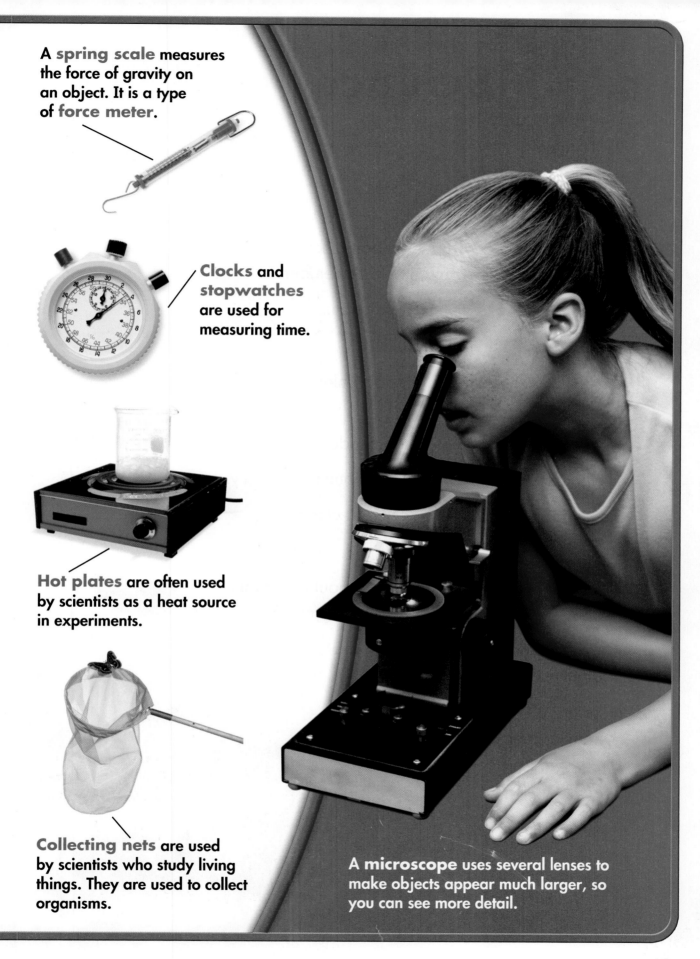

A **spring scale** measures the force of gravity on an object. It is a type of **force meter**.

Clocks and **stopwatches** are used for measuring time.

Hot plates are often used by scientists as a heat source in experiments.

Collecting nets are used by scientists who study living things. They are used to collect organisms.

A **microscope** uses several lenses to make objects appear much larger, so you can see more detail.

Safety in Science

You need to be careful when doing science activities. This page includes safety tips to remember:

- Listen to your teacher's instructions.

- Read each activity carefully.

- Never taste or smell materials unless your teacher tells you to.

- Wear safety goggles when needed.

- Handle scissors and other equipment carefully.

- Keep your work place neat and clean.

- Clean up spills immediately.

- Tell your teacher immediately about accidents or if you see something that looks unsafe.

- Wash your hands well after every activity.

- Return all materials to their proper places.

Unit A
Life Science

You Will Discover

- ways parts of a plant help it survive.
- different types of plants.
- different ways plants make more plants.
- that plants have changed over time.

Chapter 1
Plants
and
How They Grow

online
Student Edition
pearsonsuccessnet.com

How do the different parts of a plant help it live and grow?

system

coniferous

pollinate

seed leaf

germinate

deciduous

seedling

fossil

extinct

3

Explore How are plants alike and different?

Materials

grass

radish

hand lens

What to Do

1. **Observe** each plant with a hand lens. Notice the characteristics of their leaves and roots.

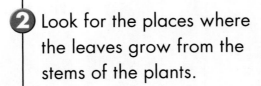

root

2. Look for the places where the leaves grow from the stems of the plants.

3. Look at the roots that grow from the stems of the plants.

root

Explain Your Results

Use what you **observed** to explain how the two plants are alike and different.

How to Read Science

Compare and Contrast

Knowing how to compare and contrast can help you understand what you read and the things you **observe.**

- We **compare** when we say how things are alike. We **contrast** when we say how things are different.
- Words and phrases such as *similar, like, all, both,* or *in the same way* are used to compare.
- Words and phrases such as *unlike* or *in a different way* are used to contrast.

Science Article

Plants and Animals

Both plants and animals are living things that need food, air, water, and space to live. Unlike most plants, most animals don't stay in the same place. They move around. Unlike animals, most plants have roots that keep them in the same place.

Plants　　　　**Both**　　　**Animals**

Ways that plants are different from animals

Ways that plants and animals are alike

Ways that animals are different from plants

Apply It!

Make a graphic organizer like the one shown. Use the information from the science article to fill it in.

You Are There!

It's a cool spring day and you are walking along a river in Alaska. Tall trees rise above the river. Why do some have flat, broad leaves, while others have sharp needles? Lots of other kinds of plants are growing here too. Even though they may look different, every plant needs the same things to live and grow. Listen. You hear a splash. An Alaskan brown bear bounds out of the trees into the river. The bear needs certain things too.

AudioText

Lesson 1

What are the main parts of a plant?

Most plants have four main parts. These parts are leaves, roots, stems, and flowers. In different kinds of plants, these parts may look similar. They may also look very different.

What All Living Things Need

Most living things, including plants and animals, need food, air, water, and space to live and grow. Animals find and eat plants or other animals to get their food. Unlike animals, plants can make their own food. To make their food, plants need energy from the Sun. Most plants also need soil.

Most plants have four main parts. These parts are leaves, roots, stems, and flowers.

Black-eyed Susans are one of the many plants you might see in a prairie.

1. ✓**Checkpoint** What do plants and animals need to live?

2. **Writing in Science** **Descriptive**
Choose an animal and a plant and describe in your **science journal** what each needs to survive.

Why Plants Need Leaves

A plant's leaves make up its leaf system. A **system** consists of parts that work together. Leaves come in many shapes and sizes. They help green plants because they make food. The food they make is a kind of sugar.

To make food, leaves use air, water, and the energy of sunlight. Carbon dioxide is a gas in air. It enters the plant through tiny holes on the underside of leaves. Water passes from soil through roots and stems and into each leaf. The leaves change the carbon dioxide and water into sugar and oxygen. Oxygen goes out from the plant through the same tiny holes on the lower surface of the leaves. The plant uses the sugar to live and grow.

Gas
Carbon dioxide enters the leaf through tiny holes on its underside.

Water
Water enters the leaf from the roots and stem.

Sugar
The leaves make sugar for food that passes through the stems to the rest of the plant.

Oxygen
Plants make and let out oxygen gas when they make sugar.

Sun
Plants need energy from the Sun to change carbon dioxide and water into sugar and oxygen.

Leaf Veins
Tiny tubes called leaf veins deliver water to the leaf. They also carry sugar made in the leaves to the rest of the plant.

Other Ways Leaves Help Plants

Leaves help plants in other ways. They help plants to balance the amount of water plants take in. If there is too much water in the plant, leaves will let some water out through the tiny holes on their underside. Plants in dry places may have leaves with waxy or fuzzy coatings to help keep water in.

A plant's leaves may also help to protect the plant from being eaten. Leaves might be poisonous, sharp, or tough to chew. Hungry animals will leave the plant alone.

✓ Lesson Checkpoint

1. List the main parts of most plants.

2. How does a leaf help a plant live?

3. **Compare and Contrast** Describe ways that leaves are alike and different. Use a graphic organizer.

Some trees have leaves that look like needles.

A pecan tree leaf is made up of many smaller leaflets that grow across from each other.

This oak leaf is more like the pecan leaves than the needle-like leaves. Yet observe how different it is.

Lesson 2

Why do plants need roots and stems?

Along with their leaves, plants need their root and stem systems to live and grow.

How Roots Help Plants

The root system of a plant is often below the ground where you cannot see it. The roots hold the plant in the ground. Roots take in water and materials called minerals from the soil. The roots also store food made by the plant.

Many plants, such as carrots and dandelions, have a large root called a taproot. The taproot grows deep into the soil. The taproot stores food for the plant. Have you ever tasted a carrot or a beet? If your answer is "yes," then you've eaten the taproot of a plant!

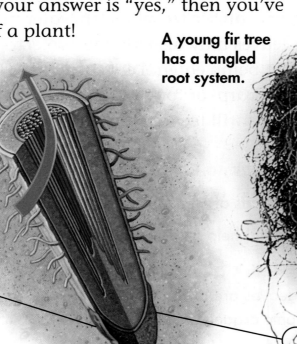

Water and minerals travel up the root through tubes to the stem and leaves.

Root hair

Water enters the root through the root hairs.

Growing tip of root

A young fir tree has a tangled root system.

10

Grasses do not have a taproot.

Roots that We Eat

Beet

Radish

Carrot

Turnip

At the tips of roots are tiny root hairs. Plants take in water through their root hairs. Root branches with their many root hairs grow far into the soil to reach water. Water travels through tubes to the plant's stem and leaves.

On summer days, the root system can be a very busy place. Sunshine and hot air can dry a plant out. The roots must take in water to replace water lost from the plant leaves.

1. ✔ **Checkpoint** How do roots help a plant?
2. **Social Studies** in Science Look up the many different ways that people around the world use roots.

How Stems Help Plants

A plant's stems hold up its leaves, flowers, and fruits. Most plant stems have tubes that move water and minerals from the roots of plants to the leaves. Other tubes carry food from the leaves of plants to the stems and roots.

The pictures show some different kinds of stems. Some stems, called stolons, are thin and grow along the surface of the ground. These stems can grow roots and a new plant. Some stems, called vines, grow parts that wrap around objects that support the plant.

Notice how thick cactus stems can be. Cactus stems swell up as they store water. The stems shrink as the plant uses water. Cactus stems also have a thick, waxy covering to help keep them from losing water. This type of stem helps the cactus plant survive in a desert.

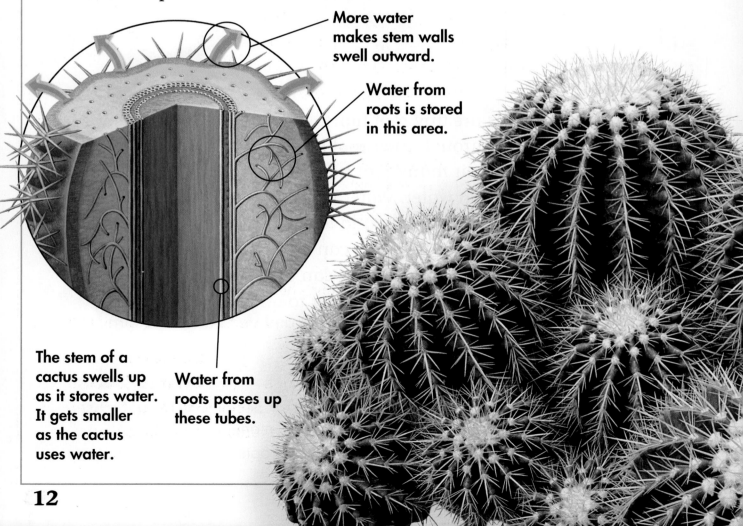

More water makes stem walls swell outward.

Water from roots is stored in this area.

The stem of a cactus swells up as it stores water. It gets smaller as the cactus uses water.

Water from roots passes up these tubes.

Stolons of this strawberry plant are for growing new plants.

Potato

Vine

Tree trunk

Parts of some stems grow underground. When you eat a potato, you eat a stem part that stored food underground. Underground stems can sprout new stems from buds such as the potato's "eyes." These parts grow upward and become new plants.

Some plants have stems with special features to help them survive. For example, some stems have thorns, spines, or stinging hairs to keep hungry animals from eating them.

The spines growing out of this cactus stem are a special kind of leaf.

✓ Lesson Checkpoint

1. How do stems help a plant?

2. How are roots and stems alike and different?

3. **Writing** in Science **Expository**
   Write a paragraph in your **science journal** that describes the special features of a cactus. Explain how these features help the cactus.

How are plants grouped?

Plants can be grouped by the kinds of parts they have.

Flowering Plants

An apple tree and a cactus do not look alike, but they both grow flowers with seeds. They belong to different groups of flowering plants. Each group has different kinds of roots, stems, leaves, and flowers. The flowering plants pictured on this page have different types of stems. The dogwood tree has a stiff, woody stem. The dogwood can grow tall. The trillium plants do not have woody stems. They grow low to the ground.

The dogwood tree survives winter because its leaves die and fall off in the fall. The leaves grow back in the spring. A tree that loses and grows leaves like this is a **deciduous** tree. Many flowering plants lose both stems and leaves in the fall. The roots live through winter and the plants grow back from the roots in spring.

Flowering trees and small flowering plants are similar and different.

Making Seeds

Flowering plants grow flowers that make seeds. Flowers have parts that make pollen or seeds. Bees, other animals, or wind **pollinate** a flower when they move pollen to the flower part that makes seeds.

After a flower is pollinated, seeds form near the center of the flower. A fruit often grows to surround and protect the seeds.

A flower's petals attract insects and other animals that pollinate the flower.

Pollen sticks to the bodies of bees as bees look for food. They carry this pollen to the part of the flower that makes seeds.

The tip of this part of the flower makes pollen.

Pollen put on the tip of this part helps form seeds down here.

1. **✓Checkpoint** Describe how a flower makes a seed.

2. **Writing in Science** **Narrative** Write a story in your **science journal** about a flower that invited a bee over for a visit. Be sure to describe the bee's thank-you gift.

Coniferous Trees

Coniferous trees grow cones instead of flowers to make their seeds. Most coniferous trees do not lose all their leaves in the fall. The leaves of most coniferous trees look like needles or brushes. Coniferous trees include pine, fir, spruce, and hemlock.

Two Types of Cones

Coniferous trees make two kinds of cones. They make small pollen cones and large seed cones. Wind blows pollen from the small pollen cones to the large seed cones. When pollen attaches to the seed cone, seeds begin to grow. A seed grows under each scale of the seed cone. When the seeds are ripe, they fall to the ground. If conditions are right, each seed can start growing into a new plant. Over time, the seeds may become trees.

Kinds of Cones

Cones form on branches near the top of conifers.

Wind blows pollen from these small cones to larger cones on other trees.

Seeds are made under the scales of this Douglas fir cone. This cone is about as big as your fist.

Larger cones grow with seeds inside.

Coniferous seeds glide to the ground.

✔ **Lesson Checkpoint**

1. What are two ways to group plants?

2. Describe two kinds of plant parts that can make seeds.

3. **Writing** in Science **Expository** Write a paragraph in your **science journal** that explains different ways flowers can be pollinated.

17

How do new plants grow?

Most plants make seeds that grow into new plants.
Sometimes a stem or root grows a new plant.

Scattering Seeds

When seeds are scattered, they are moved away from the plant. Then they have more room to grow.

Seeds are scattered in many ways. Some seeds are spread from one place to another by wind or water. Other seeds are carried to new places by animals that eat fruit with seeds. The seeds pass through the animal's body. Then they are dropped to the ground far from the plant. Some seeds are carried along when they stick to an animal's fur.

Ways That Seeds Scatter		
Wind		Wind scatters seeds that have parachutes or wings.
Water		Water scatters seeds that float, such as coconuts.
Carried by animals		Animals scatter seeds that can stick to fur.
Eaten by animals		Animals scatter seeds when they eat fruit.

You've probably seen seeds drifting through the air. Wind scatters seeds that are very light. Many of these seeds have special parts that act like tiny wings or parachutes. The seeds can drift for long distances if the wind is strong.

Special Ways of Releasing Seeds

Some types of pine cones need to be heated in a forest fire to release their seeds. The fire also removes other plants around the trees and clears space for the seeds to grow.

Each of these seeds has a tiny parachute. Wind can carry these seeds long distances where they can grow into new plants.

1. ✓ **Checkpoint** What are two ways that animals scatter seeds?

2. **Art** in Science Draw pictures of two groups of seeds. Draw one group of seeds that are scattered by animals. Draw another group of seeds that are scattered by wind. Describe how the parts of these seeds are different.

Germinating and Growing

Seeds have different shapes, sizes, and colors, but they all have the same parts. Every seed has a tiny plant inside it that can grow into a new plant. The seed is covered by a seed coat to protect this tiny plant. Every seed has one **seed leaf** or two seed leaves to provide food for the tiny plant as it grows.

Seeds need air, the right amount of water, and the right temperature to start to grow, or **germinate.** A root grows from the seed and the young plant, or **seedling**, begins to grow. The seedling uses food stored in the seed to grow.

The seedling's stem rises out of the soil. Leaves grow from the stem. The leaves use sunlight to make sugar that the plant uses for food. The seedling can grow into an adult plant that has flowers. The flowers are pollinated and new seeds form. If the seeds germinate, they grow into new plants. Then the cycle begins again.

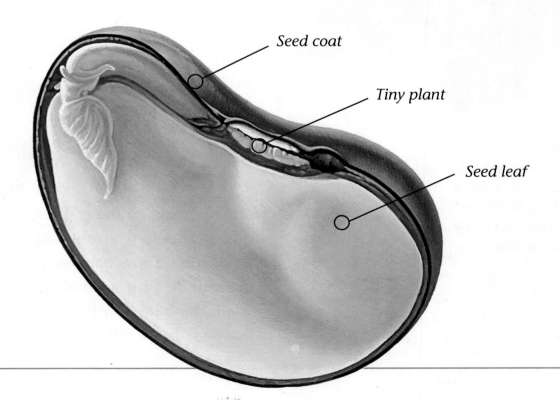

Seed coat

Tiny plant

Seed leaf

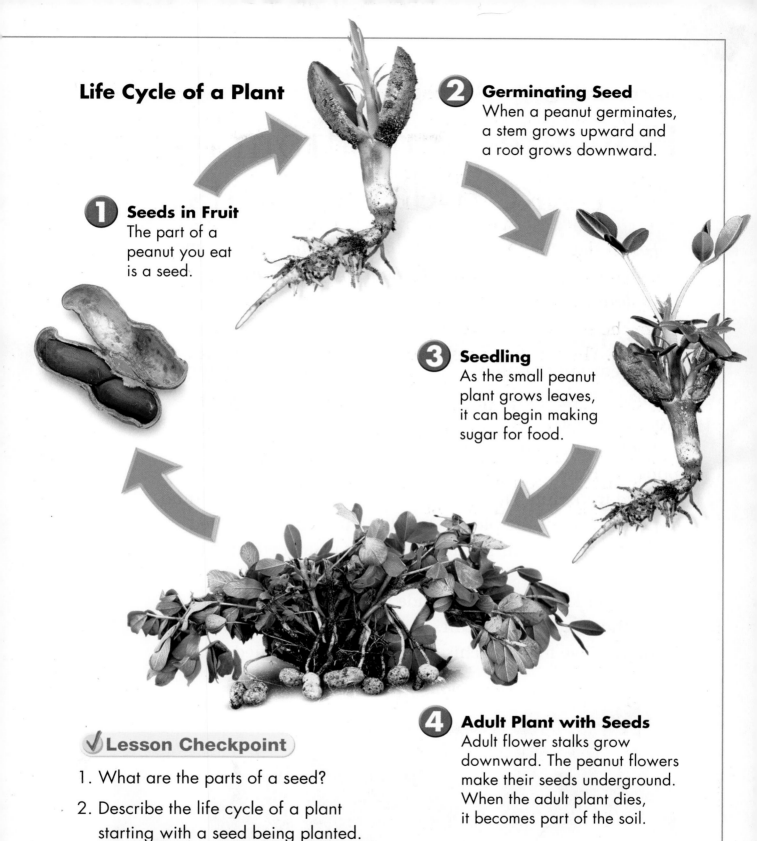

Life Cycle of a Plant

1 **Seeds in Fruit**
The part of a peanut you eat is a seed.

2 **Germinating Seed**
When a peanut germinates, a stem grows upward and a root grows downward.

3 **Seedling**
As the small peanut plant grows leaves, it can begin making sugar for food.

4 **Adult Plant with Seeds**
Adult flower stalks grow downward. The peanut flowers make their seeds underground. When the adult plant dies, it becomes part of the soil.

✔**Lesson Checkpoint**

1. What are the parts of a seed?

2. Describe the life cycle of a plant starting with a seed being planted.

3. **Social Studies** in Science Choose a vegetable that is grown in your state. Find out what farmers do to grow the vegetable and get it to market.

Lesson 5

How are plants from the past like today's plants?

Fossils show the kinds of plants that lived long ago. In some ways today's plants are similar to plants from the past that have disappeared.

Plants That Lived Long Ago

We learn about plants that lived long ago by studying fossils. A **fossil** is the remains or mark of a living thing from long ago.

Look at the fern and horsetail fossils in the pictures on page 23. How did they form? Each plant died and was pressed into mud. Next, the plant rotted away. But the mud kept the form of the plant. Over time the mud hardened into rock. The flat imprint of the plant is seen when the rock cracks open.

Another kind of fossil is made when rock replaces the parts that make up a plant. The drawings below show how it might have formed. This rock is called a petrified fossil.

Formation of Petrified Wood

Stump is buried in mud.

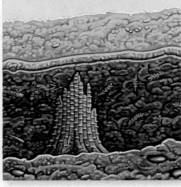
Minerals replace wood as time passes.

Rock surrounding the fossil is removed.

Plant Fossils

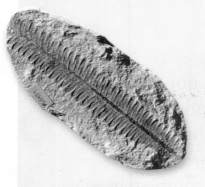

The fern that made this fossil lived about 350 million years ago.

This fossil shows a kind of fern that is extinct.

This fossil shows a kind of horsetail plant that is extinct.

This log is a fossil trunk of an extinct tree fern.

Petrified wood can form when trees are buried in the ground. Minerals replace wood in the trees. At the same time, water breaks down the wood and carries it away. Over a long period of time, the wood is replaced by stone with exactly the same shape and markings as the original wood.

Many kinds of plants that lived long ago are no longer alive. They are **extinct.** For example, ferns that live today look different from the ferns that lived long ago. Plants related to the extinct ferns and horsetail fossils shown in the photos live on Earth today.

1. **✓ Checkpoint** What can scientists learn by studying fossils?

2. **Writing in Science** **Expository** In your **science journal**, write a paragraph that explains how a plant leaf can become a fossil.

These petrified wood fossils in Arizona look like wood, but they are made of rock.

Plants Change Over Time

Plant fossils show us that the first plants did not have flowers or cones. Many were like today's ferns and horsetails. As Earth changed over time, however, plants changed too. Trees that made cones appeared. Then plants with flowers appeared. Many of these kinds of plants have completely disappeared.

Magnolias are flowering plants that first appeared when dinosaurs roamed the Earth. The world was warm and wet year-round. Magnolias grew thick leaves that they kept year-round. Their flowers bloomed for months. Magnolias just like this are alive today. Fossils show that the magnolia flower has remained unchanged for 100 million years.

As the Earth changed, so did the magnolias. Some magnolias now are deciduous. They lose their leaves in fall. Their flowers bloom all at once before the leaves appear in the spring. Even so, their leaves and flowers are similar to those of magnolias that lived long ago.

Fossils of magnolia leaves from long ago look similar to today's magnolia leaves.

Flowers of deciduous magnolias bloom all at once in the spring. After flowering, the trees grow new leaves for the summer.

The first magnolia trees were similar to many magnolias alive today. The feathered dinosaur is extinct.

✔ Lesson Checkpoint

1. What is an extinct plant?

2. How do scientists learn about plants that are extinct?

3. **Compare and Contrast** How are extinct magnolias alike and different from magnolias alive today? Use a graphic organizer to show your answer.

Investigate How fast do different kinds of seeds germinate?

Seeds from some kinds of plants germinate faster than seeds from other kinds of plants. Even seeds from just one kind of plant may germinate faster than other seeds from the same kind of plant.

Materials

paper towel and paper plate

waxed paper and masking tape

5 radish seeds

5 corn seeds

5 pinto bean seeds

5 sunflower seeds

cup with water

metric ruler

Process Skills

By **interpreting the data** you **collected** in your chart, you can analyze how different seeds grow.

What to Do

1 Fold a paper towel in half. Fold it again.

2 Make 2 lines to divide the folded towel into 4 parts. Label each part.

3 Put the waxed paper on the plate. Put the folded towel on the waxed paper. Put on the seeds. Wet the towel.

5 radish seeds   5 corn seeds
5 pinto bean seeds   5 sunflower seeds

④ Put the plate in a warm, bright place.

⑤ **Observe** and record changes for 1 week. Describe or draw the plants as they begin to grow and develop.

After the first day, keep the paper towels moist, but not wet.

5 radish seeds

5 corn seeds

5 pinto bean seeds

5 sunflower seeds

waxed paper

paper towel folded into 4 parts

Kind of Plant	Description (write or draw)	Day the First of the 5 Seeds Germinated (Day 1, 2, 3, 4, or 5)	Order in Which Different Kinds of Plants Germinated (1st, 2nd, 3rd, or 4th)	Length of Longest Stem on Day 7 (mm)
Radish				
Corn				
Pinto				
Sunflower				

Explain Your Results

1. **Interpret the data** you **collected**. Compare the radish and sunflower seeds. How did they grow and develop differently?

2. Were all the radish plants the same? Explain.

Go Further

Collect more data. Every day count and record the number of each kind of plant that has germinated. Graph your results.

27

Elapsed Time
from Seed to Fruit

If you plant a green bean seed, how soon can you eat green beans from the plant that grows? The answer is the length of time it takes for the seed to germinate, grow, and produce flowers and fruit. Different kinds of plants have different lengths of time from seed to fruit that is ready to eat.

Green bean

Cucumber

Sweet corn

Tomato

e Tools Take It to the Net
pearsonsuccessnet.com

If you plant green bean seeds on May 10, you can start eating green beans 58 days later, on July 7.

Days from planting seeds or seedling to picking ripe fruit	
green bean seeds	58 days
cucumber seeds	55 days
sweet corn seeds	75 days
tomato seedling	59 days

Use the table and calendars to answer the questions.

1 If you plant cucumber seeds on May 21, when could you start eating cucumbers?

2 If sweet corn seeds are planted on May 19, when will the corn be ready to eat?

3 When could you start eating ripe tomatoes if the seedling was planted on May 31?

Lab zone Take-Home Activity

Look at the back of seed packets or go to the library or Internet to search for seed catalogs. Find out how long it takes different kinds of seeds to grow and make fruit. Use a calendar to find what dates the fruit might be ready to pick.

Chapter 1 Review and Test Prep

Use Vocabulary

deciduous (page 14)	**pollinate** (page 15)
coniferous (page 16)	**seed leaf** (page 20)
extinct (page 23)	**seedling** (page 20)
fossil (page 22)	
germinate (page 20)	**system** (page 8)

Use the vocabulary word or words from the list above that best completes each sentence.

1. When conditions are right, a seed will start to grow, or _____.

2. A tree that makes cones is a(n) _____ tree.

3. Bees, wind, and water can _____ flowers.

4. All the leaves and their parts make up a plant's leaf _____.

5. A(n) _____ tree loses all its leaves in the fall.

6. A new plant that has just grown out of the soil is a(n) _____.

7. A new plant uses food stored in a(n) _____.

8. A(n) _____ plant no longer lives on Earth, but a(n) _____ of its remains might be found.

Explain Concepts

9. How do scientists learn about plants that are extinct?

10. Explain why all of a plant's roots and their parts are called a system.

11. What do a plant's leaves need to make sugar?

Process Skills

12. **Classify** Choose one way that plants can be sorted into two groups. Explain how the plants in the two groups are alike and different.

13. **Infer** Bees visit the flowers on apple trees to get food. How might a disease that kills bees affect the number of apples the trees make? Explain your answer.

Mind Point Quiz Show

Compare and Contrast

14. Make a graphic organizer like the one shown below. Fill in the correct information.

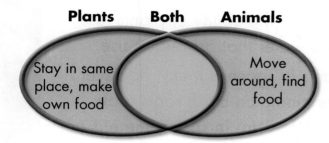

Plants   Both   Animals

Stay in same place, make own food

Move around, find food

Test Prep

Choose the letter that best completes the statement or answers the question.

15. Before a seed can become a plant, the seed must

   Ⓐ germinate.
   Ⓑ be pollinated.
   Ⓒ make food.
   Ⓓ flower.

16. A cactus stores the most water in its

   Ⓕ roots.
   Ⓖ leaves.
   Ⓗ stems.
   Ⓘ flowers.

17. What fossil is made when minerals replace plant parts, while water breaks the parts down and carries them away?

   Ⓐ imprint
   Ⓑ petrified wood
   Ⓒ extinct fern
   Ⓓ magnolia flower

18. Which of the following is an example of scattering seeds?

   Ⓕ pollen sticking to a bee
   Ⓖ wind blowing pollen
   Ⓗ apples growing on a tree
   Ⓘ burs sticking to a dog's fur

19. Explain why the answer you chose for Question 18 is best. For each of the answers you did not choose, give a reason why it is not the best choice.

20. **Writing in Science**

Expository Write a paragraph that describes the life cycle of a plant.

Plant Researcher

Do you like plants? Plant researchers study how plants live and grow.

What if food that astronauts need during long space missions runs out? Grow more aboard ship! Dr. Stutte of NASA tests ways to grow wheat aboard the International Space Station. He also tests the ability of plants to clean the air and water that astronauts use.

Growing plants in space is tricky, however. When seeds germinate on Earth roots grow down and stems grow up. In space, there is no up or down. As a plant researcher you might be called upon to solve problems like this one.

Plant researchers look for ways to grow more or stronger plants. Researchers at NASA are studying how plant seeds might grow better in space. Better traits from seeds grown in space could help farmers grow stronger plants on Earth.

Plant researchers have college degrees.

Dr. Gary Stutte

Lab zone Take-Home Activity

Draw a machine that would grow cucumbers in space where there is little gravity. Label the parts that supply the plants with water, fertilizer, carbon dioxide, and light. Write a paragraph explaining how it would work.

You Will Discover

- ways that animals are grouped.
- how an animal's body and its behavior help it survive.
- how animals grow and change.
- that many animals today resemble animals that lived long ago.

Chapter 2

How Animals Live

online
Student Edition
pearsonsuccessnet.com

Discovery Channel School
Student DVD
Discovery CHANNEL SCHOOL

How do different animals live, grow, and change?

vertebrate

trait

inherited

migrate

hibernate

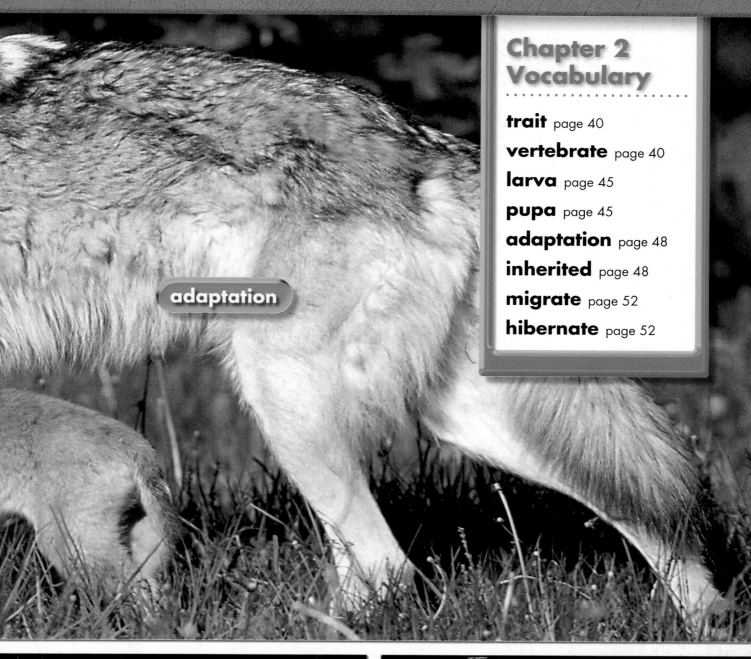

adaptation

larva

pupa

Explore How can you make a model of a backbone?

Materials

pipe cleaner

10 pieces of wagon wheel pasta

9 soft fruit jelly rings

What to Do

1 **Make a model** of a backbone. Bend the end of a pipe cleaner into a knot. String a piece of wagon wheel pasta on the pipe cleaner so the pasta rests on the knot. Next string a jelly ring.

2 Add another wheel and a ring. Keep going until you have used 10 wheels and 9 rings.

3 Bend the other end of the pipe cleaner. Make a knot to hold everything on. Can you bend your model backbone?

Process Skills

Making and using a model can help you understand scientific ideas.

Explain Your Results

How is your **model** different from a real backbone? How is your model like a real backbone?

How to Read Science

Sequence

Sequence is the order in which events take place. Clue words such as *first, next, then,* and *finally* can help you figure out the **sequence** of events. They are marked on the museum display card.

Museum Display Card

Sea Jelly

A sea jelly grows up in stages. First, an adult makes young called larvae. Next, each larva becomes attached to a rock. Then, each larva grows and becomes a polyp. Finally, each polyp grows into a group of young adults.

Apply It!

Make a graphic organizer as a **model** to show the life cycle of the sea jelly. Write each of the four events in the life cycle after your four clue words.

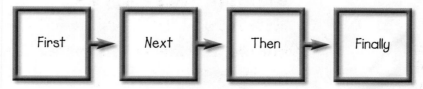

First → Next → Then → Finally

It's early morning in the forest and the birds are singing. You look down at your feet and notice ants marching by. You stand very still, listening and watching. Suddenly, you spot what looks like two dogs walking through a grassy field in the distance. As you focus your eyes you realize they are not dogs. You've spotted a wolf and her pup! Animals come in many shapes and sizes. Even though they may be different, do animals need the same basic things to live?

AudioText

How are animals grouped?

All animals have the same basic needs. Animals might be grouped by how they look, where they live, or how they act.

What All Animals Need

Nearly all animals need water, oxygen, food, and shelter to live. Animals can get water from drinking or from the foods they eat. All animals also need the gas oxygen. They get oxygen from the air or from water. Most animals that live on land have lungs to breathe in oxygen. Many animals that live in water, such as fish, breathe with gills.

Animals also need food and shelter. They get their food by eating plants or other animals. Shelters protect animals from the weather and from other animals. While some animals build or seek shelters, others use their own hard shells as their homes.

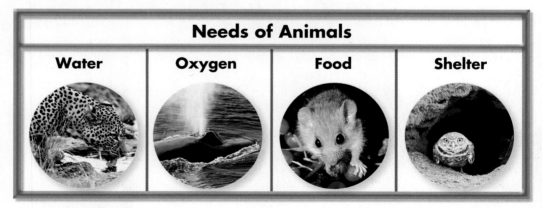

Needs of Animals

Water	Oxygen	Food	Shelter

1. ✔**Checkpoint** What do all animals need?

2. **Writing in Science** **Descriptive** In your **science journal,** write about how your favorite animal meets its basic needs.

Ways of Grouping Animals

How we group animals depends on what we want to learn about them. Animals can be grouped by where they live or how they act. They also may be grouped by how they look. A body feature passed on to an animal from its parents is called a **trait.** Traits can include things an animal does.

One animal can be placed into different groups. For example, a group of animals that eat mice can include snakes, hawks, and owls. A group of animals that fly can include hawks and owls, but not snakes.

Animals with Backbones

Another way to group animals is by whether or not they have a backbone. An animal with a backbone is called a **vertebrate.** Cats, birds, fish, and snakes all have backbones and other bones in their bodies. Their bones grow as the animals grow. Their bones give them strong support. This allows many vertebrates, such as elephants, to grow very big.

This lynx is
a vertebrate.

Groups of Vertebrates

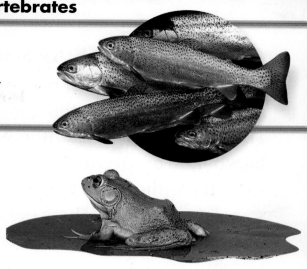

Fish

These vertebrates spend their entire lives in fresh water, ocean water, or both. Most fish have slippery scales and breathe through gills.

Amphibians

Frogs, toads, and salamanders belong to a group called amphibians. Many amphibians spend part of their lives in water and part on land. Most young amphibians live in water. They get oxygen through gills and through their smooth, moist skin. As they grow, most amphibians develop lungs that they use to breathe air.

Reptiles

Snakes, lizards, turtles, crocodiles, and alligators are reptiles. They mostly have dry, scaly skin. These vertebrates breathe air through lungs.

Birds

Birds are vertebrates with feathers and bills that do not have teeth. They breathe air through lungs. Wings and light bones help most birds fly. Their coats of feathers help them stay warm.

Mammals

The vertebrates that you probably know best are called mammals. Mammals have hair at least during part of their lives. The hair keeps them warm. Mammals breathe air through lungs and feed milk to their young.

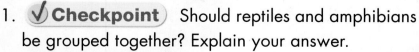

1. ✔ **Checkpoint** Should reptiles and amphibians be grouped together? Explain your answer.

2. **Art** in Science Think about two animals that share some of the same traits. Draw a picture of each animal "in action" using a shared trait.

Animals Without Backbones

Most animals do not have skeletons made of bones inside their bodies. These are the animals without backbones, or invertebrates. Sea stars, butterflies, and spiders are some invertebrates. There are many more kinds of invertebrates than vertebrates, as the chart shows.

A soft sac filled with liquid supports worms and sea jellies. A hard shell supports clams. Insects and other arthropods have a hard covering on the outside of their bodies. These kinds of structures cannot support very big animals. Most invertebrates do not grow as big as most vertebrates.

Many invertebrates are very small. Several million tiny roundworms may live in one square meter of soil. You may not notice many invertebrates, but they live all over Earth.

Kinds of Animals

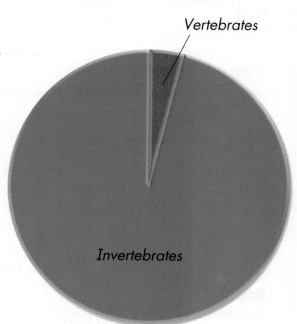

The whole circle stands for all kinds of animals. The small piece shows that kinds of vertebrates are only a small part of the total.

Kinds of Invertebrate Animals

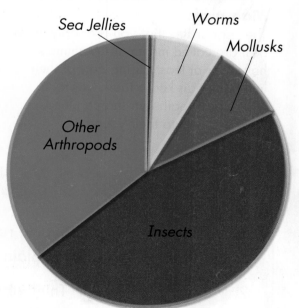

Most kinds of invertebrates are insects.

This dragonfly is an invertebrate.

Major Kinds of Invertebrate Animals

Sea Jellies	Sea jellies have soft bodies and long, stinging body parts. The body of a sea jelly is made mostly of water. A sea jelly uses its stingers to stun its prey before pulling it into its stomach. Most sea jellies live in the ocean.
Worms	Worms are animals with long, soft bodies and no legs. You've probably seen an earthworm in the soil. These invertebrates help keep soil healthy.
Mollusks	Mollusks are animals with soft bodies. Some mollusks include the octopus, squid, clam, and snail. Many mollusks have a hard shell.
Arthropods	These animals are members of the largest group of invertebrates. They wear their skeletons outside their bodies. The bodies of arthropods are made up of more than one main part and they have legs with joints. Insects, spiders, and crabs are all arthropods.

✔ Lesson Checkpoint

1. If a rattlesnake and a black widow spider both make poison, why are they put in different groups?

2. Explain why most invertebrates are small in size compared to most vertebrates.

3. **Math** in Science   There are 5 vertebrates in someone's backyard. There are 20 times as many invertebrates as vertebrates there, too. How many invertebrates are there?

Lesson 2

How do animals grow and change?

Different animals have their young in different ways. But all animals grow and change during their life cycle.

Life Cycles

An animal's life starts out as an egg. Sometimes the egg develops into a young animal inside the mother. Then the mother gives birth to a live young. For other animals, the mother lays an egg outside of her body. Then the young develops in the egg and hatches when it is ready.

When some animals hatch or are born, they look like their parents. Many other animals change a lot before they look anything like their parents.

Adult butterflies lay eggs.

1 Egg
This is a close-up view of a very small egg. The picture has been magnified, or made to look bigger.

Life Cycle Stages	
Birth	Animals are born or hatch.
Growth	Animals get bigger.
Development	Animals change into adults.
Reproduction	Animals produce young.
Death	Animals' lives come to an end.

4 Butterfly

The adult butterfly comes out of the chrysalis.

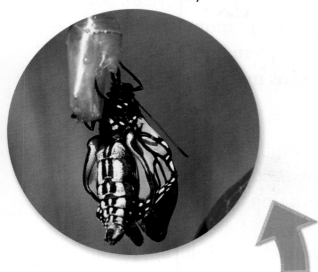

3 Pupa

Inside a hard covering, the larva's body changes.

2 Larva

The butterfly larva is called a caterpillar.

A Butterfly's Life Cycle

The egg is the first state in the butterfly's life cycle. The tiny egg is hard to see.

A caterpillar hatches from the egg. It is now a **larva.** The larva must eat a lot to survive. It starts munching on the plant where it lives.

The larva grows. It sheds its skin several times. Then the larva spins a covering around itself. A hard covering, or chrysalis, forms. The larva is now called a **pupa.**

The larva's body begins to change when it becomes a pupa. It grows wings and jointed legs. It begins to look like an adult butterfly. Soon it breaks out of the chrysalis. The adult butterfly dries its wings and flies away. After laying eggs, the butterly dies. Its life cycle is complete.

1. ✓**Checkpoint** What is the purpose of the pupa?

2. **Sequence** List the sequence of steps in a butterfly's life cycle. Use the signal words *first, next, then,* and *finally.*

Some Vertebrate Life Cycles

Vertebrates have different kinds of life cycles. Some vertebrates, like frogs, go through many changes as they grow and mature. Other vertebrates, like pandas or monkeys, do not change as much.

A Frog's Life Cycle

Just like insects, many amphibians change quite a lot as they become adults. Did you know, for instance, that a very young frog looks and acts a lot like a fish?

Look at how a frog changes during its life cycle. This frog completes all the stages of its life cycle in one summer. All frogs do not develop in the same way. In colder places, a developing frog may dig into the mud during the winter. It will not become an adult frog until the following spring or summer.

A panda cub gets a gentle nudge.

Even though it's very small, a new-born panda pup has the same body form and the same number of legs as its parents.

A Mammal's Life Cycle

Unlike amphibians and insects, young mammals do not change very much as they become adults. Many mammals look like their parents when they are born. Like you, they grow as they get older.

Most mammals develop inside their mother's bodies. When they are born, the babies drink milk from their mothers. They also have hair or fur.

It will be many years before you become an adult. A young rabbit, however, is ready to leave its nest and live on its own when it is less than three weeks old. It will be an adult at about six months.

Frog Life Cycle

2 **Tadpole**
Tadpoles hatch from the frog eggs. Tadpoles live underwater and breathe with gills.

1 **Eggs**
Mother frogs often lay hundreds or thousands of eggs in the water.

3 **Growing Tadpole**
As the tadpole grows, it starts to change. Its tail becomes shorter. Legs begin to grow. The back legs grow first.

Before a tadpole becomes an adult frog, it has to grow lungs so it can breathe on land.

4 **Adult Frog**
The adult frog lives on land and in the water. It will need to return to the water to lay its eggs.

✓ Lesson Checkpoint

1. Before a frog can live on land, how must its body change?

2. How is a mammal's life cycle different from a frog's or a butterfly's life cycle?

3. **Writing in Science** **Expository** Think about how mammals care for their young. In your **science journal,** describe why this kind of care might be helpful for most mammals.

How do adaptations help animals?

Animals have special body parts, features, and ways of doing things that help them survive in their environments.

Adaptations

Animals live in many different places on Earth. An animal needs food, water, oxygen, and shelter. A trait that helps an animal meet its needs in the place where it lives is called an **adaptation.**

The webbed feet of a pelican are an adaptation. They help the pelican swim and survive in the water where it finds its food. Adaptations, such as webbed feet, are **inherited,** or passed on, from parents to their young.

Body parts, such as feet and bills, are important inherited adaptations. There are many different kinds of adaptations. Most kinds, such as body color, differ between members of even closely related groups.

This porcupine skull shows adaptations of a plant-eating animal. Sharp front teeth cut off parts of plants. Flat teeth in the back of the jaw move from side to side, grinding tough plant material.

This hyena skull shows adaptations of a meat-eating animal. Sharp front teeth tear off meat and back teeth shred it.

The bill of a pelican has a pouch that hangs from it. When a pelican swoops into the water for food, the pouch acts like a net to help the bird catch fish.

Adaptations for Getting Food

Animals have many special adaptations for getting food. Prairie dogs and moles have feet that are especially good for digging. Hawks and eagles have feet that can hold tightly onto their food when they swoop down to catch it. Animals may also have the kind of teeth that can handle the foods they eat. Many birds have bills that help them catch and eat their favorite foods. Sometimes you can tell what a bird eats by the shape of its bill.

A long, curved bill helps the flamingo filter food from shallow water.

A short, strong bill helps the cardinal break open seeds.

A small, thin bill helps the warbler pick out insects for food.

1. ✔**Checkpoint** Give two examples of adaptations and tell how they help the animal survive.

2. **Art** in Science Think about an animal that wades into ponds and spears fish for food. Draw a picture of this animal. Include the special adaptations you think it would need to live and get food.

Adaptations for Protection

The way an animal looks can help it survive. *Camouflage* helps some animals blend into their surroundings. Camouflage helps hide the animals from predators.

Other animals have colors or markings that copy those of a more dangerous animal. This kind of adaptation is called *mimicry.*

The way an animal acts can help it survive. Many animals climb, run, hop, jump, fly, or swim away from danger. Some animals may also use poison to protect themselves. Animals such as skunks and weasels spray a bad-smelling liquid at their enemies. Many animals use body parts such as shells, teeth, claws, hooves, and bills to protect themselves.

A porcupine is covered in quills. These special hairs have sharp hooks on their tips. When the porcupine is scared, special muscles make the quills stand up. Then the porcupine can hit an attacker with its quills. The hooks pierce the attacker's skin and stay attached to it.

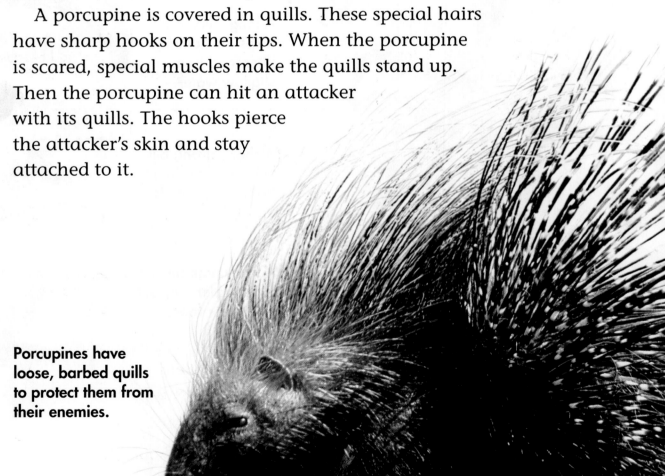

Porcupines have loose, barbed quills to protect them from their enemies.

Ways Animals Protect Themselves

Camouflage	Armor	Mimicry	Poison
Animals that can harm or be harmed by this crab spider cannot see it.	Spikes and horns protect this horned lizard.	A harmless hover fly looks like a dangerous hornet.	Lion fish have poisonous spines.
These harlequin shrimp blend in with the bright sea fans.	Pill bugs roll into a ball for defense.	A viceroy butterfly looks like a bad-tasting monarch butterfly.	Monarch butterflies taste bad because of the food they eat.
The fur color of this arctic fox changes with the seasons.	A cassowary has a tough helmet to protect its head as it runs through brush.	This king snake looks similar to the deadly coral snake.	Coral snakes bite with poisonous fangs.

1. **✓ Checkpoint** What are some ways that animals protect themselves from their enemies?

2. **Sequence** List in the correct sequence what happens when a predator attacks a porcupine. Be sure to use the signal words *first*, *next*, and *finally* in your list of steps.

Behaviors That Help Animals

Behaviors are things that animals do. Animals are born being able to do some things. These behaviors are inherited. You inherit your ability to do many things such as walk and talk.

You do not inherit your ability to read and write. You need to learn these behaviors. You do inherit your ability to learn these behaviors, though.

Baby birds are born knowing how to open their mouths for food.

Monarch butterflies have an instinct to migrate.

Instincts

An instinct is a behavior an animal is born able to do. One instinct is an animal's response to hunger. Baby birds, for example, open their mouths when they sense a parent with food is near. Some animals have an instinct to move, or **migrate,** when the seasons change. Some butterflies migrate thousands of miles to warmer weather to survive the winter.

Other animals have an instinct to **hibernate** during the cold winter months. When animals hibernate, their body systems usually slow down to save energy. Then they don't need as much food to survive.

Bats hibernate during the winter months when food is hard to find.

An adult chimp shows a young chimp how to dig for insects.

Learning

Animals learn some behaviors from their parents and other animals. For example, chimpanzees can learn how to use tools like sticks to catch insects to eat. Chimpanzees are not born knowing how to use sticks as tools. They learn how to do this by watching other chimpanzees. Young chimpanzees also learn which foods are safe to eat from their mothers and other adults.

Some young animals learn hunting behavior from their parents.

✓ Lesson Checkpoint

1. Name two types of adaptations having to do with an animal's actions.

2. Why do some animals migrate or hibernate?

3. **Social Studies** in Science
Chimpanzees live in groups and learn how to behave from other chimpanzees. Describe how humans and chimpanzees are alike in the ways that they learn.

53

This trilobite fossil is a cast. It shows what the trilobite looked like.

A cast, such as this bird-like dinosaur, is in the shape of the original fossil. It formed when a mold was filled in with rock matter over time.

How are animals from the past like today's animals?

Fossils show the kinds of animals that lived long ago. Today's animals are similar in some ways to animals of the past that have disappeared.

Animals That Lived Long Ago

Signs of past life are called fossils. Usually only the hard parts of animals become fossils. A fossil is usually not the actual bone or part. Instead, it is rock in the shape of the part.

A space in the shape of an animal in rock is called a fossil mold. Soft earth covers the remains of the animal, which wears away. This leaves a cavity or mold in the shape of the animal's parts. The earth then turns to rock over time. If the mold gets filled in with other rock materials over time, the fossil is called a cast.

This fossil cast is of a dinosaur skull about 125 million years old! It looks like the skull of a modern-day crocodile.

Long ago, this spider got trapped in sticky tree sap that hardened into amber.

Unlike the fossil remains of most dinosaur bones, the bones of this fossil saber-toothed tiger are actual bone.

Ancient Insects

Some small animals, or parts of animals, have been found in hardened tree sap called amber. Long ago, an insect might have become trapped in the sticky sap. Soon the sap would have completely covered the insect. Over a long period of time, the sap turned into a hard, yellow or reddish-brown substance called amber. Thin pieces of amber are usually clear enough to see through. What you see is the animal's actual body covering kept together for millions of years.

One other type of fossil is found in tar pits. Saber-toothed tigers and other extinct animals fell into these oily pools many thousands of years ago. The soft parts of their bodies broke down and left only the bones. These fossils are the actual bones of these animals.

1. ✓Checkpoint What are some ways that fossils form?

2. **Math** in Science If a modern-day lizard is 10 meters long and a dinosaur skeleton is 3 times as long, how long is the dinosaur skeleton?

How Animals Today Compare to Those of Long Ago

Fossils can tell us how animals have changed over time. Dinosaurs are extinct. An extinct animal is a kind of animal that no longer lives on Earth. As you can see from the pictures, some animals today look like animals of long ago.

Fossils also tell us how Earth has changed over time. The drawing on the next page shows what the Badlands of South Dakota probably looked like more than 65 million years ago. At that time, dinosaurs like *Tyrannosaurus rex* roamed the area. Plant fossils found in layers of rocks near *T. rex* fossils tell scientists that the climate was hot and wet when *T. rex* lived. Plants could grow year-round. That is why you see plants in the drawing of the *T. rex*.

T. rex's habitat has changed a great deal. The photo in the drawing shows what the Badlands look like today. Only animals that are adapted to hot, dry conditions can live there now.

Although this collared lizard is a tiny, modern-day reptile, it resembles dinosaurs of long ago.

Dinosaurs like this *T. rex* became extinct about 65 million years ago.

Today the Badlands in South Dakota are almost like a desert.

This is one artist's view of how a *T. rex* might have looked. It also shows its habitat.

✔ **Lesson Checkpoint**

1. Describe four kinds of fossils.

2. What can fossils tell us about extinct animals?

3. **Writing in Science** **Expository** In your **science journal,** write about what might have happened to *T. Rex* when its environment changed.

Investigate What can you learn from an imprint?

Imprint fossils are one type of fossil. Scientists can learn about animals that lived long ago by studying the imprints they made.

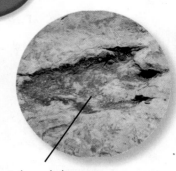

imprint made by a dinosaur

Materials

cup with prepared plaster of Paris

spoon

paper plate and paper towels

bowl of water

What to Do

1 Put plaster of Paris onto a plate.

Spread the plaster of Paris around with a spoon.

2 Wet one of your hands.

Be careful!

Do not put plaster of Paris into a sink. It can clog the drain.

3 Spread the fingers of your wet hand. Press the palm side of this hand into the plaster of Paris.

Process Skills

When you **observe** the imprint of your hand, you notice its size, shape, and texture.

4 Remove your hand from the plaster. Let the imprint dry.

Wipe the plaster of Paris off your hand. Use paper towels. Wash your hands thoroughly.

5 Make a chart to record what you **observe** about your hand and its imprint.

Appearance	
Imprint	**Hand**

Explain Your Results

1. How is your imprint like your hand that made it? How is it different?

2. **Infer** How might an imprint fossil of an animal be like the animal that made it? How might it be different?

Go Further

Use a hand lens to observe and study tiny details. If you wish, make sketches or diagrams. Use your ruler to measure your hand and its imprint.

Math in Science

Comparing Speeds of Fish

There is a great difference in the swimming speeds of fish. Generally, larger fish can swim faster than smaller fish. The bar graph below shows the greatest swimming speeds of six different fish.

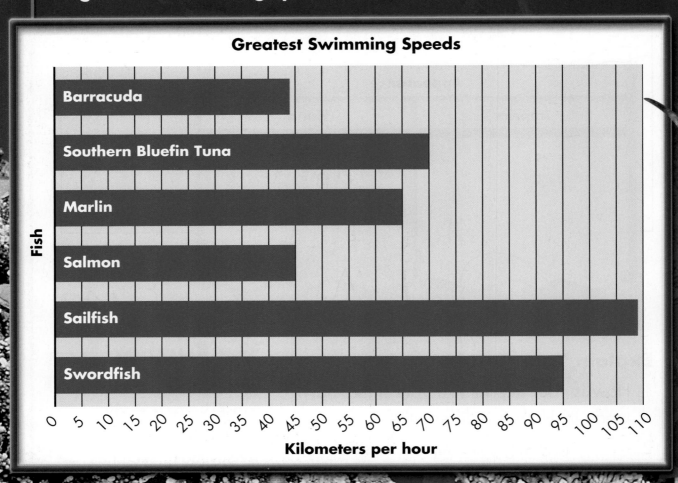

Greatest Swimming Speeds

Fish: Barracuda, Southern Bluefin Tuna, Marlin, Salmon, Sailfish, Swordfish

Kilometers per hour: 0 5 10 15 20 25 30 35 40 45 50 55 60 65 70 75 80 85 90 95 100 105 110

@ **Tools** Take It to the Net
pearsonsuccessnet.com

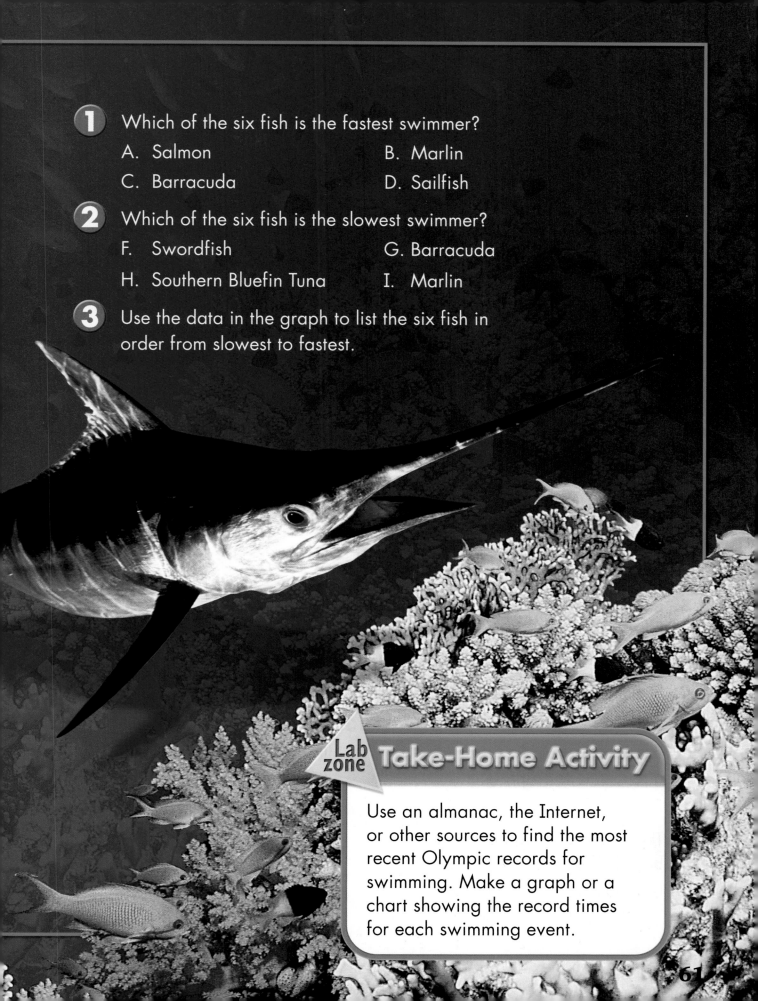

1 Which of the six fish is the fastest swimmer?

   A. Salmon   B. Marlin

   C. Barracuda   D. Sailfish

2 Which of the six fish is the slowest swimmer?

   F.   Swordfish   G. Barracuda

   H. Southern Bluefin Tuna   I. Marlin

3 Use the data in the graph to list the six fish in order from slowest to fastest.

Lab zone Take-Home Activity

Use an almanac, the Internet, or other sources to find the most recent Olympic records for swimming. Make a graph or a chart showing the record times for each swimming event.

Chapter 2 Review and Test Prep

Use Vocabulary

adaptation (page 48)	**migrate** (page 52)
hibernate (page 52)	**pupa** (page 45)
inherited (page 48)	**trait** (page 40)
larva (page 45)	**vertebrate** (page 40)

Use the vocabulary word from the list above that best completes each sentence.

1. An animal with a backbone is called a(n) _____.

2. In an early stage of life, when a butterfly eats and grows, it is called a(n) _____.

3. Some animals need much less food to survive when they _____.

4. Something that helps a living thing survive is called a(n) _____.

5. If something passes on from a parent to its offspring, it is _____.

6. The stage in the life cycle of a butterfly during which it changes into an adult is called the _____.

7. Sometimes animals move to another place, or _____, to find better food or shelter.

8. A feature passed on to an animal from its parents is a(n) _____.

Explain Concepts

9. Explain why different animals can be grouped in more than one way.

10. Why does inheriting an adaptation help offspring survive?

11. What is the difference between instinct and learned behavior?

12. Describe the changes a frog goes through during its life cycle.

Process Skills

13. **Infer** If a fossil skull has flat teeth, what do you think this animal probably ate?

14. **Predict** A hawk has feet with sharp claws on them to help it catch small animals to eat. What kind of feet would you predict a bird that swims would have?

 Sequence

15. Use the signal words to put the stages of the life cycle of a frog in the correct sequence.

First
Next
Finally

 **Test Prep**

Choose the letter that best completes the statement or answers the question.

16. Fossils tell us
- Ⓐ about animals that lived in the past.
- Ⓑ about how Earth has changed.
- Ⓒ how today's animals are similar to past life.
- Ⓓ all of the above.

17. The earliest stage in a frog's life cycle is a(n)
- Ⓕ pupa.
- Ⓖ egg.
- Ⓗ chrysalis.
- Ⓘ tadpole.

18. Which of the following is an animal without a backbone, or invertebrate?
- Ⓐ insect
- Ⓑ bird
- Ⓒ mammal
- Ⓓ amphibian

19. Explain why the answer you chose for Question 18 is best. For each of the answers you did not choose, give a reason why it is not the correct choice.

20. Writing in Science
Descriptive Suppose a hungry fox comes upon a porcupine. Write a paragraph describing what happens between the two animals.

63

Paul Sereno:
Expert Dinosaur Hunter

Paul Sereno

When he was a boy, Paul Sereno liked to go on nature hikes with his brothers. He brought home insects to add to his collection. Paul went to college to study art. However, while he was in college, Paul decided he wanted to become a paleontologist—a scientist who studies ancient life.

Paleontologists like Dr. Sereno try to find fossils to piece together the story of what life was like long ago. Dr. Sereno and his team have found many new kinds of dinosaurs.

Dr. Sereno's team made a discovery in Africa. A giant claw lying in the desert was the first clue. Dr. Sereno and his team carefully dug for more bones. They found a huge skeleton of a dinosaur. Its skull was long with crocodile-like teeth. Dr. Sereno named the new dinosaur *Suchomimus* which means "crocodile mimic."

It sometimes takes years for paleontologists to make sense of what they find. But their hard work often leads to new discoveries.

Lab zone Take-Home Activity

Using library resources and the Internet, research newly discovered dinosaurs. List them by name, type of dinosaur, and where found.

EC CRU 10 9 8 7 6 5 4 3 2 1

Chapter 3

Where Plants and Animals Live

online
Student Edition
pearsonsuccessnet.com

65

How are ecosystems different from each other?

environment

ecosystem

desert

grassland

66

Chapter 3 Vocabulary

population

community

tundra

wetland

Explore In which soil do grass seeds grow best?

How will you know in which soil grass seeds *grow best*? Should *grow best* mean the most blades of grass grow, the tallest blades grow, or the greenest blades grow? You decide. **Make an operational definition** of *grow best*. Begin with the words "Grow best means. . . ." Then say what you will observe that will tell you which *grows best*.

Materials

3 paper cups and a pencil

sandy, clay, and loam soils

grass seeds and cup with water

spoon and masking tape

Process Skills

You explained how you would decide in which soil the seeds *grow best.* When you told what you would **observe** to make this decision, you **made an operational definition**.

What to Do

1. Make 4 holes in the bottom of each cup with a pencil. Half fill the cups with soil. Put 2 spoonfuls of water in each cup.

    Label the *cups.*

2. Sprinkle $\frac{1}{2}$ spoonful of grass seeds in each cup. Lightly cover the seeds with more soil. Set the cups in a warm place with bright light.

sandy soil

clay soil

loam soil

3. Add 1 spoonful of water to each cup daily for 2 weeks. **Observe** each cup daily.

Explain Your Results

What is your **operational definition** of *grow best*? In which soil did the seeds *grow best* according to your definition?

How to Read Science

Main Idea and Details

A number of different things might all be connected to a **main idea**. These are called **details.** Learning to find the **main idea and details** helps you understand what you read. Look at the graphic organizer. The main idea is at the top. The details help support the main idea.

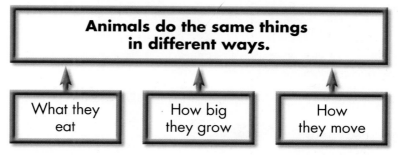

Science Article

Home Address

Animals live in different places. Some live in forests. Others live in lakes or oceans. Different animals have different body coverings. Some have fur or feathers. Others have scales. The animals' body coverings help them live where they do.

Apply It!

Make a graphic organizer like the one shown above. Use it to help you **make an operational definition** about what you read and what you have observed. Write the main idea at the top. Fill in the missing details that support the main idea from the science article.

You are standing where the ocean meets the land. You can feel the warm sunlight on your face. You hear the waves rush onto the shore. You wiggle your toes in the cool, damp sand. Birds circle above you. This is a terrific place for you to visit. What makes it a perfect place for certain plants and animals to live?

Lesson 1

What are ecosystems?

Plants and animals meet their needs in the place where they live. Living things depend on other living things and nonliving things around them.

Places for Living Things

Each living thing needs a certain environment. A living thing's **environment** is everything that surrounds it. An environment has living and nonliving parts. The living parts include plants, animals, and other living things. The nonliving parts include sunlight, air, water, and soil.

Sunlight warms the air, water, and soil to the temperature that living things need. Sunlight helps plants make food.

An environment has a climate. Climate is the weather in a place all year. One environment might have cold, wet winters and hot, dry summers. Another environment might be cold and dry all year long.

Water and soil are important parts of an environment. Water falls as rain and snow. The water enters the soil. Soils differ in the way they hold the water. Each type of plant needs a certain amount of water and a certain kind of soil.

1. **✓Checkpoint** Name four nonliving things that are part of a plant's or animal's environment.

2. **Art in Science** Draw a picture that shows the things that you need that your environment provides. Write labels on your drawing of what these things are.

Parts of an Ecosystem

Living and nonliving parts of an environment act together, or interact. These interacting parts make up an **ecosystem.**

The living parts of an ecosystem depend on nonliving parts. For example, coastal redwood trees need sunlight, soil, and air. They also need a lot of water. There is plenty of rain in winter, but little rain falls in the summer. In summer, the trees get water from fog that rolls in from the ocean.

The living parts of an ecosystem also depend on one another. For example, some sea birds eat fish from the ocean. The birds nest in the redwood trees.

Habitats

The place where a living thing makes its home is its habitat. A habitat has all the things that a plant or animal needs to live. A redwood forest can be a habitat for many plants and animals. There is light, air, water, living space, and pollinators for plants. Animals find food, water, shelter, and living space in the forest. If any of these things is missing, something will change. Some plants and animals may no longer find what they need to live. Plants and animals may die. Animals may move to a different habitat.

Interacting Parts of an Ecosystem	
Living	**Nonliving**
plants	light/heat
animals	air/water
other living things	rocks/soil

The plants, animals, and environment of this coastal ecosystem interact with one another.

This coastal California redwood tree shares its environment with other plants and animals.

Dune grass has tough roots. They help the plant survive in strong wind, bright sunlight, and shifting sand.

1. ✓ Checkpoint What is an ecosystem?

2. Main Idea and Details Read the caption about the dune grass. Give the main idea. List details that support it.

Groups Within Ecosystems

Coyotes roam the rough brush called chaparral on coastal hillsides in Southern California. All the living things of the same kind that live in the same place at the same time are a **population.** A group of coyotes make up a population.

Coyotes hunt California ground squirrels. The ground squirrels eat plants and live in burrows in the chaparral. All the populations that live together in the same place make up a **community.** The coyotes, ground squirrels, and chaparral plants are part of a community. The populations in a community depend on each other.

A coyote hunts ground squirrels.

Ecosystems Change

Ecosystems change over time. The change starts when one part of the ecosystem changes. This change causes other parts of the ecosystem to change. For example, in one winter the chaparral might get more rain than usual. Plants grow more. Ground squirrels now have more food than usual. This may cause the population of ground squirrels to grow.

The rise in the number of ground squirrels affects the coyotes. The population of coyotes can grow because coyotes find plenty of food.

If a winter has less rain than usual, plants provide less food. Less food supports fewer ground squirels. As a result, the population of coyotes remains small or decreases.

All the coyotes in one place make up a population.

Fires move quickly through chaparral. This provides space, water, and sunlight for new plants to grow.

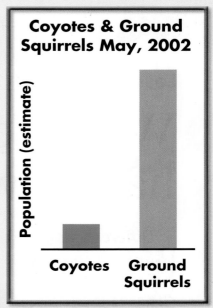

Coyotes & Ground Squirrels May, 2002

Population (estimate)

Coyotes   Ground Squirrels

More food than usual supports a large ground squirrel population.

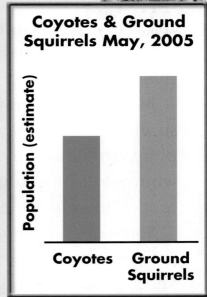

Coyotes & Ground Squirrels May, 2005

Population (estimate)

Coyotes   Ground Squirrels

If the ground squirrel population is large, the coyote population might become large too.

✓ Lesson Checkpoint

1. How do coyotes, ground squirrels, and plants interact in their environment?

2. What might happen to plants and animals if there is more rain than usual?

3. **Writing** in Science **Descriptive** Describe a population in your **science journal**. Then describe the community to which your population belongs.

75

Which ecosystems have few trees?

Different places on Earth have different climates. Some land ecosystems have climates that support only a few trees.

Grassland

Think about looking out over a wide, grassy field. A strong summer breeze makes the tops of the grasses move like waves on the ocean. A **grassland** is a kind of land ecosystem. It has many grasses and flowering plants, but few trees. A climate of cool or cold winters and hot summers supports grasslands. The climate includes little rain, so the soil is dry. Trees cannot grow well in this soil. They need more water. The trees grow mostly in the wetter soil along rivers and creeks.

Many grasses grow well in this kind of habitat. They survive because they have deep roots. These roots help the plants in many ways. When grazing animals, fire, or the cold winters kill the plants above ground, the roots survive. Deep roots also help the plants find water in the dry, hot summers.

Some grasslands get more rain than others. Tall-grass prairies grow in the wetter eastern parts of the Midwest. Short-grass prairies grow farther west where less rain falls.

Climate in the Kansas Grassland		
Average Temperature (°C)		Average Yearly Rainfall (cm)
Summer	Winter	90
20	2	

This is the Konza Prairie in Kansas. Like other parts of the Midwestern United States, it is grassland.

Winters are cool or cold in the grasslands. Deep roots help the plants store food for winter.

Many kinds of insects, such as this grasshopper, live in grasslands.

Once huge herds of bison roamed the grasslands. Now, only a few herds remain.

1. ✓**Checkpoint** What is a grassland?

2. **Main Idea and Details** Tell the main idea about grasslands. Give supporting details.

Desert—A Surprising Ecosystem

A **desert** is an ecosystem that gets very little rain. Days are often hot, but the nights are cool or even cold. Many people think of deserts as nothing but sand. However, most desert ecosystems are full of life. Desert plants and animals can live with little rainfall. Some plants, including cactuses, store water in their leaves or stems.

During the day, you might see a lizard warming itself on a rock. But many desert animals rest out of sight during the hottest time of day. Some stay in underground tunnels. Others find a shady spot under a plant. At night the desert comes alive. Animals come out of their hiding places to search for food.

Climate in a Desert		
Average Temperature (°C)		Average Yearly Rainfall (cm)
Summer	Winter	30
30	10	

Yucca plants provide shade and cover for small animals like snakes and lizards. Small birds eat the fruits.

This sidewinder rattlesnake usually hunts at night. It kills small animals for food.

This desert bobcat warms itself on a sunny rock in winter. At night, it hunts for birds and other small animals.

Map Fact

Joshua Tree National Park is a desert ecosystem in southern California. Joshua trees are a kind of yucca plant, which grows only about 6 centimeters a year. More than 78 kinds of birds nest in the park.

1. ✔**Checkpoint** Why do certain plants do well in deserts?

2. **Writing** in Science **Expository**
Write a newspaper article about desert animals. Explain why they are active at night.

Tundra—Land of Long Winters

The **tundra** is a cold, dry, land ecosystem. It is in the very northern part of the world. Parts of Alaska are tundra. Winters there are long and cold. Snow falls and cold winds blow. Summers are short and cool. The snow melts in summer, but the soil below the surface does not become soft. It stays frozen all year.

Summer days are very long in the tundra. In some places, the summer Sun shines 24 hours a day. Winter days are very short. Some places get no sunlight at all in winter.

Many plants cannot grow in this climate. For example, few trees grow in the tundra. Their roots cannot grow in frozen soil. Small plants grow here instead. These include grasses and wildflowers.

In summer, the melting snow forms ponds in the tundra. Many ducks, geese, and swans nest near these ponds. Other birds also nest in the tundra. In summer, there are millions of insects for them to eat. Most tundra birds travel to warmer places during winter.

Climate in the Tundra		
Average Temperature (°C)		Average Yearly Rainfall (cm)
Summer	Winter	
6	30° below 0	10

Caribou travel in large herds. In winter, they find food by digging through the snow with their front hooves.

What type of plant is missing in this tundra? Trees! Their roots cannot grow into the frozen soil. Grasses and wild flowers grow close to the ground.

Lichens grow in clumps close to the ground. It is the main winter food of caribou.

Wolves usually travel in groups, or packs, to hunt for food. They hunt caribou, hares, and lemmings. Other large hunters include brown bears and golden eagles.

✓Lesson Checkpoint

1. What is the coldest land ecosystem?

2. List three kinds of land ecosystems.

3. **Math** in Science   A day is 24 hours long. Nome, Alaska, has about 21 hours of daylight on July 4. How many hours of darkness does it have? Nome has 4 hours of daylight on January 1. How many hours of darkness does it have then?

What are some forest ecosystems?

There are ecosystems that have different kinds of thick forests. Each kind of forest ecosystem has its own plants and animals.

Coniferous and Deciduous Forests

Coniferous forests grow mainly in northern North America, Europe, and Asia. They grow where summers are warm and dry. Winters are cold and snowy. Spruce, fir, and pine are some coniferous trees.

Mosses and lichens can grow under coniferous trees. Few other things grow there. Many animals find food and shelter in coniferous forests.

Climates where deciduous forests grow are generally warmer than climates of coniferous forests. Deciduous forests get rain in summer and snow in winter. Oak, maple, and beech are some deciduous trees. They drop their leaves in the fall. For part of the year, sunlight reaches the forest floor. Many shrubs and other plants can grow there. These plants provide habitats for animals.

1. **✔Checkpoint** How are coniferous and deciduous forests alike and different?

2. **Writing in Science** **Descriptive** Write a short story about walking through an evergreen forest or a deciduous forest. Describe what you see, hear, and feel.

Climate in a Coniferous Forest

Average Temperature (°C)		Average Yearly Rainfall (cm)
Summer	Winter	50
8	−20	

North American Coniferous Forest

Moose eat twigs, bark, roots, and young stems of woody plants. In summer, they feed on water plants like water lilies.

Many insects and birds live in deciduous forests. Woodpeckers eat beetles that dig into tree trunks.

Climate in a Deciduous Forest

Average Temperature (°C)		Average Yearly Rainfall (cm)
Summer	Winter	160
25	5	

North American Deciduous Forest

Beavers use their sharp teeth to cut forest trees and branches. They build dams of sticks and mud across streams.

83

Tropical Forests

Where could you find a spider so big that it eats birds? These spiders live in a tropical forest near the equator. The climate in tropical forests can be warm and rainy all year long. Tall trees let little sunlight reach the forest floor. Some of the trees can be 35 meters tall—taller than a ten-story building. Plants such as orchids grow on the trees.

Most animals of the tropical forest live in the trees. Some spend their whole lives there.

Some animals, such as bats, can be found in many different tropical forests. Others live in certain forests and not in others. For example, many kinds of beetles live in only one forest in Brazil. They are found nowhere else. The tropical rainforest has huge numbers of insects. No one has ever named them all.

Woolly monkeys live in South America. They live in trees and eat fruits, leaves, seeds, and some insects.

Rainbow lorikeets live in the tropical forests of eastern Asia and Australia. These noisy birds eat nectar, flowers, seeds, and fruit.

Climate in a Rainforest		
Average Temperature (°C)		Average Yearly Rainfall (cm)
Summer	Winter	
25	25	300

These red stinkbugs live in tropical forests.

Venomous snakes, such as this palm viper, live in tropical forests. Most snakes eat frogs, lizards, and other small animals.

1. What kind of climate can tropical forests have?

2. List three kinds of forests.

3. **Writing** in Science **Descriptive** Write a paragraph in your **science journal** describing how climate affects different kinds of forests.

What are water ecosystems?

Water ecosystems can have fresh water, salt water, or both.

Freshwater Ecosystems

Freshwater ecosystems include lakes, ponds, rivers, and streams. Lakes and ponds are water surrounded by land. Rivers and streams are moving water. Rain or melting snow supplies water for most lakes and rivers. Springs that flow from underground supply water for others. Many plants and animals live in lakes and rivers.

The Everglades in south Florida is a large wetland. A **wetland** is low land that is covered by water at least part of the year. Water flows very slowly through the Everglades south to Florida Bay. This "river of grass" is very wide. But its water is very shallow. Trees, grasses, and water plants live there. Animals such as fish, bears, and birds live there, too.

Florida Everglades

Many large Florida springs are the winter homes of manatees. These slow-moving mammals eat water plants.

Alligators have sharp teeth and strong jaws. They eat fish, birds, and anything else they can catch.

1. ✓ **Checkpoint** Name four kinds of freshwater ecosystems.

2. **Technology** in Science Use the Internet to find out about the plants and animals that live in the Everglades. Make a list of these plants and animals.

Saltwater Ecosystems

Oceans cover much of Earth's surface. There is salt in ocean water. The ocean is shallow along the shore. Clams, crabs, kelp, fish, and coral live here. Otters, seals, and sea birds swim and dive for fish.

The ocean gets very deep, but most life is in the top 200 meters of water. Very small animals feed on tiny algae that make food. Large fish and whales also live here. The deep ocean is dark and cold, and it has little food. Few animals live here.

Many rivers flow into the ocean. Fresh water from the rivers can mix with salt water from the ocean. Wetlands called salt marshes can form in these areas. Plants and animals here are able to live in salty water and soil. Many plants grow in salt marshes. Some tiny animals in the muddy marsh are too small to see with just your eye. Many kinds of fishes, crabs, and other ocean animals begin their lives in salt marshes.

Life in the Oceans	
Kinds of Living Things	275,000 kinds
Longest Animal	Blue Whale, 33 meters
Longest Fish	Whale Shark, 12 meters
Fastest Ocean Animal	Sailfish, 30 meters per second

This reef cuttlefish can squirt a jet of water out of its body. This helps it escape from an enemy.

A coral is an animal about the size of an ant. It builds a hard, rocky skeleton around itself for protection. Millions of corals build a coral reef.

Map Fact

The Great Barrier Reef is a huge coral reef. It is along the eastern coast of Australia. Australia is in the southern Pacific Ocean.

Australian Great Barrier Reef

✓ **Lesson Checkpoint**

1. Where do most corals live?

2. Where is most life found in the oceans?

3. **Writing in Science** **Narrative** Find out about an animal that lives in salty water. Then write a story in your **science journal** about that animal. Title your story (Name of your animal)—This Is Your Life!

Investigate How can you show that mold needs food?

You have learned that animals of each ecosystem find the food they need where they live. In this activity you will show that in order to stay alive and grow, mold must get the food it needs. If it is in an "ecosystem" without the food it needs, it will not grow.

Materials

gloves

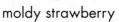
moldy strawberry

hand lens

bread slice
(without preservatives)

foil square

2 plastic bags

dropper

cup with water

Process Skills

You **interpret data** when you use data from an investigation to answer a question.

What to Do

1 **Observe** the mold on the strawberry. Draw what the mold looks like.

Be careful!

Wear gloves.

2 Lightly rub some mold off the strawberry onto the bread. Do the same for the foil.

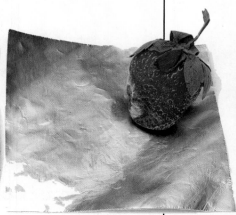

3 Put the bread in a bag. Put the foil in another bag. Use a dropper to add 10 drops of water to the 2 spots where the mold was rubbed.

4 Seal the bags. Put them in a warm, dark place.

After you seal the bags, do not reopen them.

5 After 4 days, observe the bags. Draw pictures of any mold growing in the bags.

Mold gets the energy needed for growth from the bread.

Drawings of Observations		
Mold on Strawberry	**Mold on Bread**	**Mold on Foil**

Explain Your Results

1. In which bag did mold grow?
2. **Interpret Data** Which has the food that mold needs to grow, the bread or the foil? Explain.

Go Further

Does mold need light to grow? Investigate. Use a camera to keep a record.

Math in Science

Comparing Data

The major grasslands of North America are located in six areas, as shown on the map. The tall-grass prairie, the mixed-grass prairie, and the short-grass prairie together are known as the Central Prairies.

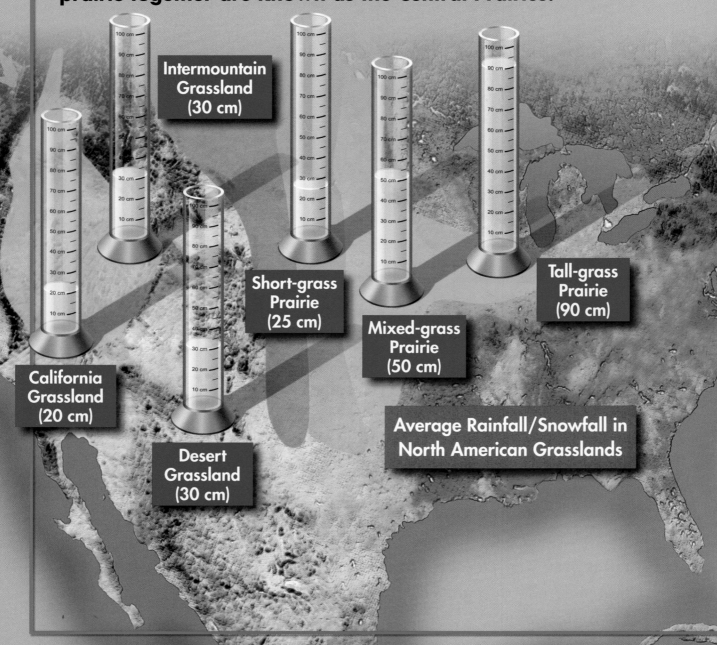

Intermountain Grassland (30 cm)

California Grassland (20 cm)

Desert Grassland (30 cm)

Short-grass Prairie (25 cm)

Mixed-grass Prairie (50 cm)

Tall-grass Prairie (90 cm)

Average Rainfall/Snowfall in North American Grasslands

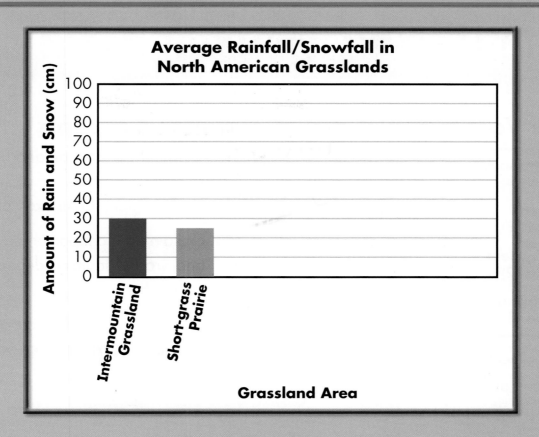

Average Rainfall/Snowfall in North American Grasslands

Amount of Rain and Snow (cm)

Grassland Area

Intermountain Grassland

Short-grass Prairie

Use the map and the graph to answer each question.

1 Copy the bar graph on grid paper and complete it. Your graph should show the data for all six grasslands.

2 Which describes how the amount of rain and snow in the Central Prairies changes?

A. increases from west to east   B. decreases from west to east

C. increases from north to south   D. decreases from north to south

3 Which grassland gets the most rain and snow? Which gets the least?

Lab zone **Take-Home Activity**

Use the library or the Internet to find data about rainfall and snowfall amounts in any type of ecosystem in North America. Show the data on a bar graph.

Chapter 3 Review and Test Prep

Use Vocabulary

community (page 74)	**grassland** (page 76)
desert (page 78)	**population** (page 74)
ecosystem (page 72)	**tundra** (page 80)
environment (page 71)	**wetland** (page 86)

Use the term from the list above that best completes each sentence.

1. Low land that is often covered by water is a(n) _____.

2. All the moose that live in one place are a(n) _____.

3. Everything that surrounds a living thing is its _____.

4. An ecosystem with hot days and little rain is a(n) _____.

5. All the populations living in the same place form a(n) _____.

6. The ecosystem that is coldest and farthest north is the _____.

7. All the living and nonliving things that interact in an area form a(n) _____.

8. An ecosystem with many grasses and few trees is a(n) _____.

Explain Concepts

9. Explain how dry soil and frozen soil affect the types of plants that grow in them. Give examples.

10. Explain how chaparral, coyotes, and ground squirrels depend on each other.

11. Explain how some desert plants are able to have enough water.

Process Skills

12. Wheat and oats are cereal grasses. **Infer** in which ecosystem these farm crops would grow best.

13. Desert snakes eat kangaroo rats. **Predict** what would happen to the population of rats if the population of snakes grew larger.

14. **Interpret data** Use the data table below. Find the difference between the greatest yearly rainfall and the least.

Forest	Yearly rainfall
Coniferous forest (Alaska)	70 cm
Deciduous forest (Maryland)	120 cm
Tropical forest (Hawaii)	1,234 cm

Main Idea and Details

15. Draw the graphic organizer below. Choose an ecosystem for the main idea. Fill in details that support the main idea.

> **All _____ ecosystems have similar features.**

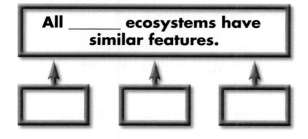

Test Prep

Choose the letter that best completes the statement or answers the question.

16. A group of trout that live in a river make up a(n)

- (A) community.
- (B) population.
- (C) habitat.
- (D) ecosystem.

17. Which ecosystem has a warm, rainy climate?

- (F) tropical forest
- (G) tundra
- (H) evergreen forest
- (I) desert

18. Which populations might live in a wetland?

- (A) corals, whales, and fish
- (B) coniferous trees, foxes, and woodpeckers
- (C) birds, alligators, and grasses
- (D) cactuses, rattlesnakes, and bobcats

19. Explain why the answer you selected for Question 16 is best. For each of the answers you did not select, give a reason why it is not the best choice.

20. Writing in Science

Expository Write a paragraph about a plant or animal and how it survives in a desert ecosystem.

Eric Stolen

"Getting wet, dirty, hot, bug-bitten and chased by critters" are things Eric Stolen loves.

Eric Stolen is a wildlife biologist at NASA's Kennedy Space Center, which includes a wildlife refuge. Mr. Stolen studies how wading birds choose a place to live and how they get food.

Mr. Stolen finds ways to study the birds without them noticing he is there. Sometimes he wades through mud. Other times he flies over the birds in a helicopter. He uses binoculars and other tools to see what the birds are doing.

When Eric was growing up, he often went camping, hiking, and boating. He became interested in nature and animals while he was in grade school. Later on, Mr. Stolen studied biology in college. He never tires of studying nature because there are so many interesting things to see and learn.

Eric Stolen

Lab zone Take-Home Activity

Spend an hour outdoors. Find a place where you can see birds or other animals. Write in your **science journal** about the animals you see and what they do.

Chapter 4
Plants and Animals Living Together

You Will Discover

- ways that plants and animals interact.
- how food energy moves through an ecosystem.
- what a healthy environment for people includes.

online
Student Edition
pearsonsuccessnet.com

97

How do plants and animals interact?

consumer

producer

herbivore

98

Chapter 4
Vocabulary

decomposer

decay

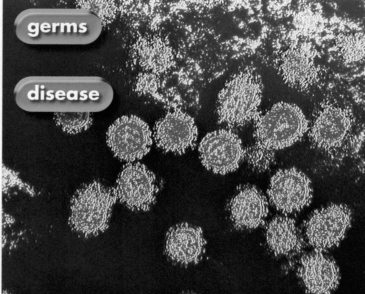

germs

disease

omnivore

carnivore   predator

competition   prey

Explore How do pill bugs stay safe?

Materials

plastic jar

soil, dead leaves, lettuce

cup with water

spoon

4 pill bugs

cheesecloth

rubber band

What to Do

1 Make a habitat for pill bugs.

2 Use the spoon to gently put pill bugs into the habitat. Add 3 spoonfuls of water. Cover the jar.

cheesecloth

rubber band

Notice how a pill bug can roll into a ball. In a ball, its hard body covering helps protect its soft belly. A pill bug also may hide in dark places to avoid enemies.

lettuce

dead leaves

layer of soil

3 **Observe** the pill bugs for 5 minutes each day for one week. Describe what they do.

Explain Your Results

1. **Infer** How might rolling into a ball help a pill bug stay safe?

2. Why might pill bugs need lettuce or other plants in their habitat?

How to Read Science

TARGET SKILL

Draw Conclusions

A good reader can put together facts and then build a new idea, or a conclusion. The conclusion should make sense and be supported by the facts. You might use a graphic organizer to show a conclusion.

Science Article

What's on the Menu

Shrews need food to be active. They find a lot of pill bugs to eat under rotting logs. One type of spider eats only such bugs. Toads, lizards, and birds eat pill bugs, too.

Apply It!

Make a graphic organizer like the one shown. Fill it in with three facts from the paragraph above. Then **infer** a conclusion. Show how the facts led to the conclusion.

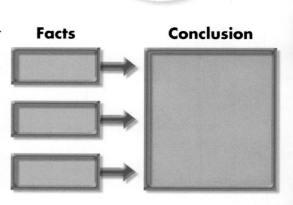

Facts   **Conclusion**

You Are There!

You are floating in clear ocean water. You look down through a face mask. You see a school of small fish. They swim left, right, up, and down. They all move together. Suddenly the school turns. You blink with surprise. When you look again, the school is gone! Where did the fish go? Why were they swimming together like that?

AudioText

Lesson 1

How do living things interact?

Living things may affect each other when they interact. The interactions can be helpful, harmful, or neither.

Ways Living Things Interact

Living things interact in different ways. Their interactions may help them survive. Study the examples in the chart. Those living in groups help each other. One kind of living thing might help another kind without being helped in return. Or different kinds might help each other.

Ways Living Things Interact		
Helping in Groups	Members of a herd protect each other.	
One Kind Helping Another	A tree helps a flower get light.	
Two Kinds Helping Each Other	While it drinks flower nectar, an insect spreads pollen among the flowers.	

1. **✔Checkpoint** List three ways in which living things might interact.

2. **Writing in Science** **Narrative** In your **science journal** describe a day during which you helped as a member of a group. Describe how the group helped you.

One bee may find flowers. Then it will fly back to the beehive and move in a certain way. This "dance" tells the other bees where the flowers are.

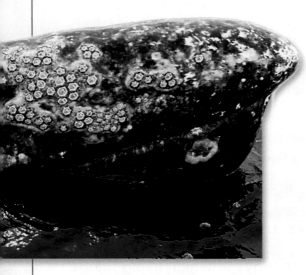

A grown barnacle is about 5 cm wide. It grabs food from the water that the whale swims through.

Living in Groups

Animals that live together might all help protect the group from predators. Together, the animals may be safer than each animal alone. For example, prairie dogs live in groups. Coyotes and golden eagles eat them. Coyotes hunt on the ground. Eagles hunt from the sky. Prairie dogs take turns standing watch at their burrow openings. If any prairie dog senses danger, it whistles. At this sound, the whole group runs and hides. All the prairie dogs stay hidden until the danger has passed.

One Kind of Living Thing Helping Another Kind

Notice the barnacles on the whale. Some barnacles swim through the ocean and attach to the skin of a whale. A barnacle usually spends its whole life attached to the same whale.

The barnacle opens and closes its shell to catch food as the whale moves through the water. The barnacles do not harm the whales. They don't help the whales either. In this partnership, only one partner is helped—the barnacle.

Helping One Another

Some kinds of living things help each other. The moth seen here shares its life with only one kind of yucca plant.

The moth helps the yucca by carrying pollen from another yucca. The yucca helps the moth by giving it a habitat and food for its young. The moth lays her eggs in the flower pods. Each larva hatches in the pods and eats some of the seeds the flower pod makes.

The cleaner fish is another example. Several kinds of small fish clean larger fish. They eat pests off the big fish. The cleaner fish gets a meal. The other fish gets clean and stays healthy.

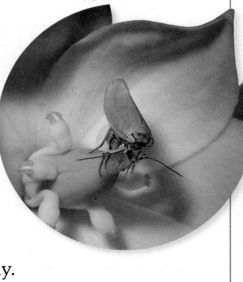

A yucca moth provides a ball of sticky pollen from another yucca. In exchange it lays its eggs in the flower.

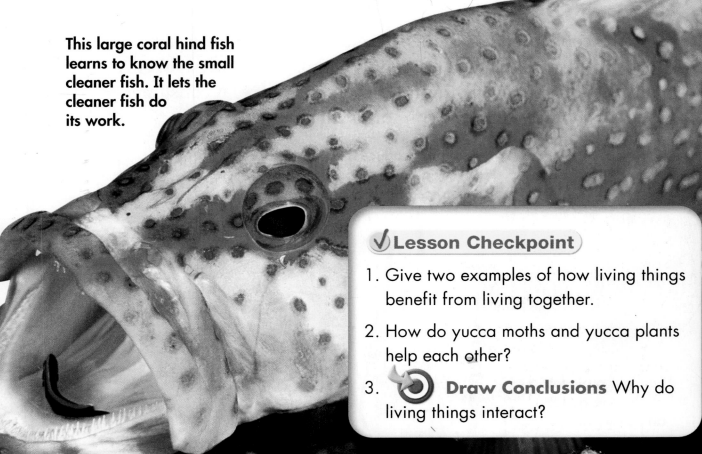

This large coral hind fish learns to know the small cleaner fish. It lets the cleaner fish do its work.

✓ **Lesson Checkpoint**

1. Give two examples of how living things benefit from living together.

2. How do yucca moths and yucca plants help each other?

3. **Draw Conclusions** Why do living things interact?

How do living things get energy?

Plants get energy from the sun. Animals get energy from plants or from other animals that eat plants.

Sources of Energy

Green plants make their own food. A living thing that makes its own food is a **producer.** Producers use energy from sunlight to make food out of matter from the air and soil.

Many living things cannot make their own food. They must get their energy from food that they eat. A living thing that eats food is a **consumer.**

Kinds of Consumers

Some consumers eat plants, others eat animals, and some eat both. A consumer that eats only plants is an **herbivore.** A consumer that eats only animals is a **carnivore.** A consumer that eats both plants and animals is an **omnivore.**

Cattails produce their own food. Every animal's food energy can be traced back to producers.

The crayfish is a consumer because it must eat food for energy.

Sunlight provides all the energy for an ecosystem.

Sheep are herbivores. They eat only plants.

A wolf is a carnivore. It eats only meat.

A bear is an omnivore. It eats both plants and animals.

Food Chains

Energy passes to living things within food chains. Food chains are groups of producers and consumers that interact in a special way. A consumer eats a producer. The producer passes energy to that consumer. That consumer may then become **prey** for another consumer. Prey is any animal that is hunted by others for food.

The prey passes energy on to a **predator.** A predator is a consumer that hunts for food. In this way, energy can move from a producer to a predator. As each living thing uses food energy, some energy is given off as heat.

The raccoon is an omnivore. It eats crayfish, other animals, and plants.

✓ Checkpoint

1. Trace the transfer of energy through a food chain that includes raccoons, crayfish, cattails, and sunlight.

2. **Art** in Science Draw a food chain that shows how grass, a cow, and a person drinking milk are connected.

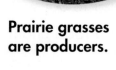

Energy in a Food Web

A food chain is simple. Energy moves from one type of living thing to another. Real life is not so simple. Energy often moves in many different ways. It might transfer from one kind of producer to many kinds of consumers. One kind of consumer might be prey for more than one kind of predator.

Energy flow in a community forms a web. A food web is made up of more than one food chain. Food webs tie a community together. Each part of a web affects other parts.

An example of a food web is found on the Great Plains. Prairie grasses grow there. They are producers. Energy flows from the grasses to the animals that eat them. These animals include prairie dogs and mice. Prairie dogs are prey for ferrets and golden eagles. Ferrets are prey for badgers. So energy can flow through the food web from grasses to golden eagles and badgers.

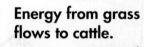

Energy from grass flows to cattle.

Energy from grass flows to prairie dogs.

Prairie grasses are producers.

Energy from grass flows to mice.

A Changing Food Web

If one part of a food web is removed, other parts change. For example, prairie dogs once built large colonies on the grassy plains. Then cattle began to feed on these same plains. This reduced the habitat for prairie dogs. Many prairie dogs also became sick and died. As a result, the number of prairie dogs was reduced.

Removing one part of the food web caused a number of things to happen. The cattle had more food, but ferrets had less. With fewer prairie dogs to eat, ferrets no longer had the food they needed. Ferrets began to die out.

This, in turn, affected predators of ferrets, such as badgers. Now badgers had to look for other food. Golden eagles and foxes also hunt prairie dogs. They too had to get more food energy from other kinds of prey, such as mice. All this can happen when one part of a food web is removed.

Ferrets eat mostly prairie dogs. Energy flows to the ferrets.

Badgers eat ferrets. Energy flows to the badgers.

Golden eagles eat prairie dogs and mice. Energy from these animals flows to the eagles.

✔ Lesson Checkpoint

1. How did reducing the number of prairie dogs affect ferrets?

2. How does the loss of prairie dogs affect eagles and foxes?

3. **Draw Conclusions** Tell what happens when a food chain is broken.

The young trees in this forest compete for sunlight and room to grow.

This male bower bird competes with other males to attract females to its nest.

Many different animals compete for water in dry places.

Lesson 3

How do living things compete?

Maybe you have tried to fit under an umbrella with another person to stay dry. You had to compete with the person for shelter. Living things often compete with one another. Usually they compete for food, water, and room to live.

Competing for Resources

Picture yourself in a dark, cool forest. The treetops form a roof high above you. Few small trees are growing. Why? They struggle to get enough energy from sunlight to grow. The small trees are in **competition** with one another. When two or more living things need the same resources, they are in competition. Since the tall trees in this forest get most of the sunlight, the small trees compete for the light that is left.

Living things compete for many kinds of resources besides light. These resources include food, water, and living space. The winners in these competitions survive. The losers might not survive.

 SciLinks **Take It to the Net** pearsonsuccessnet.com | keyword: competition code: g3p110

Predators and Prey

Many predators may compete for the same prey. Faster, stronger ones might catch more food. For example, some hunting birds may get more food by stealing prey caught by the other birds. Predators with greater ability are more likely to survive and reproduce. They pass these valuable traits on to their young.

Different types of predators may compete with each other. Lions and hyenas might want the same prey, for example. The lions hunt and kill the prey. Then the hyenas fight the lions and try to steal it.

Animals that are prey also compete. Deer that are stronger or healthier than others are more likely to protect themselves. They are better able to escape from predators.

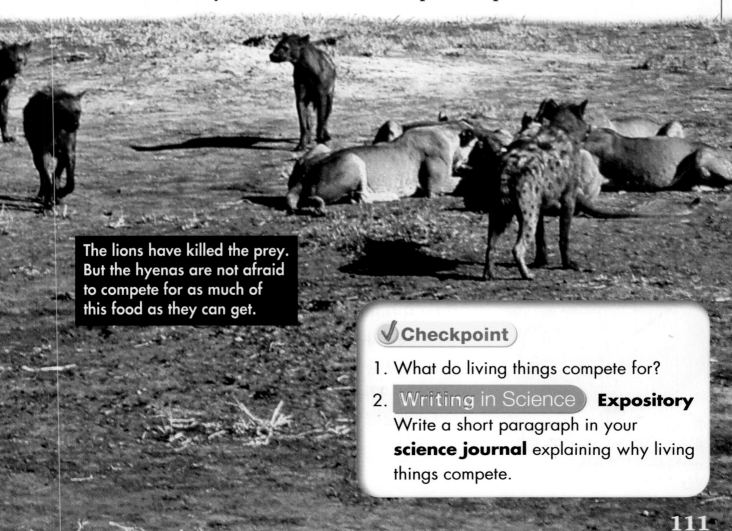

The lions have killed the prey. But the hyenas are not afraid to compete for as much of this food as they can get.

✓ Checkpoint

1. What do living things compete for?
2. **Writing in Science** **Expository**
   Write a short paragraph in your **science journal** explaining why living things compete.

Other Kinds of Competition

Some living things compete for space. Purple loosestrife is a plant that was brought to the United States. Animals here do not eat it, and it spreads easily. Purple loosestrife takes space away from other plants. Some plants are crowded out completely.

Animals and humans can compete for space. People move to places where animals live. People may see coyotes in their backyards or flocks of sea gulls on their beaches.

Living things may compete for oxygen. Algae are like plants. They provide oxygen and food for fish and other living things. If too many algae grow, some do not get enough sunlight. These algae die. Many tiny consumers of dead algae grow and use up oxygen in the water. Fish and other living things compete for the oxygen that is left.

A Competition Cycle

Lemmings are small mammals that live in the tundra. When there is plenty of grass for them to eat, the lemming population can grow quickly. Then there is less food available because so many lemmings are eating it.

After three years, too many lemmings are competing for the food. Many leave to find food elsewhere. The lemming population becomes smaller. Then the grass can grow back. The competition cycle begins again.

Purple loosestrife competes with other plants for space.

Sea gulls compete with humans for living space.

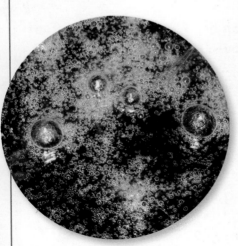

If too many algae grow, there is less oxygen for fish and other living things.

Competition between these lemmings for food can follow a cycle over time.

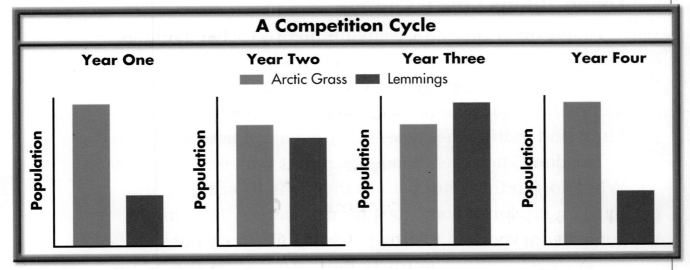

A Competition Cycle

Year One   **Year Two**   **Year Three**   **Year Four**

◼ Arctic Grass   ◼ Lemmings

There is plenty of arctic grass for lemmings to eat.

The population of lemmings grows. The amount of grass goes down.

The population of lemmings grows. There is not enough food. Many lemmings leave or die.

With fewer lemmings, the grass grows back. Once again there is enough food.

✓ **Lesson Checkpoint**

1. Why do living things compete with one another?

2. What kind of living thing usually survives in a competition?

3. **Draw Conclusions** Explain the pattern of change in the lemming population over time.

How do environments change?

Plants and animals can change their environment. Natural events, such as fire, can change the environment too. These changes affect plants and animals that live in the environment. Changes often occur in patterns.

Living Things Cause Change

People often change the environment to better suit their needs, but they are not the only ones. For example, when a beaver builds a dam, many changes occur. Water backs up behind the dam. Then a new wetland habitat grows. Fish, birds, and many other types of animals can now live there.

The dams, however, flood places that were once dry. What do you think happens to the living things that once lived on dry land? Some look for new homes. They might compete for space in nearby places. Others may not survive.

Beavers change the environment when they build their homes and dams of sticks and mud.

This place was once a grassy meadow. How has this beaver dam changed it?

Natural Events Cause Change

Natural events also change environments. For example, hurricanes can change coastlines. They wash away beaches and knock down trees. They can cause terrible floods.

Floods change environments too. They kill plants and wash away birds' nests. Floods spread thick blankets of mud. They also carry rich soil from one place to other places.

Too little water also causes changes. Little rain falls during a drought. Plants die from lack of water. If animals cannot find enough water, then they may die or move to other places.

The Mississippi River sometimes floods. The floodwater carries rich soil down the river. When floodwater drains off the land, it leaves behind a layer of soil.

High winds and water will change this environment.

Few plants, animals, or humans can live in a drought area.

✔ Checkpoint

1. Describe ways that living things and natural events can cause an environment to change.

2. **Writing in Science** **Descriptive**
   Write a paragraph or a poem in your **science journal** about one change you have seen in your environment.

115

Living Things Return

On May 18, 1980, the volcano Mt. St. Helens erupted in the State of Washington. This eruption was huge. Winds carried clouds of ash around the world.

The blast changed the local environment. It knocked over trees. It burned whole forests. Rivers of mud covered large areas.

There were few signs of life after the eruption. Over time, however, wind carried the seeds of grasses, flowers, and trees to the mountain. New plants began to grow. Soon spiders and beetles arrived. Birds returned to live in the standing dead trees. Each new change allowed more kinds of plants and the animals that depend on them to live there again. Today, even elk live on Mt. St. Helens. The mountain is filled with life once more.

In September 2004, Mt. St. Helens rumbled to life again. An active volcano can bring sudden change at any time.

Mt. St. Helens erupts.

Fires also change environments. Fires happen often in forests and grasslands. Lightning may strike a tree. A burning branch falls to the ground. Then a fire creeps along the forest floor. It removes small plants competing for space to grow. However, the plants that do not burn will have more living space. Also, ash from fires is good for the soil. It helps plants to grow.

Eruptions and fires are examples of events that cause change. The changes often kill plants and destroy animal homes. The changes, however, may improve habitats for other plants and animals.

Ground fires kill plants but help new plants grow.

✓ **Checkpoint**

1. Explain how fire is a change that can improve growing conditions for plants.

2. **Art** in Science   Draw a forest before a fire. Then draw the forest on fire. Finally, draw the forest five years later.

This young pine grows fast in an area cleaned by fire.

Very few plants remained after the volcano erupted.

New life has returned to the mountain.

This burnt stump gives a spruce seedling a place to grow.

117

Many years will go by before these Douglas fir seedlings become full-grown trees.

Smaller trees compete for sunlight because they are shaded by tall trees.

Map Fact
Forests of tall coniferous trees grow in the temperate rain forest along the coast of the State of Washington.

Patterns of Change

Living things change together. These changes often happen in patterns. Let's look at one growth pattern.

Douglas fir trees grow in cool, misty forests in the northwestern United States. Squirrels often knock the cones from the trees. The seeds from the cones sprout on the forest floor. The seedlings compete for sunlight and other resources. A few survive and grow into giant trees. Some of these giants grow old, die, and fall.

Mushrooms and other decomposers feed on the dead trees. A **decomposer** is a living thing that breaks down waste and living things that have died. This action is called **decay.** Decay returns certain materials to the soil. Decomposers cause the dead trees to slowly crumble into the soil.

Western hemlock trees live in the same forest. Seeds from their cones can land on the decaying Douglas fir logs. The decaying logs supply things that help young seedlings to grow. Also, light reaches logs in the open where the giant trees once stood. The hemlock seeds sprout and grow quickly.

SciLinks Take It to the Net
pearsonsuccessnet.com
keyword: decomposer
code: g3p118

In time, the hemlocks become tall trees. They provide homes for squirrels, spotted owls, and other animals.

When the older hemlocks are near the end of their lives, carpenter ants and decomposers go to work. The ants build nests in the decaying tree trunks. The old trunks fall to the ground. They decay and become part of the soil.

The life cycles of the trees are connected. The changes occur in a pattern that happens over and over again.

These mushrooms are decomposers. They find this dead log a good food source.

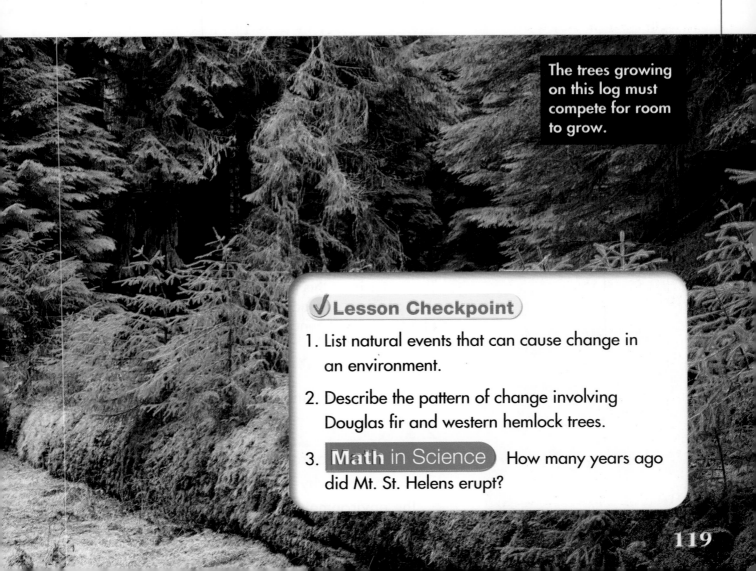

The trees growing on this log must compete for room to grow.

✓ Lesson Checkpoint

1. List natural events that can cause change in an environment.

2. Describe the pattern of change involving Douglas fir and western hemlock trees.

3. **Math** in Science How many years ago did Mt. St. Helens erupt?

Lesson 5

What is a healthy environment for people?

People find what they need for life in their environment. The environment affects how people live.

What People Need

Like all living things, people need food to live. Most people buy food at a store. That food comes from farms and ranches. Some people have the job of making sure the food we eat is safe.

People need water that is safe to drink and air that is safe to breathe. People also need shelter to protect them from the weather. Shelter helps keep people at a comfortable temperature.

People need a clean environment. Wastes must be removed. Garbage may be taken to places such as landfills.

The water from this fountain was purified, or made clean, at a water treatment plant.

 **Checkpoint**

1. Name three things people need to survive.

2. **Writing in Science** **Persuasive**
   Write a paragraph in your **science journal** explaining why we should protect the environment.

120

Food

The food you eat may come from close by. It may be grown thousands of miles away. Fresh food is shipped on airplanes, boats, and trucks. Other foods may be canned or frozen before being shipped.

Water

In some countries, people get their water from streams. In the United States, most water comes from wells or from special lakes. These special lakes are called reservoirs.

Shelter

Shelter changes according to where someone lives. In hot places, people need cool living spaces. In cold places, they need warm ones. In cities, people often live in large buildings.

Air

Fewer people live outside the cities. In these open spaces there are fewer cars and factories. As a result, the air is often cleaner.

Clean Environment

Everyone should help protect the environment. The environment affects the health of the people living in it.

Healthful Foods

To be sure you are getting all the vitamins, minerals, and other nutrients your body needs, you must eat a variety of healthful foods. This variety includes whole grains, fruits, and vegetables, as well as nuts, fish, eggs, dairy foods, and meats. Your body also needs a good amount of water each day.

To be kept healthful, food should be stored carefully. Fresh fruits and vegetables should be washed and kept in a cool place. Fish, eggs, dairy foods, and meats must be wrapped and kept cold. Using food while it is still fresh is also important.

Cooks and others who handle food must have clean hands and clean tools. Their tools include knives and cutting boards as well as mixers, bowls, spoons, and forks.

Drinking juice is a healthful choice.

Dairy products help bones grow strong.

Vegetables such as carrots and broccoli make good snacks.

Eat fruit, such as grapes, every day.

Fish contain materials your body needs to grow.

From Food to Energy

What happens to food after you eat it? The body's digestive system goes to work. It breaks foods down into a form that our bodies can use to live and grow. These are the main parts of the digestive system.

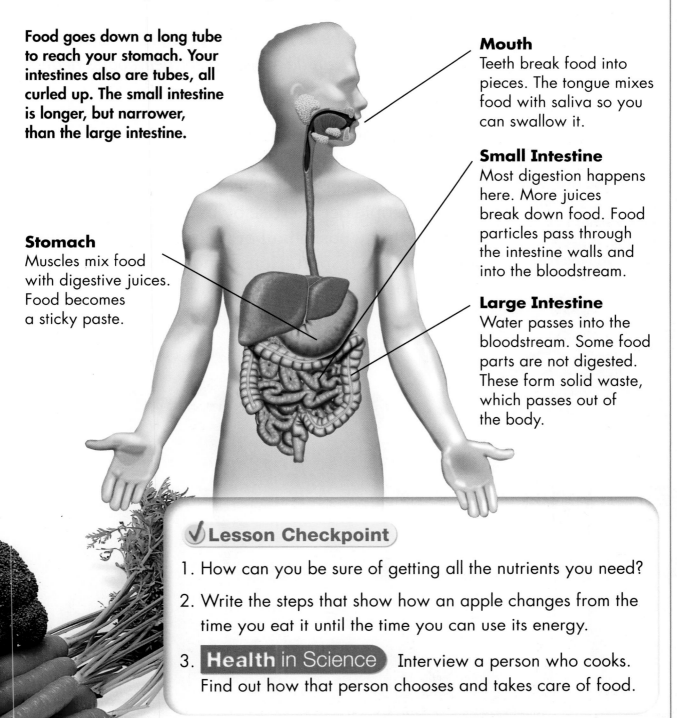

Food goes down a long tube to reach your stomach. Your intestines also are tubes, all curled up. The small intestine is longer, but narrower, than the large intestine.

Mouth
Teeth break food into pieces. The tongue mixes food with saliva so you can swallow it.

Small Intestine
Most digestion happens here. More juices break down food. Food particles pass through the intestine walls and into the bloodstream.

Stomach
Muscles mix food with digestive juices. Food becomes a sticky paste.

Large Intestine
Water passes into the bloodstream. Some food parts are not digested. These form solid waste, which passes out of the body.

✓ Lesson Checkpoint

1. How can you be sure of getting all the nutrients you need?

2. Write the steps that show how an apple changes from the time you eat it until the time you can use its energy.

3. **Health in Science** Interview a person who cooks. Find out how that person chooses and takes care of food.

123

Lesson 6

How can people stay healthy?

People want to be as healthy as possible. There are many things they can do to help keep their bodies healthy.

Exercise

Safe, regular exercise is important. People in good shape have the energy to work, play, and feel good. Exercise helps keep bodies healthy.

Some people get exercise by biking or swimming. They may play basketball or soccer. But exercise does not have to be a sport. House and yardwork can be exercise too.

When you rest, your heart beats about ninety times per minute. It beats faster when you exercise.

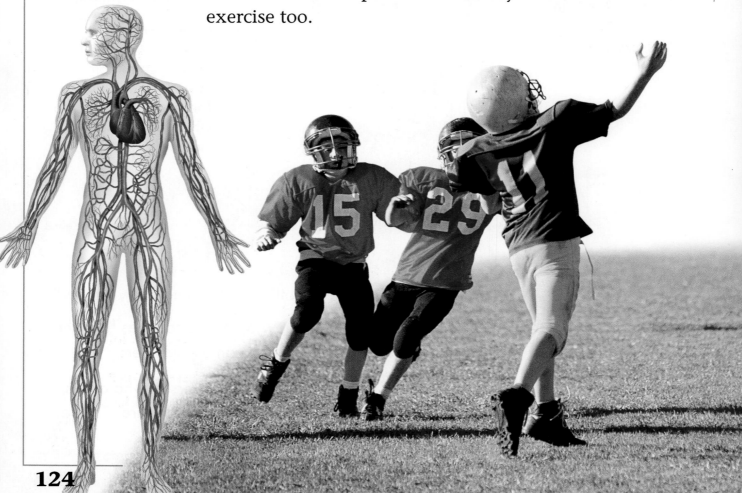

Exercise keeps a person's lungs, heart, and muscles strong. Your lungs are part of your respiratory system. They put oxygen from the air you breathe into your blood. Your heart and blood vessels are part of your circulatory system. The heart pumps blood through blood vessels. Blood carries oxygen and other materials to your muscles. Blood carries wastes away from your muscles. Exercise helps your systems work together well.

People who feel good about themselves take care of their bodies. They eat a variety of good foods. They get enough exercise and rest. They avoid things that are unhealthy.

When you breathe in, air goes down a long tube called the windpipe. The windpipe divides into two tubes. Each tube leads to a spongy lung.

The proper equipment keeps these young football players safe.

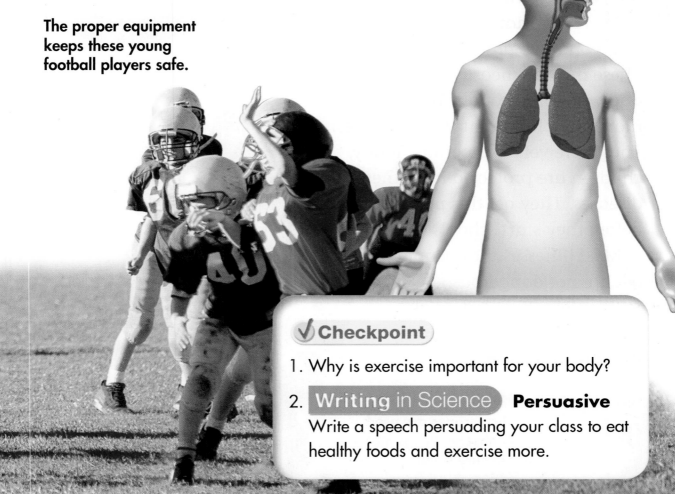

✔ **Checkpoint**

1. Why is exercise important for your body?

2. **Writing in Science** **Persuasive**
   Write a speech persuading your class to eat healthy foods and exercise more.

125

Avoiding Germs

Lin is sneezing. Shauna is coughing. Aidan has a runny nose and teary eyes. Several of their classmates are at home, sick with the flu. What are causing these illnesses? Germs.

Germs are very small living things or particles. Examples include bacteria and viruses. Many germs can make people ill. The pictures show germs that can cause disease. A **disease** is a condition in which the body or a part of the body does not work properly. You may have had one or more diseases such as the flu, chicken pox, or strep throat.

There are many other diseases that you have probably not had. These include measles, mumps, and whooping cough. Years ago, many people caught these illnesses. They were very dangerous. Today, children are protected from these diseases. They get this protection before they start school.

Most illnesses that people get are not dangerous. Still, no one likes to be sick. Everyone can help to stop the spread of germs.

This picture shows the virus that causes the flu. This picture was taken through a special, very powerful microscope.

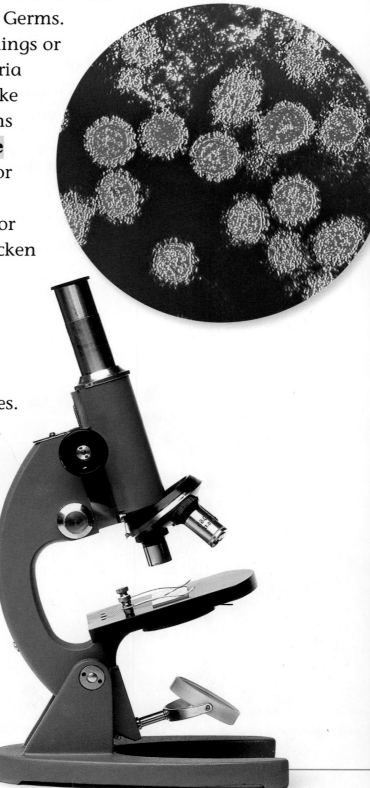

Microscopes are used to observe things that are very small.

The germs shown below cause whooping cough.

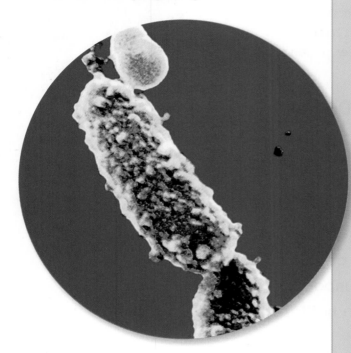

Stopping the Spread of Germs

People can help stop the spread of germs by remembering some simple rules.

- Stay home from school and work when you are ill.
- Wash your hands often, especially after using the restroom and before and after working with food.
- Cover your nose and mouth when you sneeze or cough. Wash your hands if you sneeze or cough into them.
- Clean and cover cuts and scrapes.

Wash your hands often with soap and warm water so that you don't spread germs.

The germs that cause strep throat look like tiny beads.

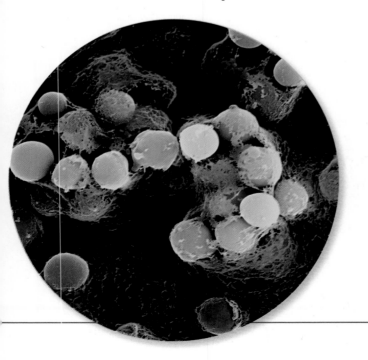

✓ Lesson Checkpoint

1. How do your respiratory and circulatory systems work together?

2. Make a list of things you can do to stop the spread of germs.

3. **Technology in Science** Choose an illness to research. Find out its causes and possible cure. Use the Internet or other technology to help in your research.

Investigate What can happen in a place without predators?

Without predators, a population of prey can starve. In this activity, your teacher will pick some students to be deer. All live in a place without predators. The deer pretend to eat the same kind of food (unpopped popcorn).

Materials

unpopped popcorn

What to Do

1 If you are picked to be a deer, line up on the side of the marked area. This is where you find food.

2 **Round A** When told, cross the area one deer at a time. Collect 5 pieces of food (unpopped popcorn) to "stay alive." Do not take more than 5 pieces.

Round	Number of Deer Alive at End of Round
Round A	
Round B	
Round C	
Round D	
Round E	

The number of rounds will depend on the number of deer and the amount of food supplied.

Record how many deer are alive at the end of each round. After each round your teacher will add food.

3 If you survive, you reproduce. Pick another student to join for the next round.

4 **Round B** Cross again and collect 5 more pieces of food.

Process Skills

You can use the **data** you **collect** during an investigation to help make an **inference**.

Deer line up here.

area where deer find food

5 Repeat until "starvation" begins. Make a bar graph to show the **data** you **collected**.

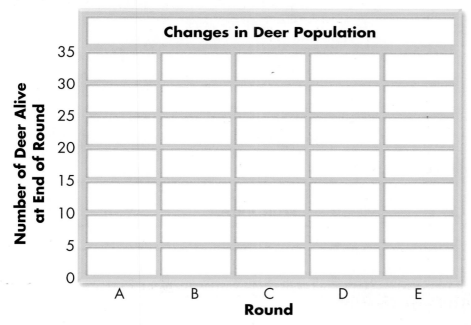

Changes in Deer Population

Number of Deer Alive at End of Round

35
30
25
20
15
10
5
0

A   B   C   D   E

Round

Explain Your Results

1. While there was plenty of food, how did the number of deer change? What finally happened?

2. **Infer** What can happen in a place without predators?

Go Further

What might happen if predators were added? Make a plan to answer this or a question of your own.

Math in Science

Health
By the Numbers

You have learned how important it is to choose the right foods for good health. It is also important to know how many Calories you need and how many are in the foods you eat.

Smiley Flakes
Serving Size 1 cup (30 grams)
Calories: 110
Total Fat: 2 grams
Cholesterol: 0 grams
Sodium: 210 milligrams
Carbohydrates: 23 grams
Fiber: 1 gram
Sugar: 1 gram

Mega Grain
Serving Size 1 cup (30 grams)
Calories: 165
Total Fat: 1 gram
Cholesterol: 0 grams
Sodium: 0 milligrams
Carbohydrates: 39 grams
Fiber: 3 grams
Sugar: 0 grams

Fresh Fruit or Fruit Juice	Serving Size	Calories
Banana slices	1 cup	133
Strawberry halves	1 cup	49
Peach slices	1 cup	66
Orange juice	1 cup	112

Milk Products	Serving Size	Calories
Whole milk	1 cup	146
Reduced-fat milk (2%)	1 cup	122
Low-fat milk (1%)	1 cup	102
Fat-free milk (Skim)	1 cup	83

eTools Take It to the Net
pearsonsuccessnet.com

Use the charts and the cereal labels to answer the questions.

1 How many more Calories are in 1 cup of whole milk than in 1 cup of fat-free milk?

2 How many Calories are in the breakfast described below?

1 cup Smiley Flakes

1 cup reduced-fat milk

1 cup strawberry halves

1 cup orange juice

3 Compare the grams of carbohydrates in the two cereals. Which has more? How much more?

4 Suppose you want to eat no more than 2,000 Calories each day. If, for breakfast, you had 1 serving each of Mega Grain, low-fat milk, banana slices, and orange juice, how many Calories would you have left for the rest of the day?

Lab zone Take-Home Activity

For one day, write down everything you eat, including the amount. Also write down the number of Calories for each food you ate. Use labels or a nutrition guide. Find the total number of Calories for the day.

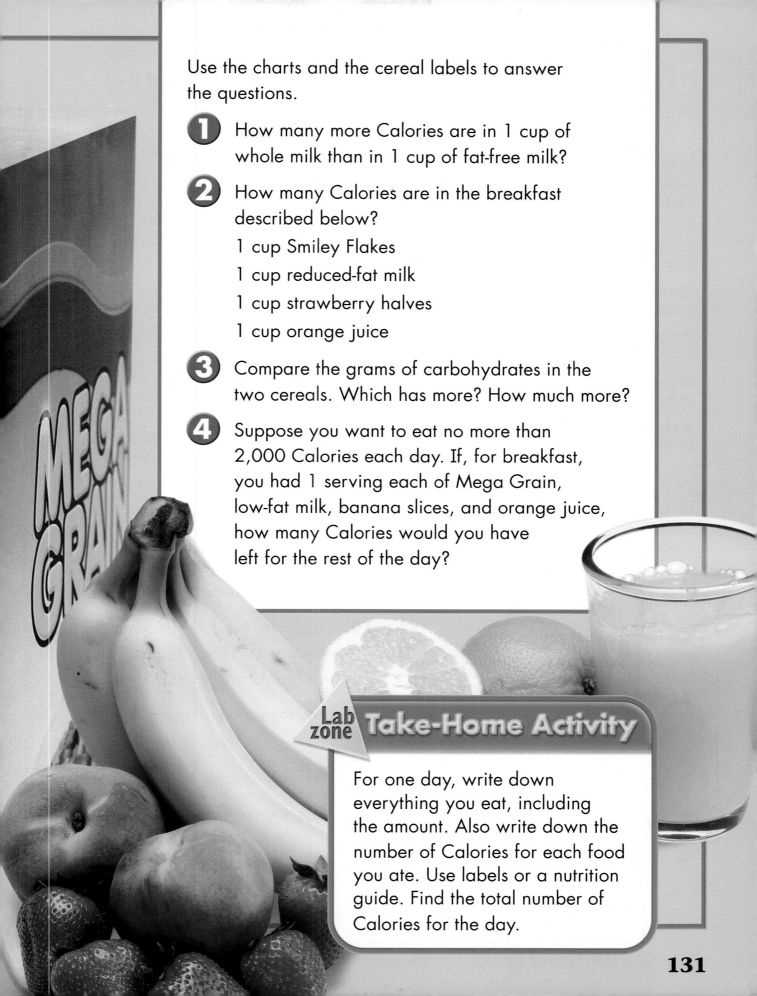

Chapter 4 Review and Test Prep

Use Vocabulary

carnivore (page 106)	**germs** (page 126)
competition (page 110)	**herbivore** (page 106)
consumer (page 106)	**omnivore** (page 106)
decomposer (page 118)	**predator** (page 107)
decay (page 118)	**prey** (page 107)
disease (page 126)	**producer** (page 106)

Write the vocabulary word or words from the list above that best completes each sentence.

1. A(n) _____ eats only animals while a(n) _____ eats only plants.

2. Bacteria and viruses are _____, which can cause _____.

3. A(n) _____ is a consumer that hunts another for food.

4. A(n) _____ is a living thing that must eat food to get energy.

5. A(n) _____ makes its own food.

6. _____ happens between living things that have a need for the same resources.

7. A(n) _____ eats both plants and animals.

8. _____ happens when a(n) _____ breaks down a living thing that has died.

9. _____ is an animal that is hunted by others.

Explain Concepts

10. Trace the flow of energy from beginning to end in the following food chain: a ferret eats prairie dogs which eat grasses and other plants.

11. Explain why some plants that are put into a new area can become dangerous weeds.

12. Explain the helpful and harmful effects ground fires have on plants in a forest community.

13. Describe ways to stay healthy.

Process Skills

14. **Classify** the following living things as producers or consumers: prairie dog, whale, purple loosestrife, barnacle, Douglas fir.

15. Predict The lemming population keeps growing. There are just enough resources. Predict what might happen to the lemmings if their population grows more.

16. Interpret Data You collect data in a field next to a stream. You trap and count 16 field mice and 10 rabbits. A beaver dam floods the field. You trap and count 7 field mice and 4 rabbits. Interpret this data.

Draw Conclusions

17. Make a graphic organizer like this one. Fill it in with three facts about whales and whale barnacles from the chapter. Then write a conclusion based on those facts.

Facts   **Conclusion**

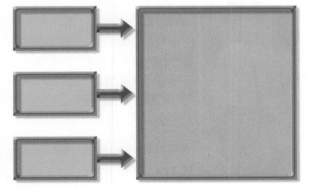

Test Prep

Choose the letter that best answers the question.

18. Which living thing helps the second living thing in the pair to survive?

Ⓐ barnacle–crayfish
Ⓑ yucca moth–whale
Ⓒ Douglas fir tree–western hemlock tree
Ⓓ raccoon–cattail

19. Which of the following is true?

Ⓐ Your lungs are a part of your circulatory system.
Ⓑ Exercise maintains health.
Ⓒ Washing your hands after coughing into them spreads germs.
Ⓓ Nutrients pass through the walls of the intestine into the stomach.

20. **Writing in Science**
Expository Write a short paragraph describing how yucca moths and the yucca plant interact.

Moon Trees

Astronaut Stuart Roosa took seeds with him into space.

Did you know there might be Moon trees growing where you live? You may be asking yourself, "What do Moon trees look like? Did they come from the Moon? Where are they growing on Earth?"

Well, Moon trees did not come from the Moon. They are trees grown from seeds that traveled to the Moon and back on the Apollo 14 mission in 1971.

Astronaut Stuart Roosa took the seeds into space. Astronaut Roosa worked for the U.S. Forest Service fighting forest fires before he joined NASA. He loved forests and wanted to protect them. He took seeds of pine, sycamore, redwood, Douglas fir, and sweet gum into space to honor the U.S. Forest Service.

A third-grade class in Indiana made this sign for their Moon tree. Astronaut Roosa's son, Col. Christopher Roosa, visited the tree with the students and their teacher.

When the seeds were brought back to Earth, scientists examined them to see if space travel had changed them in any way. Then they were planted. No one knew what the trees would look like or even if they would grow.

The Moon trees grew until they were big enough to plant outside. People all over the world began to learn about the Moon trees. They wanted one of their own. In 1975 and 1976, the little trees were sent to places around the world. Most Moon trees were sent to schools, parks, and public buildings.

Today you can find a Moon tree growing near the Liberty Bell in Philadelphia. Another grows at the White House. Let NASA know if you find that a Moon tree is growing where you live.

You can see this Moon tree at the NASA Goddard Space Flight Center in Maryland.

Lab zone Take-Home Activity

Space travel might have had what effect on the Moon tree seeds and the way they would grow? Write a paragraph.

Park Ranger

Do you like being outdoors? Would you like to work outside with plants and animals? If so, then this career might be for you.

If you visit a national park, you will probably see park rangers. Park rangers have many tasks. They help visitors decide what to see and do during a visit. They plan programs, give talks, and lead hikes. They know about the plants, animals, and history of the park.

Park rangers also help take care of visitors. Rangers keep these visitors safe. They show them where to go in the park. They help visitors who are lost or hurt. They make sure that park rules are followed.

Sometimes fires start in parks. These might be caused by visitors or by lightning. Rangers help put out fires.

Most park rangers go to college. They may start working as rangers during the summer. They later take full-time jobs.

Lab zone Take-Home Activity

Locate the National Park Service site nearest to where you live. Find out and describe what the rangers there do.

Unit A Test Talk

Find Important Words

Finding important words and their meanings in a passage can help you answer test questions. You can underline the important words as you read the passage. Some important words are underlined in the passage below.

> All animals grow and change as they go through their life cycle. The first stage of an animal's life cycle is an egg. In mammals, eggs grow and develop inside the mother and the young are born. In other kinds of animals, such as birds and insects, the mother lays eggs outside of her body. The young develop in the eggs and then they hatch.
>
> Some animals that hatch look like their parents. Baby chicks look like chickens. When a butterfly egg hatches, it is a caterpillar or <u>larva</u>. Larvae don't look like their parents. The larva develops and becomes a <u>pupa</u>. The pupa spins a covering over itself. Inside the covering, the pupa grows into a butterfly, just like its parent.

Use What You Know

To help you answer the questions, find the important words in the passage. As you read each question, decide which word choice is being described.

1. What is the first stage of an animal's life cycle?
- (A) pupa
- (B) larva
- (C) adult
- (D) egg

2. In which kind of animal do eggs grow and develop inside the mother until the young are born?
- (F) insects
- (G) mammals
- (H) birds
- (I) fish

3. What is the stage of a butterfly between a caterpillar and an adult?
- (A) larva
- (B) pupa
- (C) egg
- (D) seed

Unit A Wrap-Up

Chapter 1

How do the different parts of a plant help it live and grow?

- Most plants have roots, stems, leaves, and flowers. Each kind of part helps the plant grow, make food, or make seeds.

- Some kinds of plants have flowers. Other kinds have cones.

Chapter 2

How do different animals live, grow, and change?

- All animals begin as eggs. The eggs of some animals develop inside the mother while other animals lay eggs that hatch outside the mother.

- Some young animals look like their parents. Other young animals must go through different stages of development before they look like their parents.

Chapter 3

How are ecosystems different from each other?

- Environmental conditions determine the major types of ecosystems.

- Grasslands, deserts, tundras, and forests are land ecosystems. Water ecosystems include fresh water, salt water, or both.

Chapter 4

How do plants and animals interact?

- Animals interact by living in groups and sharing jobs. Some animals benefit by living with other kinds of animals. Animals often compete for the things they need to survive.

- Plants and animals belong to food chains. In a food chain plants produce their own food, some animals eat the plants for food, and other animals get food by eating animals.

Performance Assessment
Group Materials for Making Food

Plant leaves make food for the plant. The cards show the materials that are used to make food and the materials that are made. Place all the materials that a leaf uses to make food to the left of the leaf card. Place all the materials that the leaf makes to the right of the leaf card. What do plant leaves use to make food? What do plant leaves make?

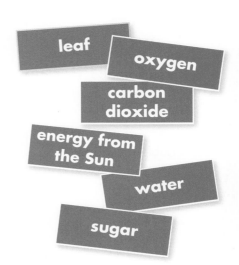

Read More About Life Science!

Look for books like these in the library.

Experiment How can a garden spider move across its web?

A garden spider weaves a web with some threads that are sticky. Prey stick to these threads. Other threads are not sticky. The spider can walk on both types and not get stuck. In this **experiment**, you make a model to find out how a garden spider reaches its prey without getting stuck in its own web.

Materials

Spider Web Pattern

regular tape

double-stick tape

eraser

toothbrush

Process Skills

Every experiment must have a **hypothesis**, a testable statement.

Ask a question.

A garden spider has stiff hairs on the ends of its legs. Do these hairs help the spider move across its web?

State a hypothesis.

If a spider has stiff hairs on its legs, then will getting stuck in its web be more likely or less likely than if it did not have these hairs, or do these hairs have no effect? Write your **hypothesis**. You will use a **model** to help test your hypothesis.

Identify and control variables.

In the model used in this experiment, the **variable** that you change is the structure of a spider's "leg" (hairs or no hairs). The variable you **observe** is whether or not the "spider" gets stuck. The structure of the "web" is a variable you keep the same.

Test your hypothesis.

1 Make a model of $\frac{1}{4}$ of the web of a garden spider. Use the Spider Web Pattern.

2 First put down double-stick tape where shown. The double-stick tape is a model of the sticky threads of a spider's web.

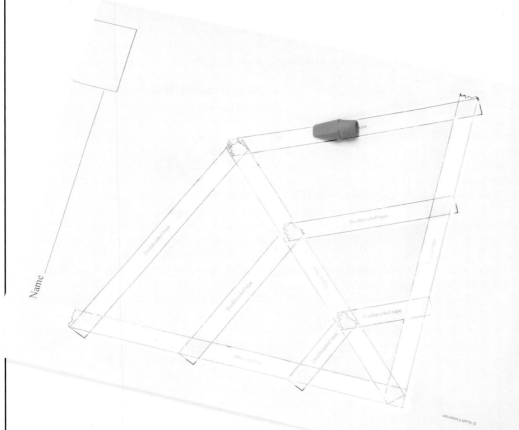

3 Next put down regular tape. The regular tape is a model of the non-sticky threads of a spider's web.

4 Put an eraser on one of the sticky outer pieces of tape. The eraser is a model of a spider's prey.

5 Start your "spider" at the center point of the web. Tap the side of the toothbrush without the brush along one of the non-sticky pieces of tape. Move from the center toward the prey. Record what happens.

6 When you reach the outer ring, tap across the sticky tape. Record what happens.

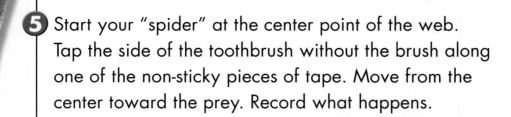

The eraser is the spider's "prey."

The toothbrush acts like a spider's leg. The side with the brush is a model of the spider's leg with stiff hairs. The side without the brush is a model of what a spider's leg would be like if the leg did not have stiff hairs.

7 Repeat steps 4 and 5, but this time use the side of the toothbrush with the brush.

Collect and record your data.

Model	Observations	
	Moving Across Non-Sticky "Thread" (regular tape)	**Moving Across Sticky "Thread"** (double-stick tape)
Without stiff hairs (side of toothbrush without brush)		
With stiff hairs (side of toothbrush with brush)		

Think of a way to use a diagram or a sketch of your model to show your observations. If your teacher wishes, explain your results orally or in writing.

Interpret your data.

What on the leg of a garden spider helps it easily reach its prey? How do you know?

State your conclusion.

Explain why a garden spider does not get stuck in its web. Compare your hypothesis with your results. **Communicate** your conclusion.

Tell how a model can help you make and test predictions. What did you learn from the model in this experiment?

Go Further

Butterfly wings are powdery. How does the powder help a butterfly escape from the sticky threads in a spider web? Design and carry out a plan for an experiment to answer this or other questions you have.

Using Scientific Methods

1. Ask a question.
2. State a hypothesis.
3. Identify/control variables.
4. Test your hypothesis.
5. Collect and record your data.
6. Interpret your data.
7. State your conclusion.
8. Go further.

Germinating Seeds

Seeds need the right conditions to germinate and grow.

Idea: Use plastic cups, potting soil, and bean seeds to find out how well seeds germinate and grow with different amounts of water.

Growing Mealworms

When mealworm eggs hatch, they look nothing like their parents.

Idea: Use mealworms and a habitat to observe and record the different stages in their life cycle.

Selecting a Habitat

Different plants and animals need different habitats to survive.

Idea: Select a plant or an animal and make a habitat in which it can survive.

A Food Chain Model

Living things are connected by their need for food.

Idea: Choose a food chain and use paper chains with names or pictures to show the connections among the living things.

Unit B

Earth Science

Chapter 5
Water

online
Student Edition
pearsonsuccessnet.com

How does water change form?

wetland

water cycle

water vapor

groundwater

evaporation

146

precipitation

condensation

147

Explore Where is Earth's water?

What if all of Earth's water would fit in a bottle?

Materials

2 L plastic bottle filled with water

4 cups

dropper and masking tape

funnel and graduated cylinder (or measuring cup)

What to Do

1 Label the 4 cups.

Earth's Water	Amount of Water (total = 2200 mL)
Atmosphere (fresh water)	about $\frac{1}{2}$ drop
Lakes, rivers, streams (fresh water)	about 4 drops
Groundwater (fresh water)	13 mL
Icecaps and glaciers (fresh water)	47 mL
Oceans and seas (salt water)	2139 mL

2 Look at the chart. Find the amount of water shown for the atmosphere. Take out that amount of water from the bottle. Put it in the atmosphere cup.

Hold the bottle with both hands.

3 Repeat for the other places water is found. Use the graduated cylinder when needed.

4 Label the bottle *oceans and seas.*

Explain Your Results

Infer Why should people use fresh water wisely?

Process Skills

Thinking about causes and effects can help you make **inferences**.

How to Read Science

 Cause and Effect

A **cause** makes something happen. An **effect** is what happens. Science writers often use clue words and phrases such as *because, so, since,* and *as a result* to signal cause and effect. The following example will help you **infer** why people should use fresh water wisely.

Science Article

Clean Streams

Factories make things for people. They often use water that gets dirty. Dumping this water into streams can harm wildlife and our water supply. As a result, the government makes laws to reduce the harm done. These laws help keep our environment clean.

Apply It!

Make a graphic organizer like the one shown. Then use it to list three causes and an effect from the science article.

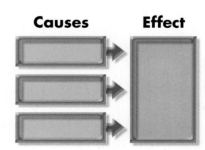

Causes   **Effect**

149

Bright sunlight gives way to rain clouds. Little splashes of water appear on the lake. Suddenly rain is pouring down all around you. Your face and clothes are quickly soaked. Too bad you don't have the waterproof feathers of a duck. Getting wet can be a bother, but what makes water so important?

Why is water important?

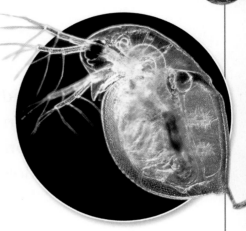

You could go without sweets or TV if you had to. But you can't give up water. You could not live more than a few days without it.

Daphnia are very tiny. This picture was taken through a microscope.

Living Things and Water

Living things from big trees to small snails need water to survive and grow. Green plants need water to make food. Fish and other animals need oxygen in water to breathe.

Water makes up about two-thirds of your body. Water is busy helping every part of your body. For example, water helps digest food into small particles. Water in your blood carries materials to every part of your body. Water also carries wastes away from every part.

Water helps keep your body at the correct temperature. What if the air temperature turns cold? Water in your body tends to hold onto its heat, keeping you warm. If your body heats up, you might sweat. The water in sweat carries heat away from your body.

Some organisms must spend their whole lives in water. Many of these creatures are very small. Daphnia, for example, are less than 1.5 mm long. Daphnia live mostly in ponds and lakes.

1. **✓Checkpoint** How does water help you live?

2. **Health in Science** Why is it important to drink water, especially after you exercise?

151

The Uses of Water

People use water in many ways. Lakes, rivers, and oceans supply us with fish and shellfish. Farmers use water to help make crops grow. Some of this water falls from the sky. But some flows through pipes to fields.

People use the power of moving water to make electricity. They build dams and power stations across rivers. Rushing water turns giant wheels inside turbines. Turbines help make electricity. This electricity can travel long distances through wires.

We also use water for transportation and enjoyment. Large ships carry goods from one place to another. Some people row on ponds or sail across oceans. Others go tubing, or swimming, or canoeing. People can have fun in the water.

Most plants take in water through their roots to grow.

1. ✔**Checkpoint** List three ways that people use water.

2. **Cause and Effect** What would happen if we did not protect our supply of fresh water?

Drinking

People need to drink water. All animals need water too. This impala slurps up a drink. The tiny bird on its horn will have some too.

Food

Water provides food. People get animals from the sea. Some fish live near the bottom of the sea. Others can be seen from boats. Boats bring back seaweed as well as fish. Seaweed is food for people and animals.

Crops and Farms

In many parts of the world, farmers irrigate land. They bring water to it. The water lets farmers grow crops in many places where no crops grew before. One third of water used in the U.S. is for irrigation.

Industry

Factories use water in many different ways. Water is used to clean foods and the insides of buildings. It is used to make paper and steel. Most of the water used in manufacturing is later put back into rivers and streams.

Electricity

Water is used to make electricity. Moving water or steam can turn large turbines. Turbines are special engines that help make power. Electric power can be used for light, heat, and to run machines.

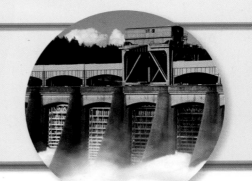

153

The Planet of Water

You could call Earth "the blue planet." That's because about three fourths, or 75 percent, of Earth's surface is covered with water.

Most of Earth's water is salty ocean water. Some of the salt in ocean water comes from rock on the ocean floor. Other salt is washed off the land into the oceans. The salt mixes with the water. You cannot drink, wash clothes, or water plants with ocean water. You cannot use this water to make products in factories.

Water is found in many places. Some water moves downward into the ground. Some is frozen into ice. Some water is found in the air as an invisible gas called **water vapor.** Clouds are made of water vapor that has changed to tiny drops of liquid water.

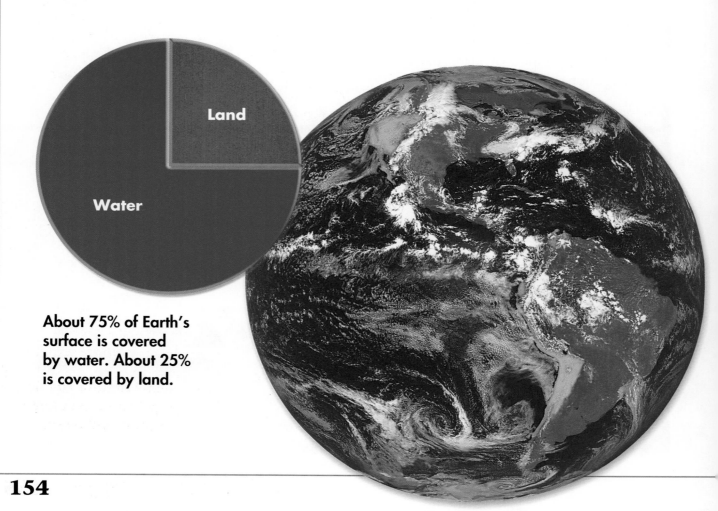

About 75% of Earth's surface is covered by water. About 25% is covered by land.

Fresh Water

There is little salt in fresh water. We need fresh water to drink. A very small amount of the water on Earth is fresh water. Most of this water is frozen as ice near the North and South Poles.

Many lakes, rivers, and streams supply fresh water. Streams run together to form rivers. Rivers can flow into and out of lakes.

Some of the fresh water we use comes from underground. Water seeps down slowly through the soil. It collects in spaces between underground rocks. This water is called **groundwater.** People dig wells to bring groundwater to the surface.

In some places, the top level of the groundwater is very close to Earth's surface. If water soaks the ground at least part of the year, the place is called a **wetland.**

Wetlands are homes for many animals. They also help prevent floods by soaking up extra water. Some water in wetlands seeps down through soil. This helps refill the groundwater supply.

A spring is a stream of groundwater that flows out of the ground.

Fresh water is frozen in huge chunks of ice. This iceberg is near Antarctica.

✓ Lesson Checkpoint

1. Why is fresh water important?

2. What are four sources of fresh water?

3. **Writing** in Science **Descriptive** In your **science journal**, write a paragraph about a time you spent near water. What did you see? What did you hear? What did you feel?

Small streams can flow together to form larger streams and rivers.

How do forms of water change?

Follow a particle of water for a year. One day the particle is rushing down a mountain stream. Later, it is frozen in pond ice. Later still, it is drifting high in the air. On its journey, water goes through many changes.

Forms Water Can Have

Cold weather can freeze water from a liquid to a solid. In some places, the weather is below 0 degrees Celsius all year long. In other places, the weather is cold just part of the year. In these places, water may freeze only when the weather is very cold.

Warm temperatures in the spring and summer keep the water in this marsh in its liquid form. What is the temperature in this marsh in degrees Fahrenheit? in degrees Celsius?

When water freezes, it takes up more space. The water in the bottle on the right has frozen. It pushes out the sides of the bottle and out of its top.

Water can also become a gas called water vapor. The process of a liquid becoming a gas is called **evaporation.** The Sun's energy evaporates surface water. Then the water becomes water vapor in the air. You cannot see water vapor, but sometimes you can feel its effects on hot summer days. On these days water leaves your skin as sweat. But sweat cannot easily evaporate if there is a lot of water vapor in the air. So you feel "sticky" from the sweat.

Water vapor in the air can turn back into a liquid. This process is called **condensation.** When the air cools, condensation turns invisible water vapor back into drops of water. Small droplets form clouds and fog. Large drops that form on plants are dew.

Cold temperatures in the winter cause the water in the marsh to freeze. What is the temperature in this marsh in degrees Fahrenheit? in degrees Celsius?

Water vapor in air condenses as dew-drops on plants.

1. **✓ Checkpoint** What are the three forms of water?

2. **Math in Science** What is the difference between the temperature of the marsh in spring and in winter? Give your answer in °F and °C.

How Water Moves Around Earth

There is only a certain amount of water on Earth. It must be used again and again. The movement of water from Earth's surface into the air and back again is the **water cycle.** The water cycle gives us a constant supply of fresh water.

Water changes form or state as it moves through the water cycle. The Sun's energy and winds cause water to evaporate and become water vapor.

Rain is just one form of precipitation.

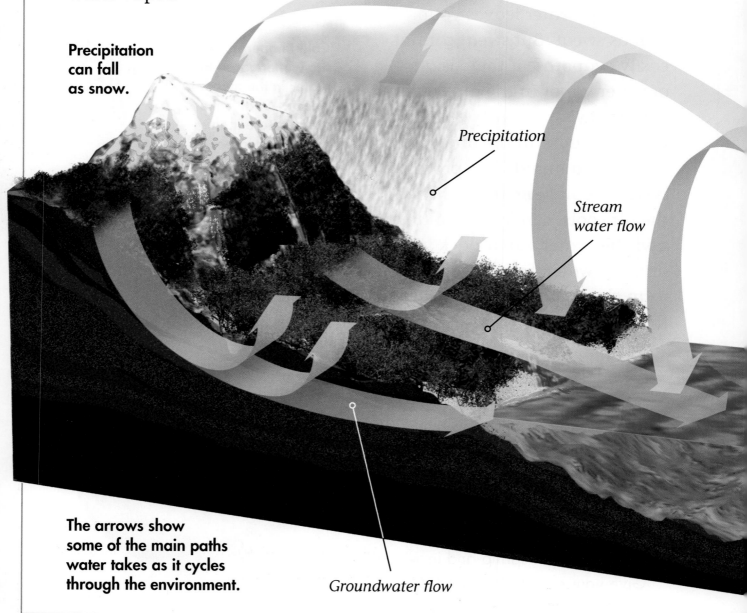

Precipitation can fall as snow.

Precipitation

Stream water flow

The arrows show some of the main paths water takes as it cycles through the environment.

Groundwater flow

Water vapor rises into cooler air, cools, and turns into water droplets or ice crystals. This process is called condensation. These water particles collect and form clouds.

When water particles in clouds grow in size and weight, they fall faster. Water that falls to Earth is called **precipitation.** Precipitation might be rain, snow, sleet, or hail.

Some precipitation seeps into the ground. There it becomes groundwater. Other precipitation falls onto streams, rivers, lakes, and oceans. Water that flows across Earth's surface is constantly moving downstream toward the ocean. A lot of ground water reaches the surface in lower areas where there are streams and rivers. This surface water evaporates. In this way, the water cycle continues all the time—everywhere.

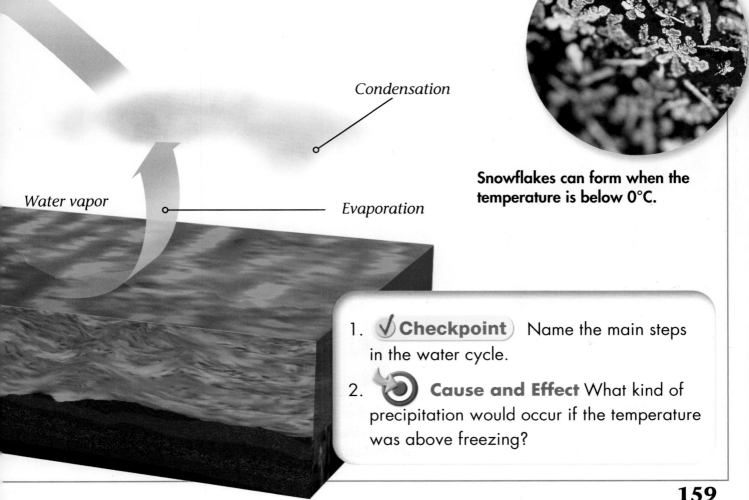

Condensation

Water vapor

Evaporation

Snowflakes can form when the temperature is below 0°C.

1. ✔ Checkpoint Name the main steps in the water cycle.

2. Cause and Effect What kind of precipitation would occur if the temperature was above freezing?

Ways to Clean Water

People need clean water. Water may contain germs that make people sick. It may contain dirt or salt that can harm machines. These things can make the water taste and smell bad. The water that people use is cleaned to remove these things.

In some places, people get water from their own wells. They must filter the water to remove dirt and chemicals.

In cities, people do not need to clean their own water. The water for most cities is cleaned in one place. First, the water is sent through pipes to a water-treatment area. There, several things may happen.

This filter cleans only the water that comes out of this faucet.

This kind of filter cleans all the water that comes into this building.

Chemicals may be added to the water. Some chemicals kill germs. Others, such as fluoride, help make teeth strong.

In some treatment plants, the water is sprayed into the air. This makes the water taste and smell better. Often, the water is stored in big tanks for a while. Tiny pieces of dirt sink to the bottom of the tank. Finally, the water is pumped through a filter. Even more dirt is removed.

The water now is clean. It can be pumped all over the city. Homes and businesses will have clean, fresh water to use.

Map Fact

The city of Chicago has two of the largest water-cleaning plants in the world. These clean between one and two billion gallons of water a day. People who live in and around Chicago use this water.

A water-cleaning plant in Chicago

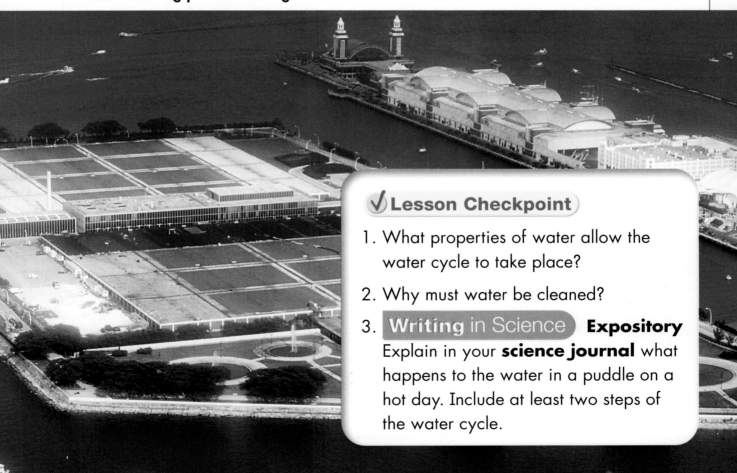

✓ **Lesson Checkpoint**

1. What properties of water allow the water cycle to take place?

2. Why must water be cleaned?

3. **Writing in Science** **Expository** Explain in your **science journal** what happens to the water in a puddle on a hot day. Include at least two steps of the water cycle.

Investigate How can you make a model of the water cycle?

Materials

ice cube

cup

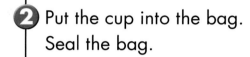

resealable plastic bag

tape

What to Do

1 Put an ice cube in the cup.

2 Put the cup into the bag. Seal the bag.

3 Tape the bag to a sunny window. **Predict** what will happen over the next 3 days.

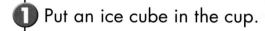

Process Skills

An **inference** about a future event is called a **prediction**.

4 Observe the bag. Record what happens. Compare your results with your predictions.

Time	Predictions	Observations
After 2 hours		
Day 2		
Day 3		

Explain Your Results

1. Make a drawing. Show how the water from the ice cube moved to the bottom of the bag. Use arrows. Use these words as labels: *melting, evaporation,* and *condensation.*

2. **Infer** What do you think would happen if the entire bag was put in a freezer?

3. Identify the different forms in which water exists in the air. How does water change from one form to another?

Go Further

How do you think you could make the water cycle happen faster or slower in the bag? Design and conduct a scientific investigation to test your prediction. Keep a record in a journal.

Snowflake Geometry

If water droplets in the clouds freeze, they form snow crystals. Snow crystals join with others and fall as snowflakes.

All snowflakes have six sides. Remember, a six-sided shape is called a **hexagon.** Many snowflakes are **symmetrical.** A symmetrical shape is exactly the same on both sides of a line, called the **line of symmetry.** There can be one or more lines of symmetry in a symmetrical shape. The snowflake below shows (with dotted lines) 3 of the possible lines of symmetry. If you were to cut out the snowflake and fold it on any one of these lines, the two sides would match.

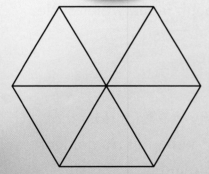

Use the shapes below to answer the questions.

A   B   C   D

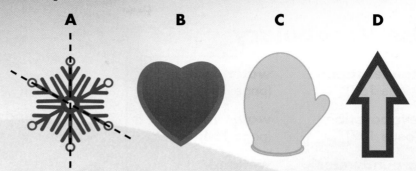

1 Which shape is NOT symmetrical?

A. shape A   B. shape B

C. shape C   D. shape D

2 Shape A is a snowflake. Two lines of symmetry are shown. How many total lines of symmetry does the snowflake have?

F. 1   G. 3   H. 5   I. 6

3 Trace the hexagon at left and cut it out. Fold the hexagon along one of the lines of symmetry shown. What is the name of the new shape? How many sides does it have?

Lab zone Take-Home Activity

Make paper snowflakes by folding and cutting. You may use the library or the Internet to find detailed instructions. See how intricate you can make snowflakes, starting with a paper square or circle!

Chapter 5 Review and Test Prep

Use Vocabulary

condensation (page 157)	**water cycle** (page 158)
evaporation (page 157)	**water vapor** (page 154)
groundwater (page 155)	**wetland** (page 155)
precipitation (page 159)	

Use the vocabulary word from the list above that best completes each sentence.

1. _____ happens when water changes into water vapor and rises into the air.

2. An area where water soaks the ground for at least part of the year is called a(n) _____.

3. The _____ moves water from Earth's surface into the air and back again.

4. When water evaporates, it turns into an invisible gas called _____.

5. Water that falls from clouds in the form of rain, snow, sleet, or ice is called _____.

6. _____ occurs when water vapor changes back into water droplets.

7. Fresh water found under the ground is _____.

Explain Concepts

8. Explain why all living things need water.

9. Describe where water is found on the Earth.

10. Why is most of Earth's water salt water?

11. Describe the changes that water goes through in the water cycle.

Process Skills

12. **Infer** Why is it important that poisonous materials do not leak into the ground?

13. **Predict** What might happen to a glass bottle if it is filled with water, capped tightly, and put in the freezer?

Cause and Effect

14. Make a graphic organizer like the one shown below. Fill in the correct effect.

Causes   **Effect**

Water is spilled on the outside door steps.	→
The outside temperature is –5°C.	→
Water freezes at 0°C.	→

 Test Prep

Choose the letter that best completes the statement or answers the question.

15. About 75 percent of Earth's surface is covered by

Ⓐ air.   Ⓑ water.
Ⓒ plants.   Ⓓ animals.

16. The step in the water cycle in which water forms water vapor in the air is called

Ⓕ evaporation.
Ⓖ condensation.
Ⓗ precipitation.
Ⓘ groundwater.

17. When the temperature of water falls below 0 degrees Celsius, the water will

Ⓐ evaporate.
Ⓑ shrink.
Ⓒ freeze.
Ⓓ condense.

18. Wetlands help refill the groundwater supply when

Ⓕ water evaporates.
Ⓖ water seeps down into the ground.
Ⓗ the winds blow.
Ⓘ water freezes.

19. Explain why the answer you chose for Question 17 is best. For each of the answers you did not choose, give a reason why it is not the best choice.

20. **Writing in Science**

Persuasive Practice writing a letter to the editor of your town newspaper. Explain why you think it is important for everyone in your town to conserve water, rather than waste it.

Oceanographer

Oceanographers learn skills to study the ocean using many special tools.

Oceanographers study the water of the ocean, the area beneath it, and the living things in it. Would you like to sail the deep blue sea? Then think about being an oceanographer. Oceanographers are scientists. They use tools to keep track of ocean temperatures, ocean currents, and life in the ocean. These scientists study the ocean as a whole, but there are many specific jobs in the field of oceanography. For example, you might want to study whales and other living things in the ocean. Then you can become a marine biologist. Do you like to tinker with tools and gadgets? Maybe you could be an engineer who designs the special equipment needed to study the underwater world.

Becoming an oceanographer requires four years of college.

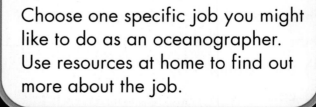

Lab zone Take-Home Activity

Choose one specific job you might like to do as an oceanographer. Use resources at home to find out more about the job.

Chapter 6
Weather

You Will Discover

- patterns of weather.
- how people measure and predict weather.
- ways people stay safe during storms.

online
Student Edition
pearsonsuccessnet.com

How does weather follow patterns?

weather

hurricane

tornado

Chapter 6
Vocabulary

atmosphere

blizzard

Explore How can you measure wind speed?

Materials

Pattern for a Wind Speed Meter

scissors

25 cm piece of string

metric ruler

tape

table-tennis ball

What to Do

1 Make a wind speed meter.

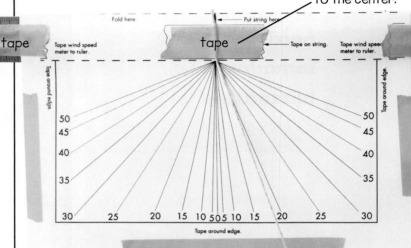

Tape the string to the center.

Fold here.

Put string here.

tape

tape

tape

Tape wind speed meter to ruler.

Tape on string.

Tape wind speed meter to ruler.

Tape around edge.

50 45 40 35

50 45 40 35

30 25 20 15 10 5 0 5 10 15 20 25 30

Tape around edge.

Tape the string to the ball.

2 Go outside. Point the ruler into the wind. Hold it level with the ground. Read the wind speed.

3 **Measure** and record the wind speed for 1 week. **Observe** at the same time each day. Look for a pattern.

You may also wish to record temperature and air pressure. Check if a thermometer and barometer are available.

Explain Your Results

Infer Suppose you use a heavier ball on the wind gauge. What else would you have to change? Explain.

Make Inferences

A writer doesn't always tell us everything. As you read, you might have to put some facts together.

When you make an **inference**, you explain an event or a thing.

- You use facts you read.
- You use your own experiences.
- You make a guess from what you observe or from what you already know.

Weather Report

The weather this morning appears sunny and warm. Winds are beginning to blow out of the northwest. The northwest region reported cloudy and cool conditions last evening. Rain began to fall there this morning.

Apply It!

Study this graphic organizer. Make a graphic organizer like this one. List the facts from the weather report in your graphic organizer. Write your inference.

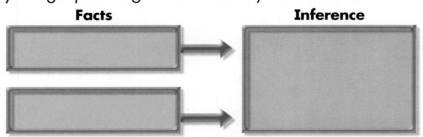

Facts   Inference

You Are There!

You are playing outside on a sunny day. Suddenly you hear a loud rumble in the sky. You look up. Huge black clouds are moving toward you. You see a flash of lightning in the distance. Uh-oh! Here comes a big change in the weather. What caused it? Time to get to safety.

Lesson 1

What makes up weather?

Weather changes all the time. Measuring weather helps people predict weather accurately.

Parts of Weather

What will the weather be like this weekend? Will it be sunny or rainy? **Weather** is what the air is like outside. It includes the kinds of clouds in the sky and the kind and amount of water in the air. It also includes the temperature of the air and how the wind is blowing.

Clouds are made of water droplets in the air. Different kinds of clouds form in different weather. Because of this, clouds can help predict what will happen to the weather. Some kinds of clouds form in sunny weather. Others form in rainy or stormy weather.

Look at clouds on a warm, bright day. The clouds are white and fluffy. On a stormy day, clouds are dark.

These cumulus clouds look a little like balls of cotton. You see these on sunny days.

These are very high, thin cirrus clouds. They are made of tiny ice crystals. You see these clouds on sunny days too.

1. ✔**Checkpoint** How do clouds look on stormy days?

2. **Writing in Science** **Narrative** Write a paragraph in your **science journal** that tells what the weather would be like on a perfect day for you. Explain why you like this weather.

175

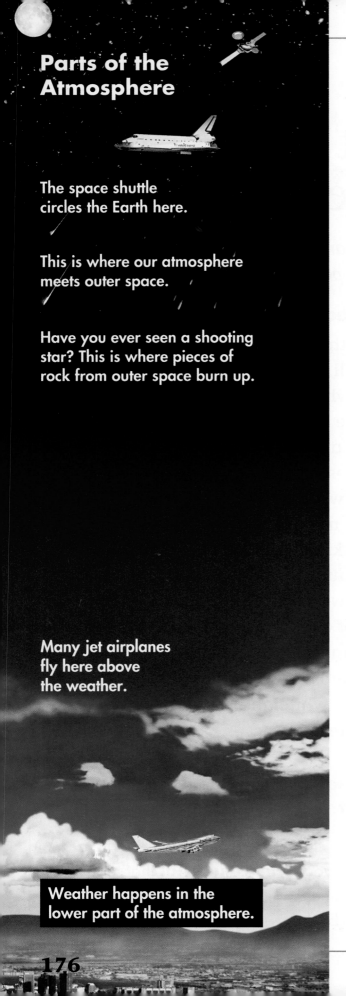

Parts of the Atmosphere

The space shuttle circles the Earth here.

This is where our atmosphere meets outer space.

Have you ever seen a shooting star? This is where pieces of rock from outer space burn up.

Many jet airplanes fly here above the weather.

Weather happens in the lower part of the atmosphere.

The Atmosphere

The **atmosphere** is the blanket of air that surrounds Earth. This air is made up of gases that have no color, taste, or odor. The temperature is different in different parts of the atmosphere. Weather happens in the lower part of the atmosphere.

The atmosphere has weight, so it presses down on Earth. This pressing down is called air pressure. When the air presses down a lot, the air pressure is high. When it presses less, the air pressure is low.

Describing Weather

You may say the weather is too hot today. Someone else might not agree. That person might like the weather. Words like *hot* mean different things to different people. But 34° Celsius (93° Fahrenheit) means just one thing. It is a fact that describes the temperature of the air. Scientists use special tools to help them describe and measure the weather.

Measuring and Predicting

Scientists can measure air pressure with a tool called a barometer. Scientists use measurements of air pressure to predict changes in weather. Weather reports often describe air pressure. Low air pressure often means that weather will be cloudy or rainy. High air pressure often means skies will be clear.

A tool called an anemometer measures wind speed. A wind vane shows the direction of the wind.

Scientists use hygrometers to measure how much water vapor is in the air. The amount of water vapor in the air is called humidity. The humidity is low when air is dry. The humidity is high when air has more water in it. Rain gauges measure liquid water. They show how much rain has fallen.

Weather tools or instruments help scientists learn more about weather. They also help scientists predict what the weather will be like.

1. **✓Checkpoint** How do tools help scientists describe the weather?

2. **Make Inferences** High pressure is moving into an area. Use this observation and what you know about air pressure to predict the weather change.

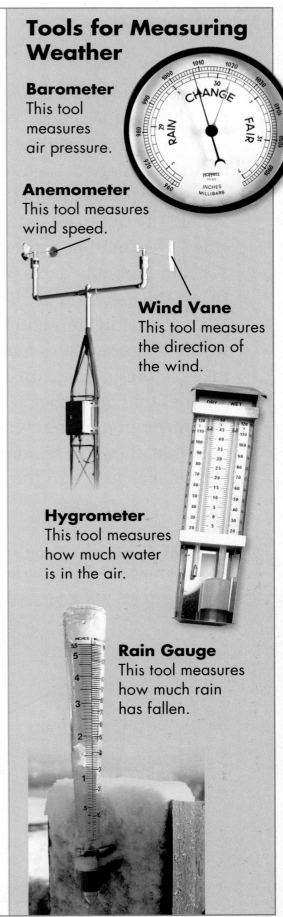

Tools for Measuring Weather

Barometer
This tool measures air pressure.

Anemometer
This tool measures wind speed.

Wind Vane
This tool measures the direction of the wind.

Hygrometer
This tool measures how much water is in the air.

Rain Gauge
This tool measures how much rain has fallen.

Weather Map

Weather tools gather weather data. Scientists show this data on weather maps. Weather maps show data for a large area. They show temperatures and storms. Some maps give information about areas of high and low air pressure.

Look at the weather map below. It shows the United States. The numbers show the temperatures in different cities. The small pictures show what the weather is like. You can probably guess what some pictures mean. The key shows the meaning of all the pictures.

Weather satellites gather weather data from all over the world. These satellites move high above the Earth. They can take pictures of large areas of the planet. They send these pictures and data back to scientists on Earth.

Information from satellites is very useful to scientists. For example, they can see storm clouds form and can tell the direction that the storms are moving.

This weather map uses pictures to interpret data that weather tools have gathered. What can you learn from this weather map?

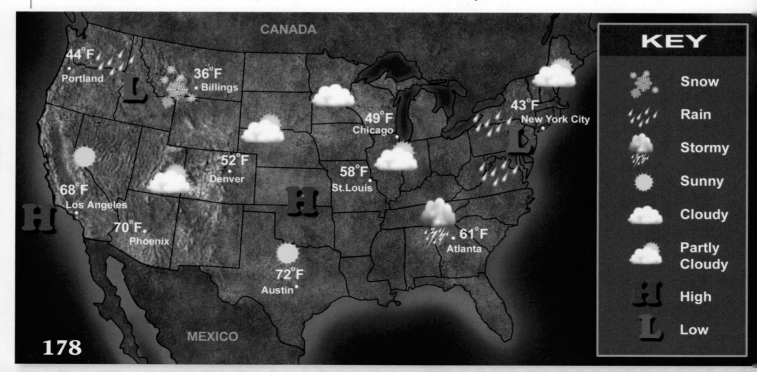

Weather satellites like this one gather weather data.

Maps made from satellite data can show the direction storm clouds are moving.

Pollution Alerts

Weather news may include smog and ozone pollution alerts. In many cities, cars and trucks help cause these alerts. The gases that leave their engines are called exhaust. On some days, a lot of exhaust stays in the air. The Sun's rays can turn that air into smog and ozone. On days with little wind, the smog and ozone do not move away.

Smog and ground-level ozone can be harmful to health. They can make people cough. Some people might not be able to breathe easily. During air pollution alerts, some people must stay inside.

The Sun's rays strike the exhaust from gasoline burned in cars and trucks. This causes smog.

✔ Lesson Checkpoint

1. What can weather maps show?

2. What is one effect that humans can have on weather?

3. **Make Inferences** If there is a smog alert, what can you infer about the weather?

179

How are weather patterns different?

Patterns of weather vary from place to place. People must protect themselves during severe weather.

Weather Patterns

Changes in weather follow patterns. Weather patterns depend on the Sun, water, and the location.

Places near oceans have different weather patterns than places far from oceans. Washington State is by the Pacific Ocean. In winter, warm, moist air from over the ocean moves over the land. There are clouds in the air. Rain falls over the western valleys.

As the clouds move east, they rise up the side of the Cascade Mountains. The clouds get colder, and snow falls. Western Washington State has a pattern of cool, wet winters.

After the air has crossed the mountains, the air does not have much moisture. Little rain or snow falls. Eastern Washington State has a pattern of cold, dry winters.

Western Washington State has a pattern of cool, wet winters.

Eastern Washington State has a pattern of cold, dry winters.

Winter in Washington State		
Locations	Average Temperature	Average Rainfall (cm)
West	5°C (41°F)	30
East	–2°C (28°F)	6

All deserts are dry. Some deserts are cold, while others are hot. Each desert has its own weather pattern.

North America has four large desert regions. The Sonoran Desert is in the southern part of Arizona and California. This desert receives some winter rain from storms that reach it from the Pacific Ocean. But most rain falls in short, heavy downpours during the hot summer. The average rainfall during the summer is 5 centimeters (2 inches). The moist air for this rain comes from the Gulf of California.

The saguaro cactus is adapted to live in the desert. The wide, shallow roots of the cactus soak up the rain. The cactus stores the water for later use.

In the hot summer the saguaro cactus stores water from storms.

Winter rain causes spring wildflowers to bloom in the Sonoran Desert.

1.  **Checkpoint** What do weather patterns depend on?

2. **Make Inferences** Moist air from the Gulf of California causes storms in the Sonoran Desert in summer. What weather does moist air from the Gulf of Mexico cause in the Midwest in summer?

Seasons in the Sonoran Desert		
Season	Average Temperature	Average Rainfall (cm)
Fall	16°C (61°F)	2
Winter	12°C (54°F)	2
Spring	24°C (75°F)	1
Summer	29°C (84°F)	5

A satellite high above Earth took this picture of the swirling winds of a hurricane.

Dangerous Storms

Thunderstorms can be dangerous. Lightning can strike people or objects. People should find shelter during thunderstorms.

A **hurricane** is a huge storm. Hurricanes form over oceans. They have winds of at least 119 kilometers (74 miles) per hour. Heavy rains, strong winds, and huge waves cause damage. Waves can lift boats out of the water and flip them over. People usually know about hurricanes before they strike.

A **tornado** is a spinning, funnel-shaped, column of air that touches the ground. Tornadoes are much smaller than hurricanes. However, their winds are stronger. Tornadoes form beneath thunderstorm clouds. They can form suddenly and without warning. When a tornado starts, people must go to safe places. They must stay away from windows.

Sudden heavy rains can cause floods. Very high waves can cause floods too. Water from flooding can block roads and damage homes. People usually have some warning that an area may flood. Then they must move to higher ground.

A **blizzard** is a winter storm. Blizzards have low temperatures and lots of blowing snow. People can get lost or stuck in the snow. They can also get too cold to move to warm shelter.

Radio and television stations send out storm safety information. The National Weather Service puts out watches and warnings. These warn people about dangerous storms. A *watch* means that a storm could happen where you live. A *warning* means that a storm is already in or near your area. Everyone who hears a warning should take action to stay safe.

Hurricanes do damage when they move over land.

Students head for home when a winter storm watch warns of a blizzard.

Most tornadoes do damage along a narrow path.

Heavy rains caused a flood that blocks this road.

✓ Lesson Checkpoint

1. What part of the State of Washington has a wet and snowy weather pattern in winter?

2. What does a severe thunderstorm warning mean? What should people do in response?

3. **Writing in Science** **Descriptive** In your **science journal** write about a storm that happened near your home. Tell how people prepared themselves or didn't before the storm came.

Investigate Can different amounts of carbon dioxide have different effects?

Carbon dioxide gas in the air helps keep Earth warm. An increase can cause a planet to get warmer. On Earth carbon dioxide has been increasing for hundreds of years. Some changes have been observed. Many scientists think if it keeps increasing, bigger changes will be observed.

Materials

safety goggles

2 cups and masking tape

funnel and graduated cylinder (or measuring cup)

BTB

2 pieces of plastic wrap and straws

Process Skills

You **interpret data** when you look closely at your data and see how it can help you to answer your questions.

What to Do

1 Prepare 2 cups of BTB.

Put 30 mL of BTB into each cup. Cover the cups with plastic wrap.

Label the cups.

Be careful!

Safety Procedure
• Wear safety goggles.
• Do not share straws.
• Use the straws to breathe out only!

2 Push a straw through the plastic wrap. Breathe out once through the straw into Cup A.

3 Repeat with Cup B but breathe out 10 times.

④ Look at the color of BTB in each cup.

⑤ **Collect data** and make a chart like the one below to show your results.

Cup	Color of BTB	
	Before Breathing into Cup	**After Breathing into Cup**
Cup A 1 breath		
Cup B 10 breaths		

Explain Your Results

1. What happened to the BTB in each cup?

2. **Interpret Data** When you breathed out, you added carbon dioxide to the BTB. Can a small amount of carbon dioxide show a different effect than a larger amount? Explain.

Go Further

How many breaths can you breathe out without observing a change? Make a plan to answer this or another question.

Math in Science

Comparing Temperatures

Places near oceans have different weather patterns than places far from oceans. The tables on page 187 compare the average high and low temperatures in two cities for January and for July. Notice that Seattle is warmer than Indianapolis in January.

July

January

Seattle

July

January

Indianapolis

@ **Tools** Take It to the Net
pearsonsuccessnet.com

Average Temperatures in January

	Seattle, Washington	Indianapolis, Indiana
Average High	8°C (46°F)	1°C (34°F)
Average Low	2°C (36°F)	−8°C (18°F)

Average Temperatures in July

	Seattle, Washington	Indianapolis, Indiana
Average High	24°C (75°F)	30°C (86°F)
Average Low	13°C (55°F)	18°C (65°F)

Use the tables and the map to answer the following questions.

1 Use the map to explain why Seattle is usually warmer than Indianapolis in January.

2 What is the average high temperature in July in Seattle? in Indianapolis?

3 What are the average low temperatures in the two cities in July?

4 Which city is usually warmer in July? Use the map to help explain why this is true.

Lab zone Take-Home Activity

Find information about the average high and low temperatures in January and July where you live. Compare these temperatures to the temperatures in Seattle and Indianapolis.

Chapter 6 Review and Test Prep

Use Vocabulary

atmosphere (page 176)	**tornado** (page 182)
blizzard (page 183)	**weather** (page 175)
hurricane (page 182)	

Use the vocabulary word from the list above that best completes each sentence.

1. A(n) _____ is a spinning column of air that touches the ground and happens quickly.

2. Temperature, wind speed, and clouds are parts of the _____.

3. A(n) _____ is a huge, strong storm that forms over the warm ocean.

4. A winter storm with low temperatures, strong winds, and lots of blowing snow is a(n) _____.

5. The _____ is made up of gases that surround Earth.

Explain Concepts

6. Why is weather important?

7. If you had tools for measuring parts of the weather, what information could you collect?

8. List some clues that indicate a change in the weather.

9. Give an example of a weather pattern and describe it in detail.

10. How does the National Weather Service help people stay safe?

11. Use the chart below to tell which city has warmer average temperatures in July. Which city has the biggest difference between the average high and average low?

	Birmingham, Alabama	Santa Fe, New Mexico
Average High in July	33°C (91°F)	29°C (85°F)
Average Low in July	21°C (70°F)	12°C (53°F)

Process Skills

12. **Predict** It is a rainy day, but the air pressure is getting higher. How might the weather change?

13. **Infer** How might weather be different if water never evaporated? Explain your answer.

 **Make Inferences**

14. Copy the table below. Fill in the missing inference.

Facts	Inference
Earth has become slightly warmer over the past 100 years.	
Many places get more or less rain than before.	

 Test Prep

Choose the letter that best completes the statement or answers the question.

15. What kind of winter weather would a city near the ocean in the western U.S. most likely have?

Ⓐ warm and rainy

Ⓑ warm and snowy

Ⓒ cold and snowy

Ⓓ cool and rainy

16. A severe thunderstorm watch means

Ⓕ a severe thunderstorm is in the area.

Ⓖ a tornado is in the area.

Ⓗ flooding could happen soon.

Ⓘ a thunderstorm might happen.

17. If a tornado forms, people should

Ⓐ go to safe places.

Ⓑ move to higher ground.

Ⓒ close windows.

Ⓓ drive to another city.

18. Most smog and ozone in cities are caused by

Ⓕ acid rain.

Ⓖ forest fires.

Ⓗ carbon dioxide.

Ⓘ burning gasoline.

19. Explain why the answer you chose for Question 15 is best. For each of the answers you did not choose, give a reason why it is not the best choice.

20. **Writing** in Science

Expository Write a paragraph that describes both helpful and harmful effects that the weather can have on people.

189

Studying Clouds From
SPACE

You know that NASA studies space. NASA also studies Earth's clouds from space. NASA satellites orbit Earth and use different tools or instruments to collect information about clouds and other parts of the Earth system, including weather. Some of the tools measure the amount of sunlight that bounces off clouds. Other tools measure how much heat is trapped by clouds and how much escapes into space.

Cumulus

Cirrus

Cumulonimbus

Stratus

Clouds are an important part of weather patterns. They are part of the water cycle. They interact with the gases that trap heat and warm Earth. NASA scientists are studying how clouds affect Earth's climate.

Many schools are helping NASA study clouds. Students and teachers at these schools observe and measure clouds and other weather conditions. They are given special times to take their measurements. These are the same times when NASA satellites are recording information for their area.

Cirrostratus

Altocumulus

Lab zone Take-Home Activity

Record your own observations of clouds and the temperature at the time of day you observed them. Collect this data for a week. Organize data into a chart. Decide if the kinds and amounts of clouds affected the temperature.

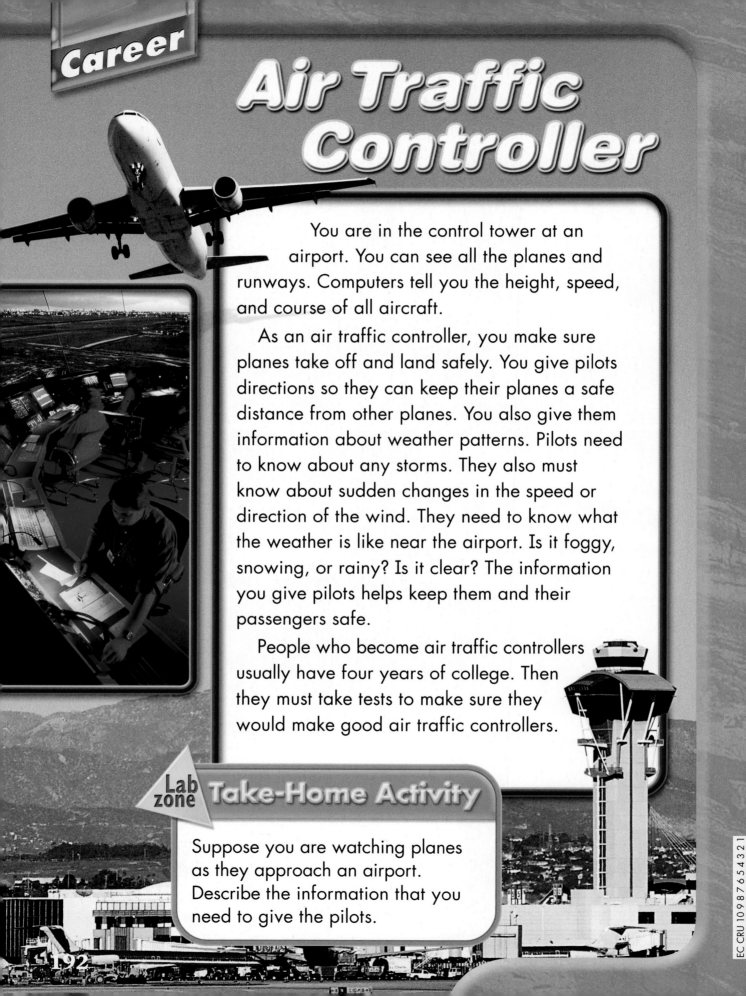

Air Traffic Controller

You are in the control tower at an airport. You can see all the planes and runways. Computers tell you the height, speed, and course of all aircraft.

As an air traffic controller, you make sure planes take off and land safely. You give pilots directions so they can keep their planes a safe distance from other planes. You also give them information about weather patterns. Pilots need to know about any storms. They also must know about sudden changes in the speed or direction of the wind. They need to know what the weather is like near the airport. Is it foggy, snowing, or rainy? Is it clear? The information you give pilots helps keep them and their passengers safe.

People who become air traffic controllers usually have four years of college. Then they must take tests to make sure they would make good air traffic controllers.

Lab zone Take-Home Activity

Suppose you are watching planes as they approach an airport. Describe the information that you need to give the pilots.

EC CRU 10 9 8 7 6 5 4 3 2 1

Chapter 7
Rocks and Soil

You Will Discover

- how to tell one kind of rock from another.
- how rocks are formed.
- what soil is made of.
- why soil is important.

online
Student Edition
pearsonsuccessnet.com

What are some kinds of rocks and soils?

rock

igneous rock

sedimentary rock

metamorphic rock

194

loam

soil

mineral

decay

The slow breaking down of the remains of living things in soil

nutrient

Material in soil that plants need to grow

Explore What can you learn from rock layers?

Wind, water, or ice can carry away sand and other materials. Often these materials are dropped in places in layers. Over time, the materials can join together to form rock. This is one reason rocks are often found in layers. In this model the layers of rock are shown by the sand, salt, coffee, sugar, and clay soil.

Materials

small measuring cup and large cup

sand, salt, coffee

sugar and clay soil

small paper clip
rubber band
piece of crayon

What to Do

1 **Make a model** of rock layers. Fill the small cup with sand. Pour it into a large cup. Put a paper clip in the sand. Place it touching the side of the cup. The paper clip stands for a fossil animal.

2 Add layers of the other materials to the cup. Place a "fossil animal" (a rubber band or a piece of crayon) in 2 of the layers.

crayon
clay soil
sugar
coffee
rubber band
salt
paper clip
sand

Process Skills

A **model** of something is different from the real thing but can be used to learn something about the real thing.

Explain Your Results

1. Which layer was added first? Which layer in your **model** is the "oldest"? How do you know?

2. **Infer** Where would you expect to find an older fossil—in an upper layer of rock or in a lower layer? Explain.

How to Read Science

Compare and Contrast

When you **compare** things, you tell how they are alike. When you **contrast** things, you tell how they are different.

- Words and phrases such as *similar, like, all, both,* or *in the same way* are clues that things are being compared.

- Words and phrases such as *different, unlike,* or *in a different way* are clues that things are being contrasted.

Magazine Article

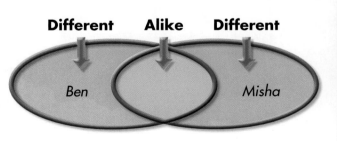

Rock Collectors

Ben and Misha both collect rocks. Ben prefers brightly colored rocks. He is a member of a rock hunters club that goes on collecting trips. Misha has a different way of collecting his favorite kinds of rocks—fossil rocks. His uncle sends Misha fossil rocks from all around the world. Unlike Ben, Misha just has to make a trip to his mailbox to add to his collection.

Apply It!

You can use a graphic organizer as a **model** to show how things compare and contrast.

Different   **Alike**   **Different**

Ben   Misha

Use a graphic organizer to show ways that Ben and Misha are alike and different in the way they collect rocks.

197

You Are There!

Be careful as you climb on the rocks. It's a good thing you have on hiking boots. They will help you climb. Can you see that some of the rocks have sharp edges? Some look rough. Others look smooth. There are differences in color. What are rocks made of and where do they come from?

AudioText

Lesson 1

How do rocks form?

Rocks are everywhere. Some are as large as a mountain. Others are smaller than a grain of sand. Minerals make up rock. Rock forms in different ways.

Rocks

Earth consists of mostly different kinds of rocks. **Rock** is natural, solid, nonliving material made of one or more minerals. A **mineral** is a natural material that forms from nonliving matter.

You can tell rocks apart by looking at their physical properties. The physical properties of rocks include color, what minerals they are made of, and texture.

The rocks you see here range in color from gray to brown. Sometimes the minerals are so small that they aren't easy to see. Texture is the size of the bits of minerals, or grains, that make up the rock. Some rocks may have grains that are big enough to see. These different sizes of minerals make rocks feel smooth, rough, or bumpy.

1. ✓ **Checkpoint** What are some physical properties of rocks?

2. **Compare and Contrast** How are the rocks shown in the pictures alike? How are they different?

Rock Groups

Rocks can be placed into three main groups. Rocks in each group formed in a certain way. Each group contains many kinds of rocks.

Igneous rock forms from a very hot mixture of melted minerals and gases. This mixture may cool slowly below ground until it hardens. Then the mineral grains may be large. If the rock cools quickly above ground or on the ocean floor, the grains may be too small to see.

Another group of rocks form from sediments, which are tiny bits of rock, sand, shells and other materials. Sediments settle to the bottom of rivers, lakes, and oceans. Over thousands of years, the sediments are pressed together and cemented into **sedimentary rock.** Sedimentary rock forms in layers—one layer at a time.

Fossils of extinct plants and animals can be found in sedimentary rocks. Their bodies were buried in sand and mud that hardened into rock. Fossils in sedimentary rock can show the history of life over time.

Fossils in Sedimentary Rock

Crinoids were ancient animals that looked like plants.

Trilobites were like modern crabs.

Ammonites looked similar to today's snails.

Metamorphic rock is rock that has been changed by heat and pressure. Shale is a sedimentary rock. Heat and pressure underground change the minerals in the shale. The shale becomes slate, a metamorphic rock. Granite is an igneous rock. It can be changed into gneiss, a metamorphic rock.

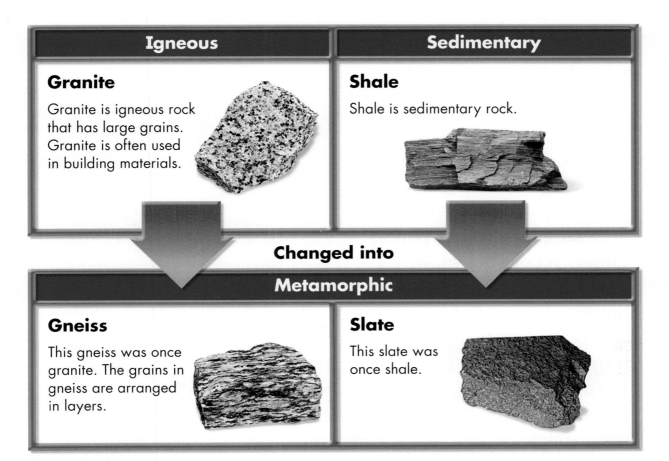

Igneous

Granite

Granite is igneous rock that has large grains. Granite is often used in building materials.

Sedimentary

Shale

Shale is sedimentary rock.

Changed into

Metamorphic

Gneiss

This gneiss was once granite. The grains in gneiss are arranged in layers.

Slate

This slate was once shale.

✓ Lesson Checkpoint

1. How is igneous rock that forms above ground different from igneous rock that forms below ground?

2. Describe clues, found in sedimentary rock, which show that living things have changed over time.

3. **Writing in Science** **Expository** List facts in your **science journal** about the three kinds of rocks. Then write a paragraph describing each of the three kinds.

What are minerals?

Minerals are the most common solid material found on Earth. Gold and silver are rare minerals. Rock salt and quartz are common minerals.

Identifying Minerals

Color is a property you notice easily about a mineral. But some minerals can be found in different colors. For example, the mineral quartz can be pink, purple, yellow, brown, white, or black. Other minerals always have the same color.

A better way to identify a mineral is by the color in its powder form. When you rub a mineral across a rough surface, it may leave a streak mark or powder. The color of these effects are always the same even if two pieces of the mineral are different colors.

Luster is a property that shows how a mineral reflects light. Minerals can be metallic, pearly, silky, greasy, glassy, or dull.

The mineral magnetite has the property of magnetism. Objects that contain iron are pulled to the magnetite.

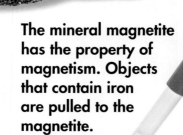

Vinegar fizzes on limestone that contains the mineral calcite. The fizzing happens because the vinegar reacts with the calcite. The reaction gives off carbon dioxide.

Properties of Minerals

Mineral	Color	Luster	Streak	Hardness
Mica Mica breaks into flaky pieces when struck.	black, gray, green, violet	pearly on surfaces	white	can be scratched with a knife
Molybdenite This mineral is one of the strongest and most commonly used heat-resistant metals.	silvery	metallic	bluish gray	can be scratched with a fingernail
Crocoite Much of this mineral comes from Australia.	reddish-orange	very shiny	orange-yellow	can be scratched with a coin

Another way to identify a mineral is to test its hardness. Some minerals, such as talc, are so soft you can scratch them with your fingernail. The hardest mineral is diamond. It can be scratched only by another diamond.

Some minerals can be identified by their appearance. Gold, for example, appears sometimes in nugget form. Other minerals can be identified by taste, smell, or touch.

1. ✓**Checkpoint** What are ways to identify minerals?

2. **Compare and Contrast** How are rocks and minerals alike? How are they different? Use a graphic organizer to show your answer.

How the Body Uses Minerals

These are some ways that the body uses minerals.

Mineral	How Used
Calcium	Helps form bones and teeth and helps cause muscles to contract
Chromium	Helps change digested food into energy
Copper	Helps form skin and other tissues
Iron	Carries oxygen in blood to all parts of the body
Potassium	Helps nerves and muscles work
Phosphorus	Helps release energy and form bones and teeth
Sodium	Helps control water levels and carry messages through nerves

How We Use Minerals

It is almost impossible to go through a day without using minerals. The cavity-fighting fluoride in your toothpaste came from the mineral fluorite. The glass you look through in your window came from the minerals quartz, soda ash, and limestone. The salt in your food is the mineral halite. The metal in your spoon is a mineral. Even the graphite that you write with in your pencil is a mineral. Almost everything we use is made from minerals or contains minerals.

Minerals Keep Us Healthy

People also need minerals to keep their bodies healthy and full of energy. Many of these minerals are found in plants. Green leafy vegetables, such as spinach, contain calcium. Iron is found in fruit and green vegetables. Sodium in vegetables such as celery, and potassium in fruits work together to help transmit nerve impulses and control muscles. Almost everything we eat has some minerals in it.

✓ Lesson Checkpoint

1. What is a mineral?
2. Why are minerals important to your health?
3. **Writing in Science** **Expository** In your **science journal** list five things you did today that used minerals. Use a chart with two columns. Head the first column, *Activity*. Head the second, *Mineral*.

Other Ways We Use Minerals

Halite

The mineral halite is crushed and then ground up. We use it to flavor and preserve food. (We know this mineral as table salt.)

Copper

The mineral copper is found in igneous rock. The rocks are mined from the ground. When the rocks are crushed and heated, the copper becomes separated from the rock. Then, the copper can be made into objects such as pots and pans.

Fluorite

The mineral fluorite is found in many rocks, such as granite. The rocks are crushed and the fluorite is separated out. Then, it is used to make many products such as toothpaste.

Lead

Lead is found in a mineral known as galena. The rocks are crushed and heated to produce lead. Lead is put into aprons such as the ones shown to protect people while X-ray pictures are taken.

Iron

Iron is a mineral found in the rock called hematite. The rocks are crushed and heated. Then, iron in the melted material is separated out. Iron is mixed with other materials to make steel. Steel is used for many tools and machines.

Earthworms mix up the topsoil as they dig through it. That improves the soil.

We depend on topsoil to grow our food.

Soil must pack down hard and stay firm so that houses built on it don't shift.

Why is soil important?

Soil is an important part of the system that supports all life on land. Soil and parts of soil have different properties.

Parts of Soil

Soil is the thin layer of loose material that covers most of Earth's land. Soil is not simply dirt. Natural processes develop soil over a long period of time. It takes hundreds of years for nature to rebuild lost topsoil. Soil has the material plants need to grow.

Squeeze a handful of soil and see that it's more than bits of rock. Soil might clump together because it holds water and material that was once living.

Living things in soil break down the remains of plants and animals. This process is called **decay.** Decay releases things plants need in order to grow. Each of these things is a **nutrient.** Some minerals also release nutrients. Water and nutrients support most plants on land, including crops. When you think about it, soil is more valuable than gold!

Soil Layers

Soil is organized into layers. Different places have layers of different thicknesses and color.

Topsoil

Topsoil is the top layer. Topsoil includes rock particles mixed with the dark products of decay. The decayed parts of plant and animal remains are called humus. Humus contains much of what plants need to grow.

Subsoil

Subsoil is under topsoil. It is often lighter in color than topsoil. It doesn't have as much humus as topsoil. Subsoil includes pieces of broken rocks. Tree roots grow into the subsoil. Water from precipitation may be in this layer.

Bedrock

As this rock breaks down, it provides raw material for making new soil.

1. ✅ **Checkpoint** What is soil made of?

2. **Math** in Science Suppose it takes 1,500 years for 1 centimeter of soil to form in a certain place. How long would it take for 2 centimeters of soil to form? Show your work.

Comparing Soils

Soil is not the same everywhere. Soil near your home may be different than soil at your school. The kind of soil depends in part on the types of rock particles that help make up the soil. Sand, silt, and clay are the three main types of particles found in soil. They differ in size. Sand particles are the largest. Clay particles are the smallest.

Sand
Large spaces in sand allow water to easily pass through. Roots of many plants in sandy soil may not have time to soak up the water. Sandy soil feels rough and gritty.

Silt
The medium-sized particles in silt are more closely packed together. Although water passes through silt, silty soil also holds water well.

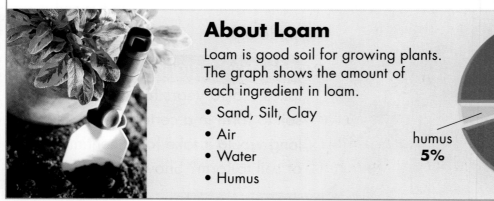

About Loam
Loam is good soil for growing plants. The graph shows the amount of each ingredient in loam.

- Sand, Silt, Clay
- Air
- Water
- Humus

sand, silt, clay **45%**

air **25%**

water **25%**

humus **5%**

All soil has the same four ingredients. Weathered rocks containing minerals make up most of the soil. Humus makes up another part. Humus is made up of decaying plants and animals. Humus is a very important part of soil. Air and water fill in the spaces between particles of rock and humus.

Most soils are a mixture of sand, silt, and clay. Soils with this mixture are called **loam.** Loam also contains humus, which has many minerals and other nutrients. Loam soil with its minerals, humus, air, and water is a very good mixture for growing most plants. Loam soils hold onto water loosely enough for plant roots to soak it up.

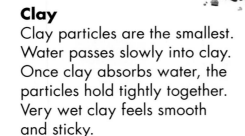

Clay
Clay particles are the smallest. Water passes slowly into clay. Once clay absorbs water, the particles hold tightly together. Very wet clay feels smooth and sticky.

✔ **Lesson Checkpoint**

1. Explain the importance of soil.

2. Compare the ability of sand, silt, and clay to hold water.

3. **Social Studies** in Science Find information about states that have many large farms. Find out which fruits, vegetables, and grains grow in each area.

Lab zone Guided Inquiry

Investigate How much water can soil hold?

Materials

small measuring cup

3 clear plastic cups and 3 foam cups

sandy, clay, and loam soils

hand lens and pencil

paper towel and scissors

spoon and masking tape

graduated cylinder (or measuring cup)

water

Process Skills

By **measuring** carefully, you can find out which type of soil can hold the most water.

What to Do

1. Get 60 mL of each type of soil.

   sandy soil
   loam soil
   clay soil
   Label the cups.

2. **Observe** the soil samples with a hand lens. Describe their properties (color, texture).

   sandy soil
   loam soil
   clay soil

3. Punch 10 holes in the bottom of each foam cup.

4. Set each cup on the paper towel and trace around the bottom. Cut out the 3 circles you traced and put one inside each cup, over the holes.

5 Put each of your soil samples into a different foam cup. Pack down the soil using a spoon.

inside view

outside view

clay soil

clay soil

paper towel

foam cup

plastic cup

6 Put each foam cup inside a clear plastic cup. Pour 50 mL of water on each soil sample. Wait 10 minutes. Use a graduated cylinder to **measure** the amount of water in the clear plastic cups. Record your **data**.

Type of Soil	Amount of Soil (mL)	Amount of Water Added (mL)	Amount of Water Collected in 10 Minutes (mL)
Sandy soil			
Clay soil			
Loam soil			

Explain Your Results

1. Describe the color, texture, and other properties of each soil you **observed**. What do you think each is made of?

2. Based on your **measurements**, which type of soil holds the most water? the least?

Go Further

In which soil would desert plants grow best? Make a plan to answer this or another question you may have.

Living Soil

Soil is made mostly of bits of rock. But it contains a lot of other things, too. Students at different schools wanted to explore the living things in soil. You might be surprised by what they found and how "alive" the ground is under your feet.

Students at Maple Creek School dug 10 samples of soil. They looked at each sample carefully. They counted the numbers of different animals in the soil samples. Their table on page 213 shows the totals. They found more ants than any other kind of animal. Students at Forest Grove School also dug 10 soil samples and counted animals. Their table is also on page 213.

Soil Animals at Maple Creek School

Beetles	Ants	Spiders	Earthworms
55	430	32	189

Soil Animals at Forest Grove School

Beetles	Ants	Spiders	Earthworms
24	235	48	95

Use the tables above to answer the questions.

1 How many animals were found in the samples at Forest Grove School?

A. 299　　　　　B. 402

C. 706　　　　　D. 1,020

2 How many more ants were found at Maple Creek School than at Forest Grove School?

F. 205　　　　　G. 665

H. 195　　　　　I. 470

3 How many earthworms were found all together?

A. 284　　　　　B. 174

C. 274　　　　　D. 94

Lab zone Take-Home Activity

With an adult, get a small shovel full of soil. Spread it out on a driveway, outdoor table, or sidewalk. Be sure to wear gloves. Keep a record of the animals you find. Don't harm the animals. Remember to return them and the soil to the place you found them.

Use Vocabulary

decay (page 206)	**mineral** (page 199)
igneous rock (page 200)	**nutrient** (page 206)
loam (page 209)	**rock** (page 199)
metamorphic rock (page 201)	**sedimentary rock** (page 200)
	soil (page 206)

Use the vocabulary word from the list above that best completes each sentence.

1. Rock made up of layers of sediment that have hardened is _____.

2. Most of the land is covered with a thin layer of loose material called _____.

3. A(n) _____ is a natural material that makes up rock.

4. When living things _____, they break down, or rot.

5. Soil that is a mixture of sand, silt, clay, minerals, and decayed matter is called _____.

6. Any kind of solid, nonliving material found on Earth and made of minerals is a(n) _____.

7. Each type of small particle that plants take into their roots is a(n) _____, found in good growing soil.

8. Rock that has changed to another type of rock by heat and pressure is _____.

9. Rock that forms when melted Earth materials cool and harden is _____.

Explain Concepts

10. What is one way that sedimentary rock forms?

11. Explain why a bone is not considered a mineral.

12. Describe the layers of soil from top to bottom.

Process Skills

13. Predict Which would dry faster after it rains: a sandy beach or a grassy field? Give a reason for your answer.

14. Model Make a model or a drawing that shows the different layers of soil.

15. Infer You observe that a mineral sample can be scratched with a coin. What do you infer about the hardness of the mineral?

Compare and Contrast

16. Make a graphic organizer like the one below. Fill it in to compare and contrast sandy soil and clay soil.

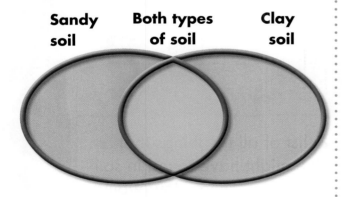

Sandy soil Both types of soil Clay soil

Test Prep

Choose the letter that best completes the statement or answers the question.

17. All rocks contain
- (A) loam.
- (B) minerals.
- (C) water.
- (D) sediments.

18. In what rocks are fossils most often found?
- (F) sedimentary
- (G) igneous
- (H) metamorphic
- (I) all of the above

19. The layer of soil just below the topsoil is
- (A) loam.
- (B) decayed matter.
- (C) rock.
- (D) subsoil.

20. Writing in Science

Persuasive Write a letter to a member of a city council that discusses why rich farmland is valuable to everyone in the community.

Dr. Elissa R. Levine

Dr. Levine's interest in soil began when she was a child.

Dr. Levine is a Soil Scientist for NASA's Goddard Space Flight Center. She has been interested in soil for a long time. She once said, "When I was little my mother sat me in the soil and showed me all kinds of interesting things to look at and play with. I've been interested in the soil ever since."

Dr. Levine gathers information from pictures taken by satellites that travel high over Earth. The pictures tell about our environment. She also studies the ways that soil changes all around the world. She is trying to find the causes of these changes.

Dr. Levine also teaches about soil to students all over the world. The students gather data about soil. Dr. Levine uses the information to make computer models of the soils. She has found that soil connects all the other parts of our environment together.

Lab zone Take-Home Activity

Make a list of all the things that Dr. Levine might have found in soil when she was a child. How would each thing help the soil?

EC CRU 10 9 8 7 6 5 4 3 2 1

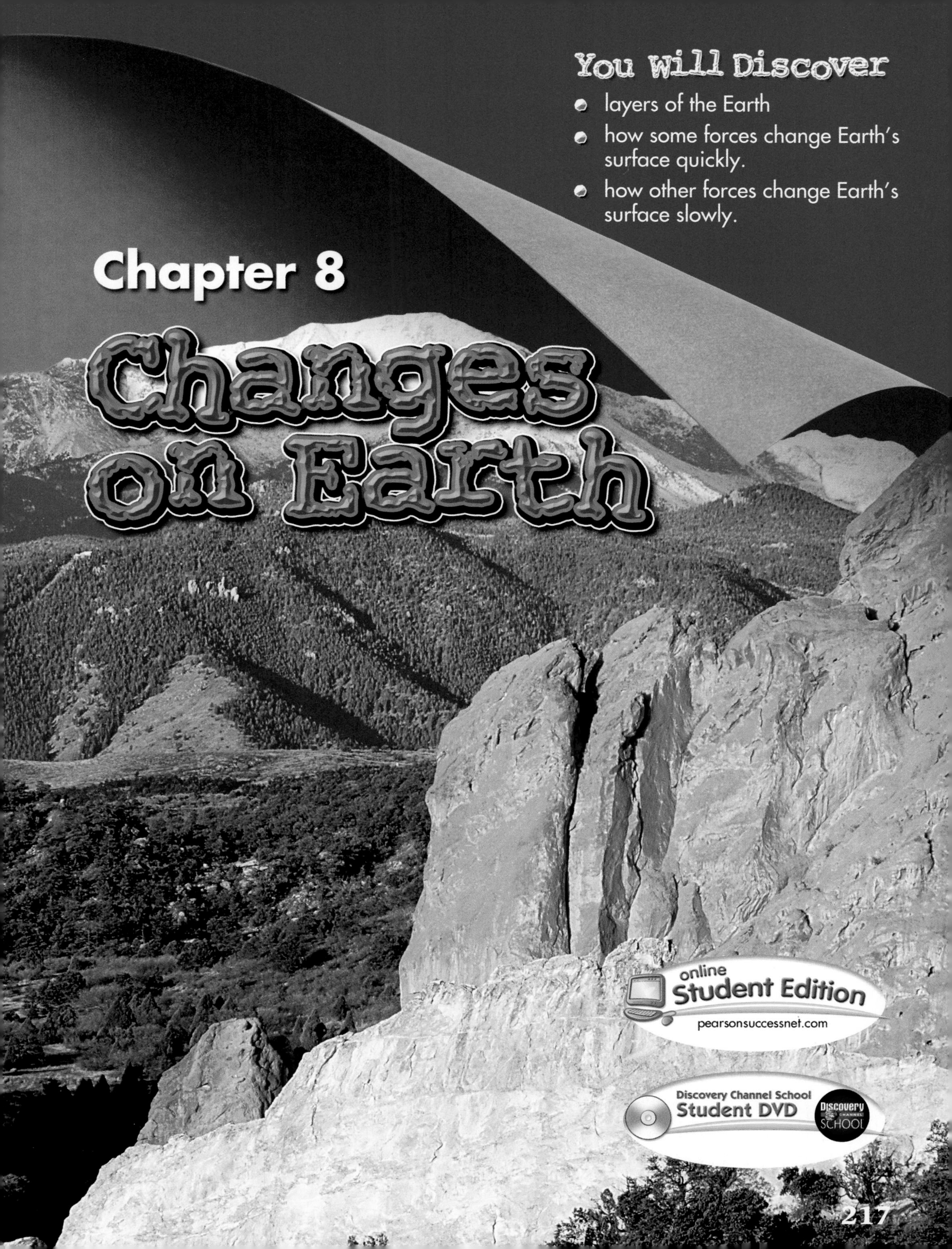

You Will Discover

- layers of the Earth
- how some forces change Earth's surface quickly.
- how other forces change Earth's surface slowly.

Chapter 8

Changes on Earth

online
Student Edition
pearsonsuccessnet.com

Discovery Channel School
Student DVD
Discovery Channel School

How do forces cause changes on Earth's surface?

magma

lava

landform

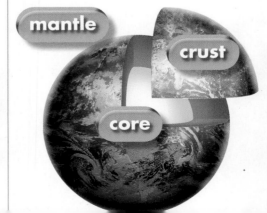

mantle

crust

core

218

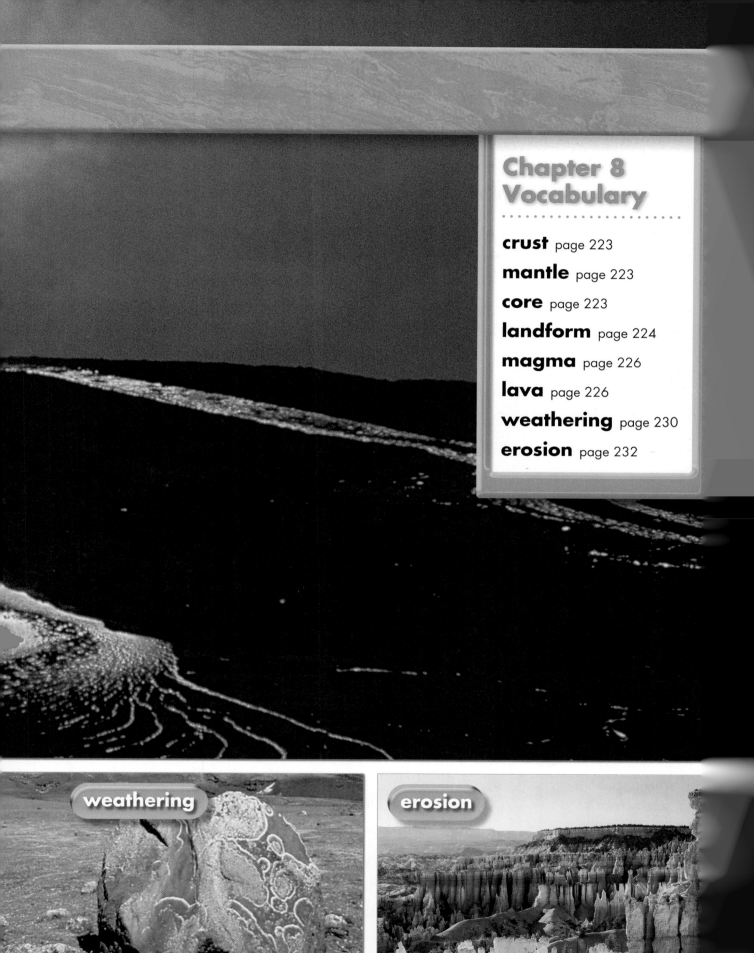

weathering

erosion

219

Explore How do some mountains form?

Materials

clay

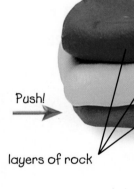

waxed paper

What to Do

1 Make a **model** of one way mountains can form. First, make flat layers of clay. Then, stack the layers on waxed paper.

2 Next, push on the ends of the clay. Keep the clay on the waxed paper.

surface of the Earth

Push!

Push!

layers of rock

In real life this change would be too slow to see.

Do not change what you record just because your results are different from those of someone else.

3 Finally, record what happens to your model. Make a sketch or diagram.

Explain Your Results

1. This model shows a way some mountains form. Think about the layers of rock in this type of mountain. Do you think the layers will be mostly tilted or mostly level? Explain.

2. Compare and contrast your model and a real mountain. How does **using the model** help you learn about real mountains?

Process Skills

When scientists **use a model** to help learn about a real thing, they compare and contrast the model and the real thing.

How to Read Science

Sequence

A **sequence** is a series of actions that take place in a certain order.

- A writer might use clue words such as *first, then, next,* and *finally* to show a sequence.

- An artist might use numbers and labels in a drawing to show a sequence.

Science Article

Eruption

How does a volcano erupt? First, pressure and heat melt rock within the Earth. This material is magma, a hot, thick liquid mixed with gases. Then, some of the material rises through cracks in the rock above it. Next, the liquid rock and gases build up pressure on the rock at the surface. Finally, the pressure gets so great that liquid rock, gases, and bits of rock come out of the ground.

Apply It!

Make a sequence to **model** how a volcano forms. Place information you read into a graphic organizer like this one.

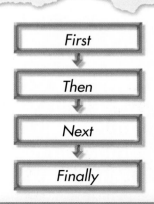

First

↓

Then

↓

Next

↓

Finally

🔊 You Are There!

What is that billowing cloud on the horizon? What is making that rumbling sound? Is there a storm forming over there? No, it's a volcano erupting! The cloud above the volcano rises miles high. The Sun disappears behind the huge plume of smoke and ash. What force could cause such a tremendous change?

AudioText 🔊

Lesson 1

What are Earth's layers?

If you could remove a big chunk of Earth, you would see that it is made up of layers.

Mantle

Crust

Core

Earth's Layers

Earth can be divided into three main layers. You live on the outer layer of Earth—the **crust.** Earth's crust is made of different kinds of rock. The thickness of the crust varies from place to place. Its thickness under the continents is about 37 kilometers (23 miles). That may seem pretty thick. If you compare all the Earth to a peach, however, the Earth's crust would be just the skin.

Beneath the crust lies the **mantle.** Earth's mantle is made of very hot igneous and metamorphic rock. It may flow like oozing toothpaste.

The **core** is the innermost layer of Earth. It is made of metal. The core is hot enough to melt. The center of the core is packed together so tightly, however, that it remains mostly solid. The much larger outer part of the core is a very hot, dense liquid.

1. **✓Checkpoint** What is Earth's core like?

2. **Writing in Science** **Expository** Compare Earth's layers to the parts of a peach. Make a labeled drawing in your **science journal**. Then, write a paragraph that compares the two.

223

Shapes on Earth's Surface

Does the land near you have mountains, hills, and valleys? Each is an example of a **landform.** Landforms are the solid features formed on Earth's crust. Other features include bodies of water.

Many forces shape landforms. These forces come from above and below Earth's crust. Moving water, though, is the main force. For example, rivers can act like saws. Pebbles and sand in the moving water slowly cut through rock. Flooding rivers deposit pebbles, sand, and silt on their banks. These processes help shape valleys. Notice how many of the landforms below were shaped by water.

Glacier
A glacier is a large, moving body of ice. It forms in cold places where snow and ice pile up year after year. It slowly moves downhill.

Valley
A valley is a low, narrow area on the crust. Some valleys are formed by rivers, while others are formed by glaciers.

Plateau
A plateau is a plain that is higher than the land around it.

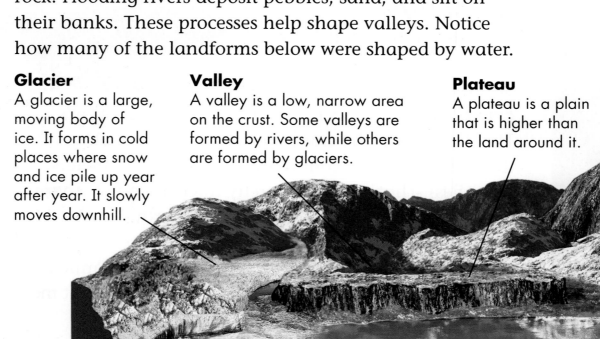

Ocean
The ocean is the salt water that covers almost three-fourths of Earth's surface.

Coast
The coast is land next to the ocean, which helps to shape the coastline.

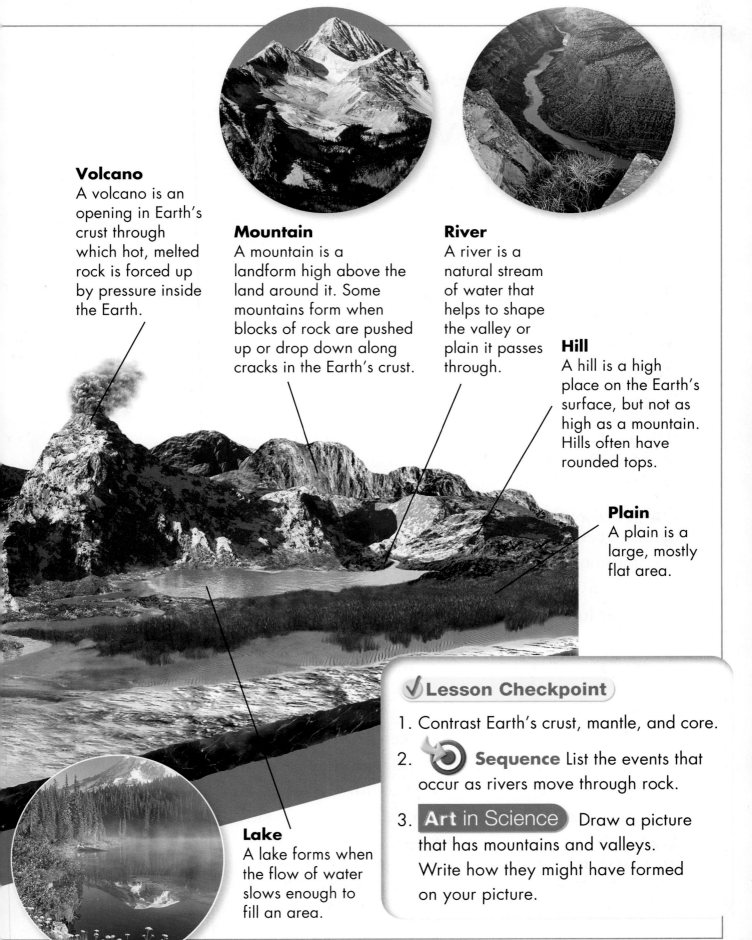

Volcano
A volcano is an opening in Earth's crust through which hot, melted rock is forced up by pressure inside the Earth.

Mountain
A mountain is a landform high above the land around it. Some mountains form when blocks of rock are pushed up or drop down along cracks in the Earth's crust.

River
A river is a natural stream of water that helps to shape the valley or plain it passes through.

Hill
A hill is a high place on the Earth's surface, but not as high as a mountain. Hills often have rounded tops.

Plain
A plain is a large, mostly flat area.

Lake
A lake forms when the flow of water slows enough to fill an area.

✓ Lesson Checkpoint

1. Contrast Earth's crust, mantle, and core.

2. **Sequence** List the events that occur as rivers move through rock.

3. **Art in Science** Draw a picture that has mountains and valleys. Write how they might have formed on your picture.

What are volcanoes and earthquakes?

Volcanoes and earthquakes cause rapid and sometimes dangerous changes in the landscape.

How Do Volcanoes Form?

Volcanoes begin deep within the mantle where **magma** forms. Magma is hot, pasty rock that moves within the mantle. Magma close to the suface melts and flows easily because the pressure is less. Magma can gush out of weak spots in the crust, aided by the pressure of gases it contains. A volcano is an opening out of which this hot material erupts.

An eruption is like opening a can of shaken soda. Bubbles of gas separate from the liquid and force the liquid out. Material that erupts from a volcano contains ash, cinders, and hot, molten rock called **lava.** As lava cools and hardens, it becomes igneous rock. That's brand-new crust! If the rock builds to great heights, a mountain or island forms.

Volcanoes

Magma collects in large pockets called magma chambers. As magma leaves the chamber, it moves up a tunnel or central vent. Sometimes, magma escapes from the central vent and erupts from side vents. Most magma, however, erupts at the top of the volcano through a bowl-shaped crater.

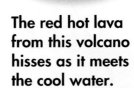

The red hot lava from this volcano hisses as it meets the cool water.

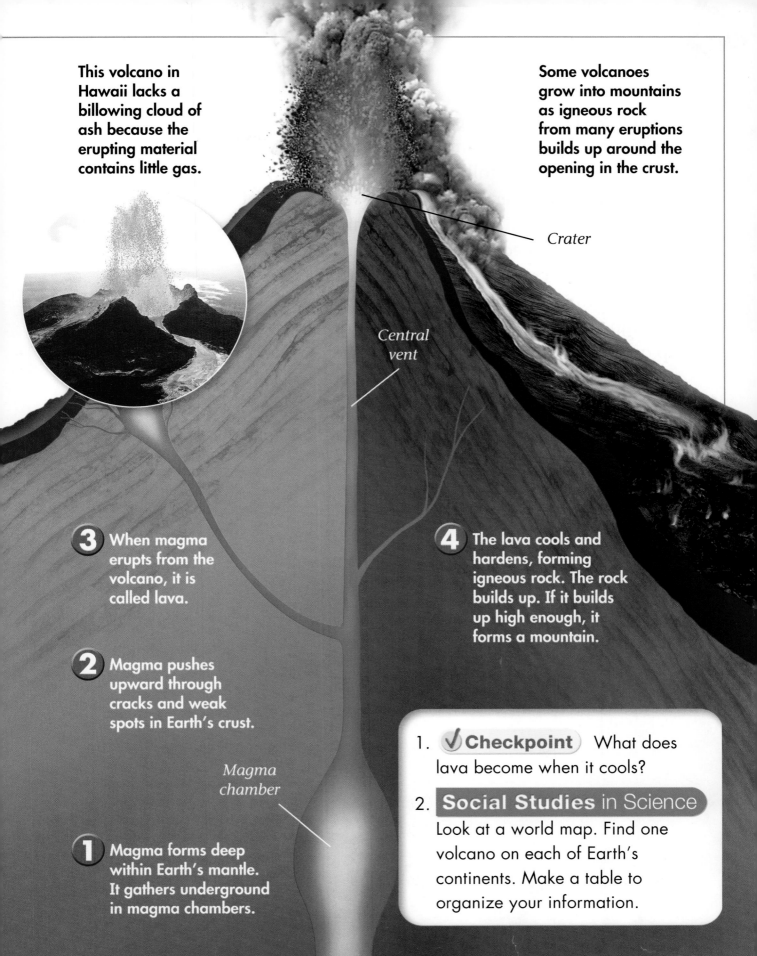

This volcano in Hawaii lacks a billowing cloud of ash because the erupting material contains little gas.

Some volcanoes grow into mountains as igneous rock from many eruptions builds up around the opening in the crust.

Crater

Central vent

3 When magma erupts from the volcano, it is called lava.

4 The lava cools and hardens, forming igneous rock. The rock builds up. If it builds up high enough, it forms a mountain.

2 Magma pushes upward through cracks and weak spots in Earth's crust.

Magma chamber

1 Magma forms deep within Earth's mantle. It gathers underground in magma chambers.

1. ✔**Checkpoint** What does lava become when it cools?

2. **Social Studies** in Science
Look at a world map. Find one volcano on each of Earth's continents. Make a table to organize your information.

227

Earthquakes

Have you ever built a play house out of flimsy cardboard? A sudden bump sends vibrations through the house and it can fall over. In a similar way, sudden shifts between parts of Earth's crust cause the ground to vibrate in all directions. This shaking is an earthquake. Most earthquakes happen along faults. A fault is a large crack in the Earth's crust.

The vibrations of an earthquake move as waves through the Earth. Waves move back and forth and up and down along Earth's surface. These waves can cause cracks in the Earth's surface. Rubble can pile up in areas where the crust moved.

The 15-second Loma Prieta earthquake in 1989 destroyed this road in Oakland, California.

Earthquake Damage

The damage an earthquake causes depends on how close the earthquake is to the surface and how long the crust shakes. Also, the closer an earthquake is to a city or town, the more damage it can cause to buildings, bridges, and underground pipes.

An earthquake can cause landslides. Landslides are just what you might think they are. They are downhill movements of rocks and earth. The loose surface of the land slides down a slope.

Landslides can happen on the ocean floor or on land. Undersea landslides can form giant waves. Landslides on hills and mountains can ruin homes and destroy roads. They can bury large areas.

Vibrations from an earthquake cause cracks such as this one.

Parts of this parking garage snapped during a 1994 earthquake.

Loose soil and rock slid down this hillside during a landslide.

✓ Lesson Checkpoint

1. Compare and contrast magma and lava.

2. Where do most earthquakes happen? Why?

3. **Sequence** Use a graphic organizer to show the steps in the eruption of a volcano.

229

The growing roots of this tree in Arizona are helping to break the rock apart.

What are weathering and erosion?

Weathering and erosion are forces that change the surface of the Earth.

Weathering

Landforms change constantly. For this to happen, rocks in landforms must first break apart. **Weathering** is any action that breaks rocks into smaller pieces.

Weathering changes can be very slow. Some may take less than a year. Others might take centuries. Weathering goes on all the time.

Plants sometimes cause weathering. Their roots can grow into cracks in rocks. As the roots grow, they can split and break up the rocks.

Water can soak through soil. The water changes the minerals in rock below the soil. The rock is weakened and it begins to break apart.

While in a glacier, this rock became smaller and smoother as forces acted upon it.

When water freezes and thaws, it can cause weathering. Water can get into cracks in rocks. When water freezes, it expands, or grows larger. The ice pushes against the sides of the cracks. Over the years, the rocks may break apart.

Ice weathers rocks in another way. A glacier is a huge amount of ice that moves slowly over Earth's crust. As a glacier moves, it carries rocks with it. The rocks and ice scrape against the ground. The huge force of this action grinds valleys wide and smooth. When a glacier melts, weathered rocks of all sizes are left on the ground.

1. ✔Checkpoint Describe weathering, giving three examples.

2. **Math** in Science Look at the pictures of rocks on this page. How much bigger is a boulder than a cobble? How much smaller is a sand grain than a pebble? How many sand grains could you line up along a meter stick?

Sizes of Rocks

Weathering breaks rocks into smaller and smaller pieces. Water wears many rocks to a smooth and rounded shape. The following lists the order of size from largest to smallest.

Boulder 300 mm

Cobble 100 mm

Pebble 30 mm

Sand 1 mm

Silt Each is a tiny speck!

Clay You need a microscope to see clay particles!

It took millions of years for waves carrying sand and pebbles to carve a hole in this cliff.

This island formed as sand settled from moving water. Waves will continue to shape it.

The whole side of this hill has moved down.

Erosion

Sometimes weathered material stays in place. Sometimes it is picked up and slowly or quickly carried to other places. The movement of weathered material is **erosion.** Water, wind, gravity, and glaciers can cause erosion.

Erosion by Water and Wind

Water causes erosion in many places. Rainwater can carry away soil from farm fields. Waves cause erosion along shorelines. Rivers carry bits of rock from place to place. Sand and mud flow over a river's banks during a flood.

New islands can form as a result of erosion. This happens when rivers carry rock and bits of soil to the ocean. These particles build up over time. Some form islands just off the coast. Wind and waves continue to shape these islands.

Erosion by wind is common in dry regions, such as deserts. Wind can carry dry sand and soil to other places. Few tall plants grow in deserts, so there is little to stop the particles from blowing around. The particles bump into rocks and break off tiny grains. Over time, more grains are broken off. The rocks slowly change.

Erosion by Gravity and Living Things

Gravity can cause erosion. Gravity pulls rocks and soil downhill. This material moves slowly on gentle slopes. Weathered material can move quickly on steep slopes. A mudflow is the quick movement of very wet soil. A rockslide is the quick movement of rocks down a slope.

Living things can cause erosion. Ground squirrels tunnel through soil. Worms mix and move soil. Ants move soil to make underground nests. Erosion continues as water and air move through the tunnels.

Map Fact

Water erosion shaped these rocks in Bryce Canyon in Utah. The shapes that look like creatures are called "hoodoos."

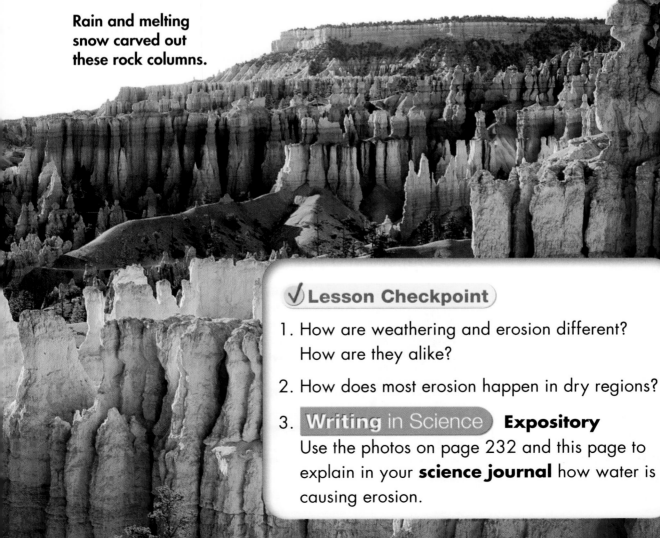

Rain and melting snow carved out these rock columns.

✓ Lesson Checkpoint

1. How are weathering and erosion different? How are they alike?

2. How does most erosion happen in dry regions?

3. **Writing** in Science **Expository**
Use the photos on page 232 and this page to explain in your **science journal** how water is causing erosion.

233

Investigate How can you observe erosion?

Materials

safety goggles

small paper cups and pencil

tub and spoon

sand, mud, rocks

eraser and ruler

water

Process Skills

Recording your careful **observations** in a chart is one way of **collecting data**.

What to Do

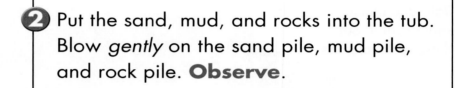

① Poke 4 holes in the bottom of a paper cup. This is your Rain Cup.

Poke from the inside!

Rain Cup

Be careful! Wear safety goggles!

② Put the sand, mud, and rocks into the tub. Blow *gently* on the sand pile, mud pile, and rock pile. **Observe**.

③ Use an eraser to prop up the back edge of the tub. Fill a small paper cup $\frac{1}{2}$ full with water. Hold the Rain Cup 4 cm above the sand. Quickly pour water into the Rain Cup. Observe. **Collect data**. Record your observations in a chart.

	Amount of Erosion by Wind and Water	
	Effect of Blowing	**Effect of Moving Water**
Sand		
Mud		
Rocks		

4 Repeat step 3 for the mud pile and the rock pile.

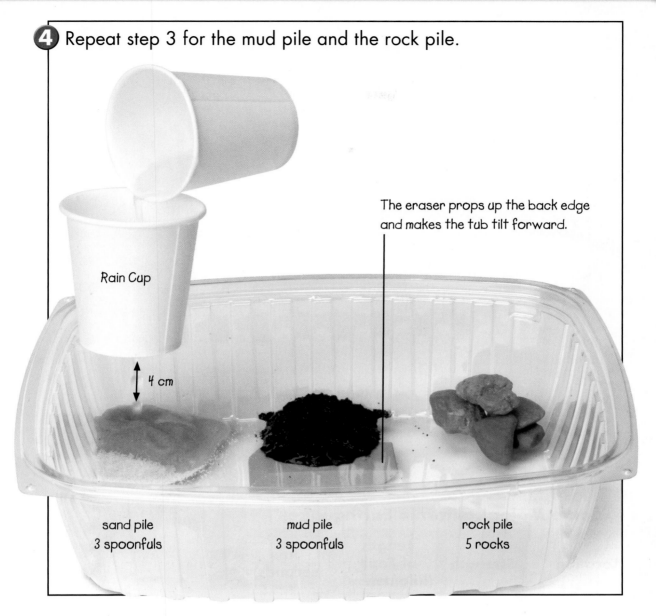

Rain Cup

4 cm

The eraser props up the back edge and makes the tub tilt forward.

sand pile
3 spoonfuls

mud pile
3 spoonfuls

rock pile
5 rocks

Explain Your Results

1. **Interpret Data** Which caused more erosion, blowing air or moving water? Which was eroded the most, the sand pile, the mud pile, or the rock pile? Which was eroded the least?

2. How is your **model** like what happens in the real world? How is it different? How can your model be used to learn about erosion?

Go Further

How could you change your model to prevent water or wind erosion? Think of a way to solve the problem. Then use your model to test your solution.

Math in Science

Measuring an Earthquake

"The earthquake measured 6.7 on the Richter scale." Did you ever hear a news reporter talk about an earthquake this way? The number tells how strong the earthquake was. The strength of an earthquake depends on how much the rocks along the fault moved and how long the earthquake lasts.

In the table below, 9 earthquakes are listed in order of their strength, from least to greatest.

Some Major California Earthquakes			
Location	**Strength**	**Length of Fault (kilometers)**	**Time (seconds)**
Whittier Narrows	5.9	6	3
North Palm Springs	5.9	20	4
Borrego Mountain	6.5	25	6
Northridge	6.7	14	7
Loma Prieta	7.0	40	15
Landers	7.3	70	24
Kern County	7.5	75	27
San Francisco	7.7	400	110
Fort Tejon	7.8	360	130

Use the table on page 236 to answer these questions.

1. Which earthquake was the strongest?
   A. San Francisco
   B. Kern County
   C. Loma Prieta
   D. Fort Tejon

2. Which earthquake lasted the least amount of time?
   F. Whittier Narrows
   G. Fort Tejon
   H. Landers
   I. Northridge

3. Which earthquake happened along the longest fault?
   A. North Palm Springs
   B. Borrego Mountain
   C. Fort Tejon
   D. San Francisco

4. Which of these statements is true?
   F. Shorter faults produce stronger earthquakes.
   G. Longer faults produce weaker quakes.
   H. Stronger quakes last longer than weaker quakes.
   I. Weaker quakes last longer than stronger quakes.

Lab zone Take-Home Activity

Use the library to find data about these earthquakes: Chile, 1960; Alaska, 1964; Kuril Islands, 1963; Indonesia,1938; and Kamchatka, 1952. Arrange the earthquakes in a table like the one shown. How do these quakes compare with those that struck California?

Chapter 8 Review and Test Prep

Use Vocabulary

core (page 223)	**lava** (page 226)
crust (page 223)	**magma** (page 226)
erosion (page 232)	**mantle** (page 223)
landform (page 224)	**weathering** (page 230)

Use the vocabulary word from the box above that best completes each sentence.

1. Hot, molten rock on Earth's surface is _____.

2. Earth's _____ is the innermost layer of the planet.

3. A hill, a mountain, and a valley are each a(n) _____.

4. The thinnest layer of Earth is the _____.

5. Hot, molten rock that forms deep underground is _____.

6. Magma forms in Earth's thickest layer, which is called the _____.

7. The breaking of rocks into smaller pieces is _____.

8. The moving of weathered materials is _____.

Explain Concepts

9. Which is a better model of Earth's layers, a raw egg or a hard-boiled egg? Explain your choice.

10. Explain how weathering and erosion change Earth's landforms.

11. How do volcanoes change Earth's surface?

12. Compare and contrast erosion that wind causes and erosion that water causes.

Process Skills

13. **Classify** Classify each of the following as either weathering or erosion.
    - (A) a river carrying silt flooding its banks
    - (B) water freezing in the crack of a cliff
    - (C) mud sliding down a hill

14. **Model** Make a series of four drawings to show how a volcano builds up over time.

15. Infer A fault lies between a town with a few buildings and a city with many skyscrapers. The town is 10 miles from the fault. The city is 5 miles from the fault. Infer which area might have the most damage in an earthquake.

Sequence

16. Make a graphic organizer like the one below. Fill in the spaces to show the steps that water may take to weather rocks.

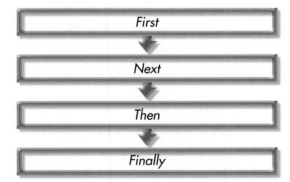

First

Next

Then

Finally

Test Prep

Choose the letter that best completes the statement or answers the question.

17. Why is Earth's core solid when it is hot enough to melt?

Ⓐ It is in the middle of the planet.

Ⓑ It is smaller than the mantle.

Ⓒ It is made of igneous rocks.

Ⓓ It is under great pressure.

18. What makes water a powerful cause of weathering?

Ⓕ It is a liquid.

Ⓖ It takes up more space when it freezes.

Ⓗ It evaporates.

Ⓘ It rains all the time.

19. Why is erosion by wind so effective in deserts?

Ⓐ Deserts are very moist.

Ⓑ Deserts are very dry.

Ⓒ Deserts are landforms.

Ⓓ Deserts do not have living things.

20. Writing in Science

Narrative Think of being in San Francisco in 1906. That year, a violent earthquake shook the city. Write a paragraph about your experience in this earthquake. Tell what happened during the earthquake and in the week following it.

Dr. Jean Dickey

Dr. Jean Dickey uses views of Earth from space to measure Earth's movements.

As a child growing up in Pennsylvania, Jean Dickey, like her mother, had a strong interest in math and science. While she was still in college, she worked at the Argonne National Laboratory. This laboratory does work in many areas of math and science.

Today, Dr. Dickey is a physicist at NASA's Jet Propulsion Laboratory. One of Dr. Dickey's recent projects was to investigate why Earth appears to be bulging around its middle. That's right! Earth is getting about 1 millimeter "fatter" near the equator each year. After much study, Dr. Dickey and others found two causes for Earth's "weight gain." One is the rapid melting of glaciers. Another is a change in the size and shape of Earth's oceans.

Dr. Dickey's group is also responsible for keeping an eye on Earth's movements in space. They measure and record even the smallest shifts in Earth's place in space. This information is used to help navigate spacecraft.

Lab zone Take-Home Activity

Draw and color a cartoon that shows what is happening to Earth around the equator. Include sentences that explain why it is getting larger.

EC CRU 10 9 8 7 6 5 4 3 2 1

Chapter 9
Natural Resources

You Will Discover

- ways we use natural resources.
- the difference between renewable and nonrenewable resources.
- ways you can help conserve natural resources.

online
Student Edition
pearsonsuccessnet.com

241

How can people use natural resources responsibly?

natural resource

renewable resource

nonrenewable resource

242

conservation

recycle

Explore How can you classify resources?

A resource is something people use. All the materials on this page come from or are made from resources.

Materials

grape

paper

wool cloth

aluminum foil

cup with water

plastic bottle

solar energy

solar energy

What to Do

1 **Classify** each resource in the List of Resources. Does it belong in group A, B, or C?

2 Look at each material in the Materials list. Match each with the resource it comes from.

List of Resources
grapevine
river
trees
bauxite (mined from the ground, contains aluminum)
sheep
sunlight
petroleum (oil, pumped out of the ground, used to make plastic)

Group A
Cannot be replaced

Group B
Can be replaced within a fairly short time

Group C
Cannot be used up

3 Now classify each material into a group based on the resource it comes from.

plastic bottle

wool cloth

aluminum foil

paper

solar energy

water

grape

Explain Your Results

Explain how you **classified** the resources and materials.

Process Skills

When you sorted the materials into the groups, you **classified** them based on the type of resource they came from.

How to Read Science

Compare and Contrast

When you **compare** things, you tell how they are alike. When you **contrast** things, you tell how they are different.

- Words such as *similar, like, all, both,* or *in the same way* are clues that things are being compared.
- Words such as *different, unlike,* or *in a different way* are clues that things are being contrasted.

Science Article

Worm Tunnels

Soil in which earthworms live is not like other soil. Earthworms dig tunnels in soil. As a result, plants grow in a different way.

Plant roots grow more quickly down tunnels. Rainwater and air that roots need move easily through them too. Also, earthworms leave body wastes in tunnels. These have a lot of nutrients that plants need to grow.

Unlike soil with worms, soil without earthworms cannot support plants as well.

Apply It!

Study the graphic organizer below.

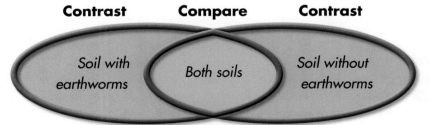

Contrast   Compare   Contrast

Soil with earthworms   Both soils   Soil without earthworms

Make a graphic organizer like the one shown. Use it to **classify** ways that these two soils are alike and different.

You are walking through a lush, green forest. A soft cushion of needles keeps your footsteps silent. You smell the trees. You hear chipmunks twittering in the branches. Birds dart back and forth. This is a beautiful place. But the trees may soon be cut down for lumber and paper. Can we keep our forests and still have the products we need?

AudioText 🔊

Lesson 1

What are resources?

Everything we use comes from materials found on Earth. Some of these materials can be replaced, but others cannot. Some resources are never used up.

Resources That Can Be Replaced

The things we need come from natural resources. A **natural resource** is an important material from the Earth that living things need.

Trees are a natural resource. People cut down trees for wood. Wood is used to build new houses. Wood chips are turned into pulp. Pulp is made into paper. Paper products include boxes, newspapers, and books.

People can plant new trees to replace those cut down. If the new trees get the sunlight, air, and water they need, they can grow big enough to be cut down. A resource that can be replaced in a fairly short time is called a **renewable resource.** Trees are a renewable resource.

These logs at a lumber or paper mill came from trees.

Lumber mills saw tree trunks into boards that are used to build new houses.

1. ✔**Checkpoint** What makes some resources renewable?

2. **Writing in Science** **Expository** In your **science journal** make a table with two columns. Title one column *Wood.* Title the other *Paper.* Use the table to list things found in your home made from each. Then, write two paragraphs about how your family uses wood and paper products.

Resources That Cannot Be Replaced

Many natural resources come from below the ground. Miners dig into the ground to get rocks called ores. Ores contain metals and other minerals that people use. Copper, iron, and aluminum are some useful metals. Hematite is an ore that contains the metal iron.

Steel is made from iron. Steel is used to make nails, cars, and many other products. There is only so much iron ore in the ground. Once we use it up, it cannot be replaced. A resource that cannot be replaced is a **nonrenewable resource.**

Coal is a nonrenewable resource. Like oil and natural gas, coal is a fuel. When it is burned it releases useful energy. The energy from these fuels can be used to heat buildings. The energy can power cars and planes. We can get more fuel by digging more of these materials from the ground. But supplies of these fuels are limited.

Using Resources	
Resource	**Uses**
Oil	Gasoline, paint, plastic, shampoo
Coal	Electricity, heat, paint thinner, insecticides
Iron ore	Machines, bicycles, autos, buildings

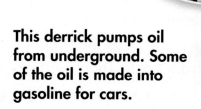

This derrick pumps oil from underground. Some of the oil is made into gasoline for cars.

When we use up an ore, mineral, or fuel resource in one place, we must find them in a new place. Mining and drilling can leave permanent marks, such as the open pit mine in the picture. Getting natural resources from Earth can change its surface.

Hematite is an ore that contains iron.

An Endless Supply of Resources

Some natural resources are not used up. Plants need sunlight, air, and water to grow. We need air to breathe and water to drink. These resources are not used up. Sunlight, air, and water are resources that are always available on Earth.

This coal formed in the Earth from plants that lived millions of years ago.

A huge crane loads coal into a dump truck at a mine.

✔ Lesson Checkpoint

1. List two nonrenewable resources.

2. Why is coal a nonrenewable resource?

3. **Compare and Contrast** How are renewable and nonrenewable resources alike? How are they different?

Dirty water is piped into a wetland in Florida. It will become clean enough to be piped back into a river.

Water from homes is filtered through sand in ponds like these. Farmers use the recycled water for their orange trees.

How can we protect our resources?

We must protect natural resources by not using them up or damaging them.

Using Resources Responsibly

When people walk instead of riding in a car, they save fuel. When they choose products that have less packaging, they save paper and plastic. There is less garbage. Saving in these ways is called conservation. **Conservation** is the wise use of natural resources so that people do not waste them or use them up.

Conserving Water

You can conserve water by using less of it. You can turn off the water while brushing your teeth and take shorter showers.

One way that communities conserve water is to clean used water. Wetlands can clean used water. First, the dirty water is piped into wetlands. Soil filters out harmful particles. Then, plants and tiny living things break down the particles. Finally, the water is clean enough to flow back into a river and be used again.

Conserving Soil

Soil needs protection from erosion. Some farmers plant crops around hills instead of up and down the hills. The curved rows of plants hold back rainwater. Soil soaks up water instead of being washed away. Farmers also plant trees by fields to keep soil from blowing away.

As people in cities need more room, they often build new houses on nearby farmland. Buildings and roads cover the soil. There is less farmland. Landfills may also take up famland space.

We can conserve soil in our own yards. We can put yard clippings and leaves where they decay instead of sending them to a landfill. The decayed material turns into compost. You can add compost to garden soil for fertilizer.

We could allow these leaves to decay into compost. Then they would add nutrients to soil.

Contour plowing keeps soil from washing away.

1. **✓ Checkpoint** Describe ways people can conserve water.

2. **Writing in Science** **Expository** Research ways to make a compost pile that will become fertilizer. In your **science journal** write a paragraph to explain it.

Using Up Land Space for Trash

Everything we use is made from natural resources. For example, plastic milk jugs are made from oil. Food cans are made from metals such as steel and tin. When we no longer need these products, we throw them away. They become trash. The trouble with our trash is that it never really goes away. A truck often hauls trash to a landfill. A landfill is a large area in which trash is buried. Trash rests on top of a liner so that pollution does not leak into groundwater. Once in place, we no longer have to see, smell, or worry about our garbage making us sick. But it still exists and the landfills continue to grow.

We put more than two hundred million tons of trash each year into landfills like this one.

What is in a Year's Worth of My Trash?	
Materials	**Mass (in kilograms)**
Paper	250
Plastic	80
Metal (steel cans)	40
Metal (aluminum cans)	10
Glass	40
Food scraps	80

Landfills are filling up and closing down. The number of landfills has fallen from 8,000 in 1988 to less than 2,000 today. Our need for land in which to bury our trash continues to grow. Most people, however, would rather see land used for other purposes.

One way we are reducing the need for landfill space is by burning garbage in special furnaces. Burning garbage also gives off energy that can heat buildings and generate electricity. However, the smoke from the burning must be cleaned. If the smoke is not cleaned, it can harm the air we breathe. Special smoke cleaners are expensive.

Another way we are lessening the need for landfill space is by reducing the amount of trash we make. If we were not doing this, we would have needed 100 new landfill areas. What are ways we are reducing the amount of trash we make?

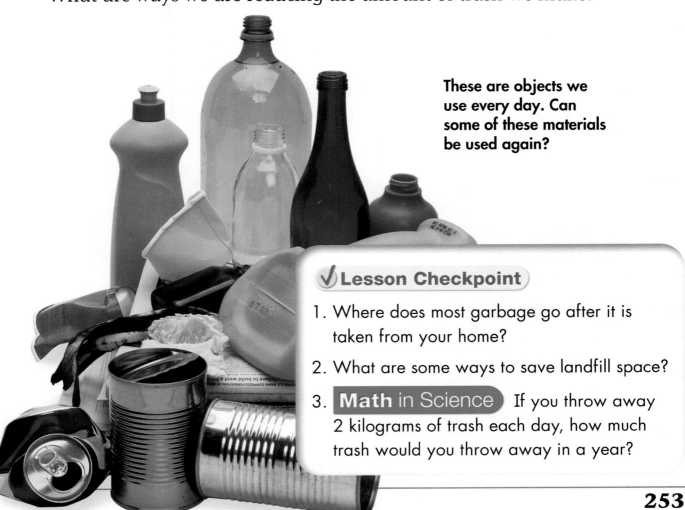

These are objects we use every day. Can some of these materials be used again?

✔ Lesson Checkpoint

1. Where does most garbage go after it is taken from your home?

2. What are some ways to save landfill space?

3. **Math** in Science If you throw away 2 kilograms of trash each day, how much trash would you throw away in a year?

What are ways to use resources again?

Many things can be used more than once. Old materials can be used to make new things. Reusing and recycling conserves land, keeping it from becoming landfill space.

Using Resources Again

When you reuse things, you conserve resources. For example, you can reuse cloth napkins, but not paper ones. You can reuse empty jars to store leftover food. Or you can give toys and clothes you have outgrown to others to use.

Another way to conserve resources is to recycle things that contain useful material. You **recycle** when you change something so that it can be used again. The useful resources that went into making objects can then be made into new products. Many of these new products are made from recycled metal, glass, plastic, or paper.

① Sort Glass
Recycled glass bottles and jars are separated by color. They are broken into small pieces.

② Ship to Glass Company
Pieces of glass are put into boxes. The boxes are shipped to a glass reprocessing company.

Let's follow the process used to recycle things that contain glass. Workers at the recycling plant sort glass by color. Common colors are clear, brown, and green. The bottles and jars are then broken into pieces called shards. Shards are shipped to glass companies. Glass shards must be passed under a magnet to remove metal caps and rings. Shards are then crushed into grain-sized particles called cullet. The cullet is cleaned and dried. Now the cullet is ready to be turned into new glass things. It is melted in furnaces and blown by machines into glass bottles and jars. Some is flattened into windowpanes. If glass is recycled, it can be used over and over again.

1. ✓Checkpoint What are the four main types of materials that are recycled?

2. **Compare and Contrast** How is recycling glass the same as recycling water? How does recycling glass differ from recycling water?

Process Crushed Glass
Glass bits are crushed into grain-sized particles. They are cleaned and dried.

Make New Glass Bottles
The bits are melted and reformed into glass bottles or jars.

255

This park bench was made from recycled plastic. It will last for about 50 years.

This wall is made of old tires and aluminum cans held together with mud and straw.

A reused plastic barrel makes a terrific flower pot.

Using Recycled Materials

Reusing and recycling are not new ideas. Your great-grandparents might have bought flour in cloth sacks. They cleaned the empty sacks, cut them, and sewed them into rags, towels, and even clothing!

Today, recycling is easier than ever. Many communities collect items to be recycled when they collect the regular garbage. Places such as movie theaters and office buildings have special containers for bottles and cans. Grocery stores collect used plastic shopping bags that can be recycled.

Conserving recycled material requires buying or using products that include it. For example, you can shop for products made out of recycled material. Your next sleeping bag might include stuffing made out of shredded plastic bottles. Your next sweater might be knit out of yarn recycled from old garments. Or you can play on playgrounds that have a surface made out of shredded car tires.

This playhouse was made from recycled plastic milk bottles.

The Three *R's*

What's a good way to remember what you've learned to protect natural resources? Just think about the three *R's*—reduce, reuse, and recycle. *Reduce* the amount of resources you use and the trash you make. *Reuse* old things in new ways. *Recycle* everything you can. Every time you practice one of the three *R's*, you are helping to care for Earth.

Stuffing in this sleeping bag and yarn in this sweater are from recycled materials.

✓Lesson Checkpoint

1. Why is it important to recycle?

2. What are the three *R's*?

3. **Art** in Science Draw or make a model showing how you might reuse something in an unusual way.

Investigate Where are some freshwater resources?

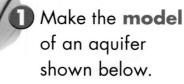

When it rains, some water soaks into the ground. This water collects in aquifers, layers of underground rock, gravel, and sand. People drill wells to get this water. People also get water from lakes and rivers.

Materials

safety goggles

container and gravel

paper cups and water

metric ruler

pencil and tape

spray nozzle and piece of nylon

plastic bag

Process Skills

When you **collect data**, you can make and use a table or a chart to help record your **observations**.

What to Do

1 Make the **model** of an aquifer shown below.

2 Slowly add water until the lake is 1.5 cm deep.

Use a pencil to poke 5 small holes in the bottom of a cup.

3 Make it rain. Hold the cup with holes over the land. Move the cup as your partner pours a cup of water into your cup. **Observe** the water level.

5 cm

Water above ground forms lakes and rivers.

land

lake

water level

gravel

1.5 cm

You are modeling the effect on an aquifer of a year of heavy rains.

More Lab zone Activities Take It to the Net
pearsonsuccessnet.com

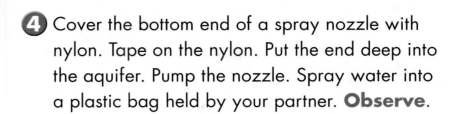

4 Cover the bottom end of a spray nozzle with nylon. Tape on the nylon. Put the end deep into the aquifer. Pump the nozzle. Spray water into a plastic bag held by your partner. **Observe**.

water between rocks

Be careful! Wear safety goggles!

You are modeling the effect of very heavy pumping.

5 Record your observations in a chart. Make and label a sketch or diagram of your model.

	Observations		
	Changes in Height of Water Table (increased, decreased, no change)	**Changes in Depth of Lake** (increased, decreased, no change)	**Explanation of Your Observations** (How do you know? Why do you think so?)
Rain			
Pumping			

Explain Your Results

1. **Infer** Think about a real aquifer. How might rain and pumping from wells affect the water level?

2. What problems might be caused by too much pumping? How might the problems be solved?

Go Further

Change your model. Show how pollution could enter the aquifer.

Recycling

Almost everything we throw away can be recycled. But we do a better job recycling some things than other things.

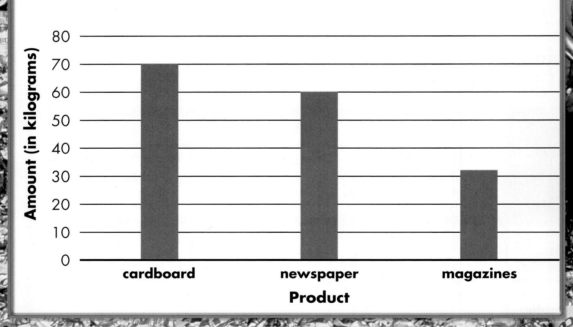

Amount of Paper Products Recycled for Every 100 Kilograms

The bar graph shows how much of three different paper products we recycle. We recycle 70 kilograms of cardboard boxes from every 100 kilograms we make. We recycle 60 kilograms of newspapers from every 100 kilograms we make. But we recycle only 32 kilograms of magazines from every 100 kilograms we make.

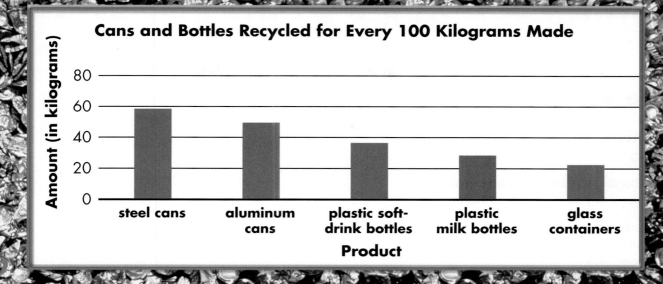

Cans and Bottles Recycled for Every 100 Kilograms Made

Amount (in kilograms)

80
60
40
20
0

steel cans | aluminum cans | plastic soft-drink bottles | plastic milk bottles | glass containers

Product

This bar graph shows how many kilograms of cans and bottles we recycle from every 100 kilograms we make.

Use the graph to answer the questions.

1 About how many kilograms of glass containers do we recycle from every 100 kilograms made?

A. about 58 kilograms

B. about 32 kilograms

C. about 28 kilograms

D. about 22 kilograms

2 Which container is recycled most?

F. steel cans

G. aluminum cans

H. plastic soft drink bottles

I. plastic milk bottles

3 From every 100 kilograms of aluminum cans we make, about how many kilograms do we **not** recycle?

A. about 50 kilograms

B. about 20 kilograms

C. about 80 kilograms

D. about 100 kilograms

Lab zone Take-Home Activity

Recycling 1 glass jar saves enough energy to run a TV for 3 hours. Find how many glass jars you have in your kitchen. How many hours of TV-watching in your home would recycling the jars pay for in energy savings?

Use Vocabulary

conservation (page 250)	**recycle** (page 254)
natural resource (page 247)	**renewable resource** (page 247)
nonrenewable resource (page 248)	

Use the term from the list above that best completes each sentence.

1. Trees, iron ore, water, and air are each a _____.

2. A natural resource that can be replaced in a fairly short period of time is a _____.

3. When we change something so it can be used again, we _____ it.

4. A resource that cannot be replaced once it is used up is a _____.

5. The saving and wise use of Earth's resources is called _____.

Explain Concepts

6. Explain the difference between a renewable resource like trees and a nonrenewable resource like iron ore.

7. What is the difference between a limited resource like iron ore and a limitless resource like air?

8. What are ways to conserve soil?

9. How is making compost out of yard wastes and food scraps one solution to the garbage problem?

10. Why is conserving natural resources important to everyone?

11. Why should people try to buy products made from recycled materials?

Process Skills

12. We get milk from cows and wool to make clothing from sheep. **Infer** whether milk and wool are renewable or nonrenewable resources. Explain your answer.

13. Copy the table below on a sheet of paper. Then **classify** each kind of trash as paper, plastic, or metal.

Trash	Classification
Milk carton	
Soft-drink can	
Magazine	
Laundry detergent bottle	

Compare and Constrast

14. Make a graphic organizer like the one below. Write in each part ways to show how reusing and recycling are similar and different.

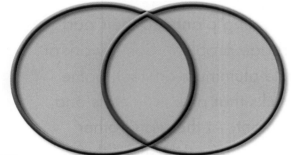

Reusing   **Both Reusing/ Recycling**   **Recycling**

Test Prep

Choose the letter that best completes the statement or answers the question.

15. Which of the following is a renewable resource?
- (A) coal
- (B) oil
- (C) aluminum
- (D) sunlight

16. Which of the following does NOT conserve soil?
- (F) planting different crops
- (G) planting trees along the edges of fields
- (H) plowing up and down hillsides
- (I) adding compost to soil

17. Which of the following is a nonrenewable resource?
- (A) soil
- (B) iron ore
- (C) water
- (D) trees

18. Many power plants use coal to make electricity. Which of the following is a way you could help conserve coal?
- (F) Ride a bicycle instead of riding in a car.
- (G) Leave the television on when going outside.
- (H) Turn off lights when leaving a room.
- (I) Plant a flower garden using compost.

19. Explain why the answer you selected for Question 18 is best. For each of the answers you do not select, give a reason why it is not the best choice.

20. **Writing in Science**
Narrative Write a story about a person who saw how natural resources were not being protected and did something about it.

Recycling Plant Worker

Workers sort paper to be recycled.

Recycled paper has become a roll of paper to be used again.

Many people work to conserve our natural resources. They have many different kinds of jobs. This is just one of them. But remember, conserving resources is a job you can do every day by using resources wisely.

Workers at recycling plants do their part to battle the garbage problem. Some work at plants that recycle aluminum or steel. Some workers drive trucks that pick up metals and take them to the plant. At the plant, other workers operate machines that shred the metal into small pieces. Still other workers melt and reshape the metal into new products.

Most recycling plant workers need at least a high school education.

Lab zone Take-Home Activity

Paper, aluminum and steel cans, and plastic are recyclable. List the steps you take or would take to recycle these materials in your home.

Unit B Test Talk

Choose the Right Answer

To answer a multiple-choice test question, you need to choose an answer from several choices. Read the passage and then answer the questions.

Evaporation changes water to an invisible gas called water vapor. **Condensation** changes water vapor into tiny drops of liquid water. These processes are parts of the water cycle.

Water also causes **weathering** by breaking rocks into smaller pieces. Water then carries the weathered rock to different places.

There is always the same amount of water on Earth. However, it is important to conserve fresh water and not waste it.

Use What You Know

To choose the right answer, eliminate answer choices that you are sure are incorrect.

1. In the passage, the word "condensation" means
   - Ⓐ liquid water changes into water vapor.
   - Ⓑ water vapor changes into liquid water.
   - Ⓒ liquid water changes into solid ice.
   - Ⓓ solid ice changes into liquid water.

2. In the passage, the word "weathering" means
   - Ⓕ causing weather patterns.
   - Ⓖ changing water vapor into clouds.
   - Ⓗ carrying pieces of rock to different places.
   - Ⓘ breaking rocks into smaller pieces.

3. Which of the following statements about water is true?
   - Ⓐ The amount of Earth's water always changes.
   - Ⓑ Water can change Earth's surface.
   - Ⓒ Condensation changes liquid water to water vapor.
   - Ⓓ Evaporation changes water vapor to liquid water.

Unit B Wrap-Up

Chapter 5

How does water change form?
- Living things need water to survive. People use water in many ways.
- Heating and cooling changes water between the forms of liquid, solid, and gas.

Chapter 6

How does weather follow patterns?
- Ways in which the sun heats the Earth and influences the water cycle cause weather patterns.
- Knowing about weather patterns helps people predict the weather and be safe.

Chapter 7

What are some kinds of rocks and soils?
- Rocks differ on the basis of how they form and what minerals they are made of.
- Soil covers most of Earth's land and is made of bits of rock, water, and humus.

Chapter 8

How do forces cause changes on Earth's surface?
- Forces within the Earth cause volcanoes and earthquakes to change Earth's surface quickly.
- Earth's surface can be changed slowly or sometimes quickly by weathering and erosion.

Chapter 9

How can people use natural resources responsibly?

- People can plant trees to replace ones they cut down and do things to make soil healthy and useful again.

- People can conserve natural resources by reducing the amount of resources they use and trash they make. They can also reuse and recycle materials.

Performance Assessment

Identify Changing Forms of Water

Water can be a solid, a liquid, or a gas. What changing forms of water can you identify? Place ice cubes and water in a plastic cup. Put the cup in a warm place and observe it over time. What forms of water were in the cup when you started? How did the forms change?

Read More About Earth Science!

Look for books like these in the library.

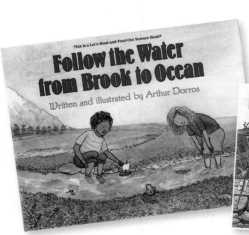

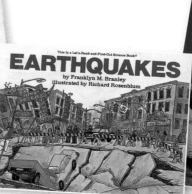

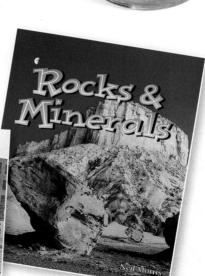

Experiment What settles first?

As a river flows to an ocean, it can carry particles of soil. The soil particles may be small, large, or in between. Some of them may settle out of the water quickly and are not carried far. Some may settle out of the water very slowly. These may be carried a long distance.

Materials

3 small measuring cups

small gravel, sand, clay soil

hand lens

plastic bottles with caps

funnel and water

Ask a question.

How do particles in water settle out?

State a hypothesis.

If particles are larger, then do those particles settle faster, slower, or at about the same speed as smaller particles? Write your **hypothesis**.

Identify and control variables.

The **variable** you change is the size of the particles. The variable you **observe** is how fast the particles settle. Every other part of the experiment must be **controlled**, or kept the same.

Control the amount of each type of particle. Use equal amounts of gravel, sand, and clay soil. Control how long the bottles are shaken. Shake all bottles the same length of time. Control when the particles start to settle. Stop shaking all the bottles at the same time.

Process Skills

Experiments have a **variable** you change, a variable you **observe**, and variables you **control**.

More Lab zone Activities Take It to the Net
pearsonsuccessnet.com

Test your hypothesis.

1 Measure 30 mL of gravel, 30 mL of sand, and 30 mL of clay soil. Observe the particles. Use a hand lens. Observe their size, shape, and color. In a chart, record their sizes (smallest, medium-sized, largest).

2 Put each kind of particle into a different bottle. Use a funnel. Fill each bottle $\frac{3}{4}$ full with water.

3 Screw the caps on tightly. **Predict** which particles will settle out fastest. Along with 2 others in your group, begin shaking the bottles.

Hint: If the funnel jams, tap it or shake it.

gravel

sand

clay soil

$\frac{3}{4}$ full with water

4 At the same time, stop shaking the bottles.
Put them on a table. Observe what happens.

5 Record the order in which the contents settle.

6 Repeat twice. Do a total of 3 trials. Compare your results
with your prediction and with those of other groups.

Collect and record your data.

Type of Particles	Size of Particles (smallest, medium-sized, largest)
Small gravel	
Sand	
Clay soil	

More Lab zone Activities Take It to the Net
pearsonsuccessnet.com

Interpret your data.

Complete the charts. Analyze the information. Compare the sizes of the particles and how fast they settle.

Type of Particles	Speed of Settling (fastest, medium, slowest)				
	Predicted	Trial A	Trial B	Trial C	Overall
Small gravel					
Sand					
Clay soil					

Why do you think scientists repeat experiments?

Type of Particles	Size of Particles (smallest, medium-sized, largest)	Speed of Settling (fastest, medium, slowest)
Small gravel		
Sand		
Clay soil		

State your conclusion.

Cooperate with others in your group. Discuss your results. Consider the explanations of others. Respect their ideas. Draw a conclusion from your data. Does it agree with your hypothesis? **Communicate** your conclusion.

Go Further

What would happen if soil particles of different sizes were mixed together? Make a prediction based on the results of this activity. Design and carry out a plan to investigate.

Full Inquiry

Predicting Weather

Weather patterns help people predict the weather, but predictions can be wrong.

Idea: Compare your observations of the weather with weather forecasts from TV and radio stations, and newspapers to see how accurate they are.

Comparing Soils

Soils have different amounts of sand, silt, clay, and humus.

Idea: Use a hand lens to compare soil samples in your area.

An Earthquake Model

Most earthquakes happen along breaks in Earth's crust.

Idea: Use clay, heavy cardboard, and objects to model what happens to Earth's crust, roads, and other objects during an earthquake.

Recycling

Recycling conserves landfill space and resources.

Idea: Use information about your community's recycling program to make a display with examples of what can be recycled and ways to sort it.

Using Scientific Methods

1. Ask a question.
2. State your hypothesis.
3. Identify/control variables.
4. Test your hypothesis.
5. Collect and record your data.
6. Interpret your data.
7. State your conclusion.
8. Go further.

EC CRU 10 9 8 7 6 5 4 3 2 1

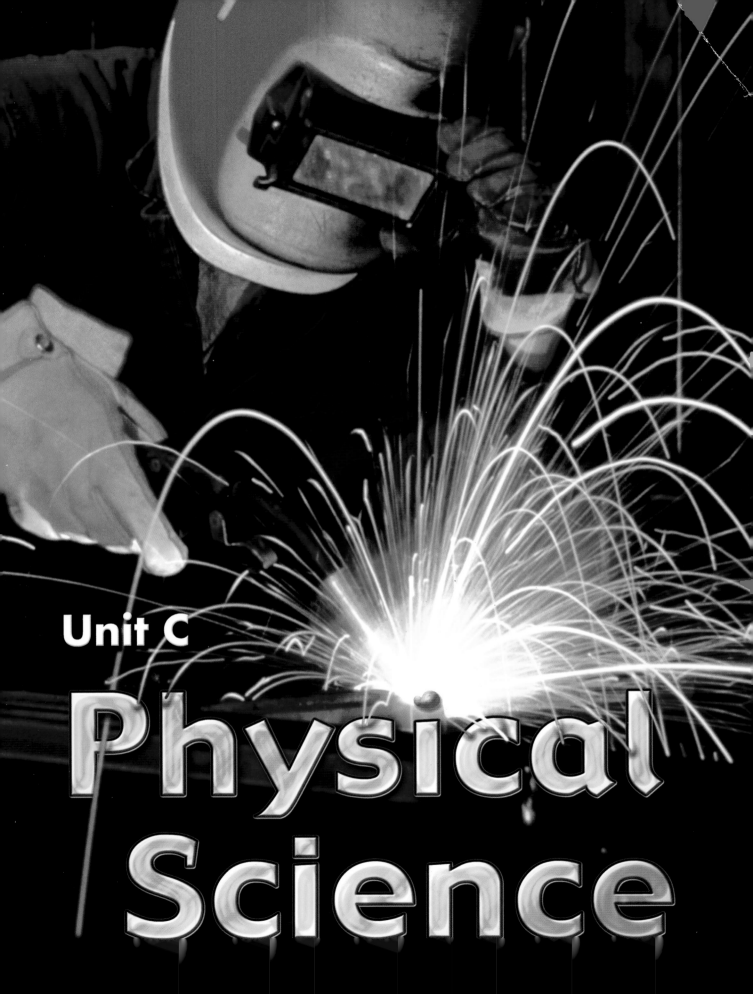

Unit C

Physical Science

Chapter 10 Matter and Its Properties

Directed Inquiry	Which material has a surprising property?
Guided Inquiry	How can you measure some physical properties of matter?
Activity Flip Chart	How can you compare the densities of different liquids? How can you change the buoyancy of an object?
Quick Activity Transparencies	How can we describe matter? How are properties of matter measured?

Chapter 11 Changes in Matter

Directed Inquiry	How can matter change?
Guided Inquiry	How can properties help you separate a mixture?
Activity Flip Chart	How can you separate a mixture? How can water and vinegar change a penny?
Quick Activity Transparencies	What are physical changes in matter? What are some ways to combine matter? What are chemical changes in matter?

Chapter 12 Forces and Motion

Directed Inquiry	How can you describe motion?
Guided Inquiry	How much force will you use?
Activity Flip Chart	How does a pendulum work? Can you design a catapult?
Quick Activity Transparencies	What happens when things change position? How does force affect motion? How do simple machines affect work?

Chapter 13 Energy

Directed Inquiry	Can electricity produce light and heat?
Guided Inquiry	Do freshwater ice and saltwater ice melt the same way?
Activity Flip Chart	How does light travel? How can you see electrical charges at work?
Quick Activity Transparencies	What is energy? How does energy change form? What is heat energy? What is light energy? What is electrical energy?

Chapter 14 Sound

Directed Inquiry	How can you see sound vibrations?
Guided Inquiry	How well does sound travel through different materials?
Activity Flip Chart	How can you change the sound you hear? How does matter affect sound?
Quick Activity Transparencies	What causes sounds? How does sound travel?

Unit C

Full Inquiry	How does energy affect the distance a toy car travels?
STEM Project	Design a Wedge

Chapter 10
Matter and Its Properties

You Will Discover

- how to observe and describe matter.
- the different states of matter.
- ways to measure different properties of matter.

online
Student Edition
pearsonsuccessnet.com

Discovery Channel School
Student DVD

What are the properties of matter?

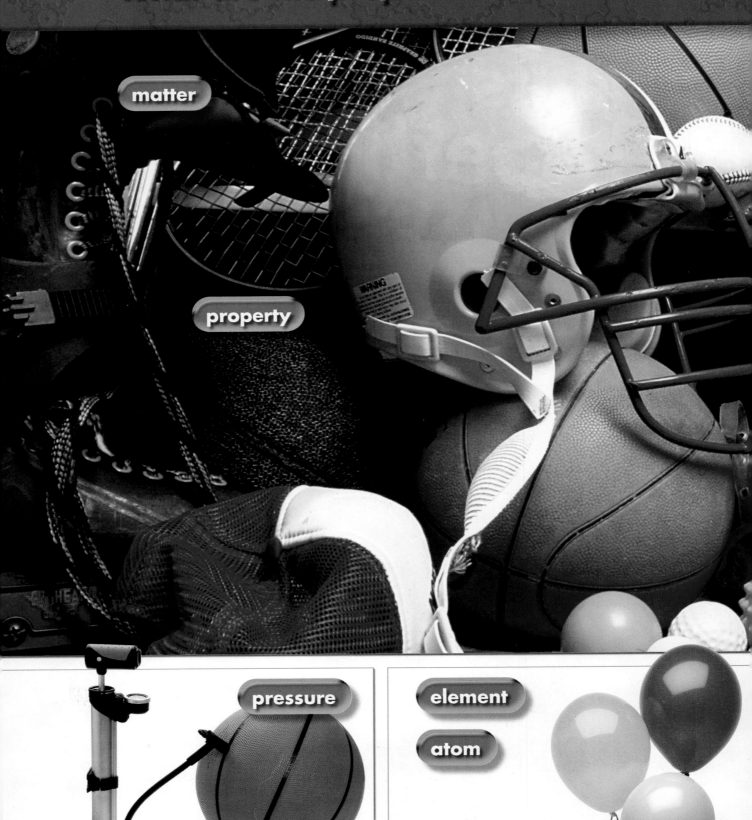

matter

property

pressure

element

atom

Chapter 10 Vocabulary

periodic table

Periodic Table of Elements

State at Room Temperature
= Solid   = Liquid   = Gas

density

buoyancy

mass

volume

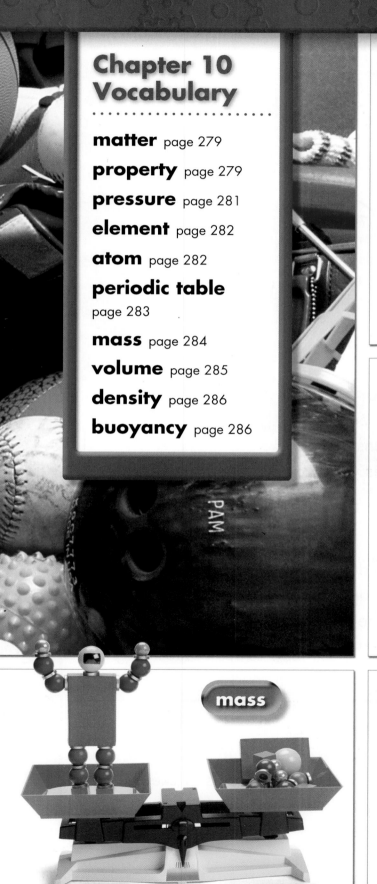

Explore Which material has a surprising property?

Materials

safety goggles

resealable plastic bag

water

tub

3 sharpened pencils

What to Do

Seal bag!

half full

Hold over tub!

1 Put water in the plastic bag.

What do you think would happen if you push a pencil into the bag?

2 Slowly push a pencil into the bag. **Observe**. Based on your observations, **infer** why the result occurred.

Discuss the results with other students. Think about their explanations.

3 Based on your observations, **predict** what will happen if you push the pencil point out the other side. Try it.

Push 2 more pencils into the bag. See if you get the same results.

Explain Your Results

Compare your **prediction** in step 3 with your **observation**. Draw diagrams or sketches to show your prediction and your result.

Reading Skills

Cause and Effect

- A **cause** makes something change. An **effect** is the change you **observe**. Sometimes science writers use clue words and phrases such as *because, so, since,* and *as a result* to signal cause and effect.

- With careful **observations**, you might **predict** an effect that a certain cause will have.

Science Article

The Matter with Juice

Justin poured some juice from a bottle into a glass. Because juice is a liquid, its shape changed when it was in the glass. He decided to measure how much juice he had, so he poured it into a measuring cup. Then he decided to make a solid, so he put the juice into a mold and put sticks in it. He put the mold in the freezer. As a result, he had a frozen juice bar!

Apply It!

Make a graphic organizer like the one shown. Then use it to list two **causes** and two **effects** from the science article.

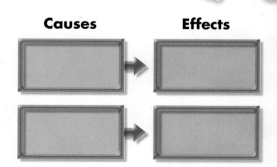

Causes   **Effects**

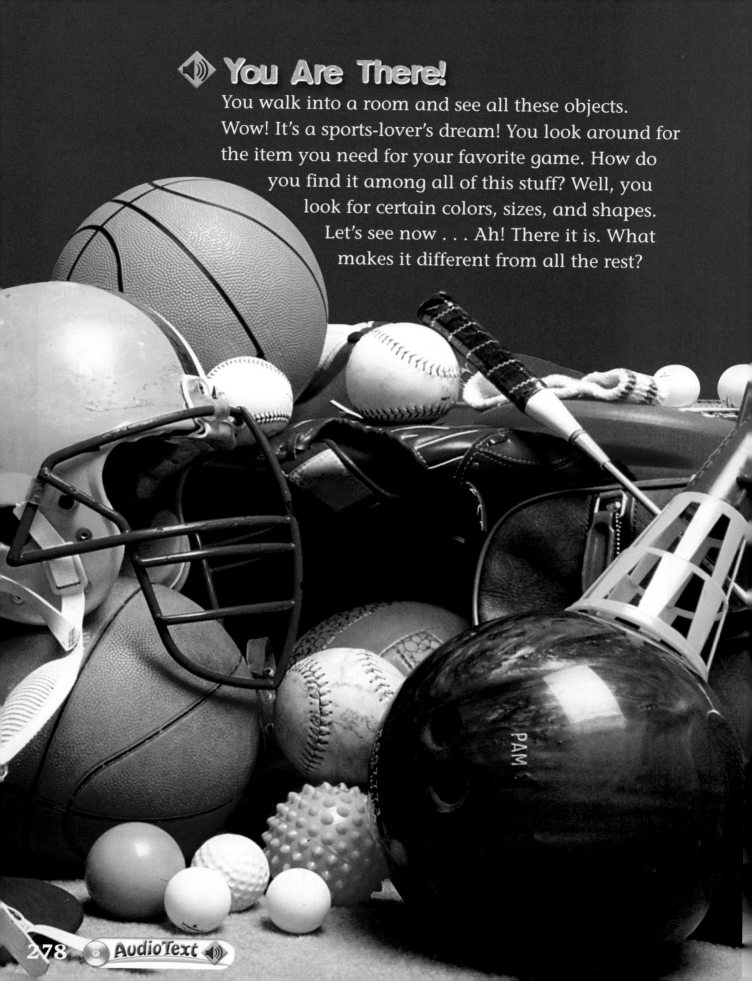

🔊 You Are There!

You walk into a room and see all these objects. Wow! It's a sports-lover's dream! You look around for the item you need for your favorite game. How do you find it among all of this stuff? Well, you look for certain colors, sizes, and shapes. Let's see now . . . Ah! There it is. What makes it different from all the rest?

Lesson 1

How can we describe matter?

Everything you can see, smell, or touch is matter. Many things that you cannot see, smell, or touch are matter too.

A World of Matter

All of the objects you see around you are made of matter. **Matter** is anything that takes up space and has mass. You can feel the mass of objects as weight when you pick them up. When you blow up a balloon, you see that even air takes up space.

A **property** is something about matter that you can observe with one or more of your senses. A ball looks round and feels smooth or bumpy. It could be hard or soft. The sound of it bouncing off the floor tells you more about the ball's properties. For other kinds of matter, such as a flower, your sense of smell tells you about other properties.

These balls, the hockey puck, the baseball mitt, and the air inside the tennis ball are matter.

1. ✔ **Checkpoint** What is *matter*?

2. **Writing** in Science **Expository** Draw two columns titled *Object* and *Properties*. Fill in the box with the properties of some things you see. Choose one object and write a paragraph using the information in the Properties column. Exchange your paragraph with a classmate. Try to guess each other's object.

States of Matter

All the matter around you is a solid, a liquid, or a gas. Each kind of matter is made of very small particles. These particles are so small that you cannot see them, even under a magnifying lens. The particles always move. In some kinds of matter they just jiggle. In other kinds they slide past one another or bounce around.

Solids

The bowling ball is a solid. You can put it over a small opening to a large container. But the ball won't change shape and fall through the opening. Like other solids, the ball keeps its shape. The particles of a bowling ball, or any other solid, are held tightly together. They jiggle or vibrate very fast. However, they stay firmly in place.

Liquids

Look at the orange juice being poured into a glass. The juice is a liquid. It will take the shape of the glass into which it is being poured. The particles of orange juice, or any other liquid, are loosely held together. The particles can flow past one another. If you pour the orange juice from the glass into another container, the juice will change shape again. However, the juice will take up the same amount of space in the new container.

Orange juice is a liquid. The particles of juice are loosely held together.

A bowling ball is a solid. The particles of the ball are firmly held together.

Gases

The air being pumped into the basketball is a gas. When you pump air into a ball, the air fills the space. Like other gases, air has no shape. The tiny gas particles are not held together. They bounce off one another as they move freely. Unlike solids and liquids, the amount of space that air takes up changes. The air spreads out, or expands, to fill whatever space is available.

As air is pumped into a ball, the air at first expands. It starts to push against the inside of the ball. This pushing is called **pressure**. As the ball is filled, the air becomes more compact. It presses together. You can feel the pressure by pushing on the ball before and after air is added.

1. ✓**Checkpoint** What are three states of matter?

2. **Cause and Effect** How does melting ice into water, and then letting the water evaporate, change the state of the ice?

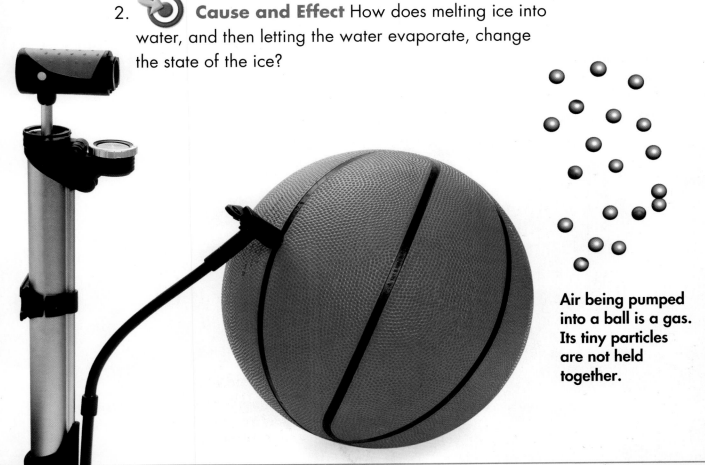

Air being pumped into a ball is a gas. Its tiny particles are not held together.

Parts of Matter

Suppose you could break a chunk of gold into smaller and smaller pieces. Each piece of gold is still the matter we call gold. Gold is an element. An **element** is matter made of a single type of particle too small to see. A chunk of gold is made only of particles of gold.

Most matter, however, is made out of many types of particles combined together in different ways. The smallest particle of an element that has the properties of that element is an **atom.** Gold is made up of atoms of gold. Clay, however, is made up of different kinds of atoms. These atoms act together to give clay its properties.

A particle of clay is made of different kinds of atoms. The atoms act together to give clay its properties.

Clay pots are made of particles of clay.

The helium that fills these balloons is an element.

282

Science experiments show that there are more than 100 different elements. Scientists arrange these elements in a **periodic table** of the elements. Elements are arranged based on their properties. Examples include how they respond to heat and other elements. This table is shown below.

Empedocles

Empedocles [em PED uh KLEEZ] lived in ancient Greece. He and others thought that earth, air, fire, and water were the four elements that made up all matter.

Periodic Table of Elements

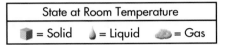

State at Room Temperature
= Solid   = Liquid   = Gas

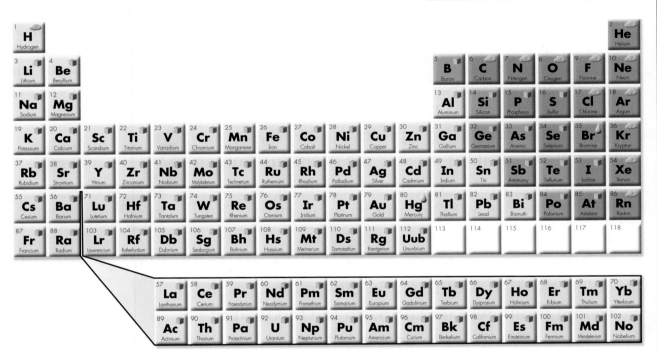

In the periodic table, elements in the same column have similar properties.

✓ Lesson Checkpoint

1. Explain why most objects you observe are not elements.

2. What about elements is used to arrange them in the periodic table of the elements?

3. **Social Studies** in Science Use library resources to find out about atoms. Find out who first used the word *atom*.

Lesson 2

How are properties of matter measured?

You can observe many properties of matter through your senses. You also can use tools to measure some properties of matter.

Tools for Measuring Mass

One property of matter is mass. An object's **mass** is the amount of matter it has. Solids, liquids, and gases all have mass. A balance is a tool to measure mass. The balance shown has two pans at the same level. The mass of the toy on left the is the same as the mass of the toy's pieces on the right.

A metric unit for mass is the gram (g). Larger amounts of matter are measured in kilograms (kg). There are 1,000 grams in a kilogram. The mass of a baseball bat is about 1 kg.

An object's mass is the same everywhere. An object's weight is different in different places. Its weight is different on Earth, on the Moon, and in space. The scales in doctors' offices and grocery stores measure weight.

A balance measures mass, or the amount of matter an object has. The whole toy has the same mass as its parts.

This table shows the mass of some common objects.

Mass of Common Objects	
paper clip	1 g
dime	2 g
pencil	5 g
mug	400 g
stapler	500 g

Tools for Measuring Volume

Another property of matter is volume. An object's **volume** is the amount of space that the object takes up. Solids, liquids, and gases all have volume. To measure the volume of a liquid, you might use a measuring cup or a graduated cylinder.

The basic metric unit for measuring liquid volume is the liter (L). A measuring cup might show marks for smaller parts of a liter called milliliters (mL). There are 1,000 milliliters in a liter.

Solids also have volume. You can measure the volume of a solid such as a rock, using water. A rock will keep its shape in water. But it pushes water out of its way. Put some water in a measuring cup. Record the level of the water. Slide the rock into the water. Record the new water level. Subtract the two levels to find how much water the rock pushed aside.

The volume of the water in this measuring cup is 500 mL.

The volume of the milk in this jug is about 2 L.

The volume of the orange juice in this bottle is about 1 L.

The volume of the water in this water bottle is about 500 mL.

1. ✓ **Checkpoint** How are an object's mass and weight different?

2. 🔄 **Cause and Effect** What effect would cutting a piece of wood in half have on the total mass of the wood?

Measuring Density

Density is another property of solids, liquids, and gases. **Density** is a measure of the amount of matter in a certain amount of space. The bowling ball and the rubber ball shown are the same size. They have the same volume. The bowling ball is harder to lift. It has more mass in the same amount of space. The bowling ball has greater density.

You can study the density of an object by observing how it floats in a liquid or a gas. This property is **buoyancy.** For example, rocks have little buoyancy in water. They sink. Rocks have a higher density than water. A balloon filled with helium is buoyant in air. A helium balloon floats upward. Helium has a lower density than air.

This ball is the same size as the bowling ball. How could you tell which has more matter in it?

How do you compare the density of solid objects? To do this, you need to measure the mass and the volume of the objects. If the objects have the same volume, the object that has the greater mass has greater density.

Knowing the density of matter helps scientists tell different kinds of matter apart.

Pennies

Marbles

Paper boat

Cork

These objects differ in their density compared to water. Predict which objects will sink and which will float.

An object will float in water if it has less density than water. It will sink if it has greater density than water.

1. ✔ **Checkpoint** What is *density?*

2. **Writing in Science** **Expository** Write a paragraph in your **science journal** that explains how to tell which of two liquids has less density.

Tools for Measuring Other Properties

1 cubic unit

Fill the box with cubes to find its volume.

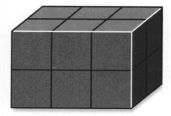

12 cubes fill the box. The volume is 12 cubic units.

Size is another property that can be measured. Length, for example, is the distance from one end of an object to the other end. Metric rulers and tapes are used to measure length. The basic metric unit of length is the meter. Shorter lengths are measured in centimeters (cm) or millimeters (mm). There are 100 cm in a meter. There are 1,000 mm in a meter. Much longer distances are measured in kilometers. There are 1,000 meters in a kilometer.

Other tools and units can be used to measure the volume of solid objects. A cubic unit is a cube that is used to measure volume. To find the volume of a box, you can find how many cubes of one size would fit inside the box. A cube that measures 1 centimeter on each side has a volume of 1 cubic centimeter. If 12 of these cubes fit inside a box and fill it up, the volume of the box is 12 cubic centimeters.

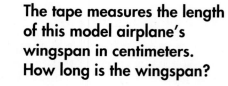

The tape measures the length of this model airplane's wingspan in centimeters. How long is the wingspan?

A hand lens makes this pillbug much easier to see.

The lens lets you see small units on the ruler clearly in order to measure with accuracy.

Some objects are too small to see easily. For instance, you may need a hand lens or magnifying glass to observe and measure the properties of a pillbug. If you put a metric ruler under the lens, you can more easily measure the length of the pillbug.

✓Lesson Checkpoint

1. Describe how you would measure the volume of a liquid.

2. How could you measure the volume of a box?

3. **Math** in Science What is the basic metric unit for length? What units are used to measure shorter lengths?

Investigate How can you measure some physical properties of matter?

Materials

sponge and small notepad

wooden block, small box, dot cube

metric ruler

balance and gram cubes

What to Do

1 Use the ruler to **measure** the length of the notepad. Measure to the nearest centimeter. Record the length.

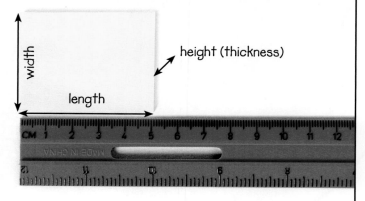

width

height (thickness)

length

2 Follow the directions in step 1 to find the width of the notepad. Then find its height.

3 Measure the mass of the notepad. Balance the note pad with gram cubes. Record the mass.

4 Repeat steps 1 to 3 to find the measurements of the wooden block, small box, number cube, and sponge.

5 Compare your measurements with those of other groups. Repeat your measurements.

Object	Length (cm)	Width (cm)	Height (cm)	Mass (g)

Explain Your Results

1. **Interpret Data** Which object has the most mass? Which has the least mass?

2. Were your **measurements** the same as those of other groups? When you repeated your measurements, were they the same? Why do you think measurements might be different?

Go Further

How can you measure larger objects? What units can you use for measuring? Can you invent a new way to measure? Choose a question and make a plan to answer it.

Math in Science

Measuring Properties

Different tools and different units are used to measure volume, length, and mass.

The volume of liquid in the measuring cup is 90 milliliters. The graduated cylinder has the same amount of liquid in it.

The small marks on the ruler mark off millimeters. There are 10 mm in 1 cm, so you can count by tens to find the length in millimeters. The paper clip is 30 mm long.

Eraser

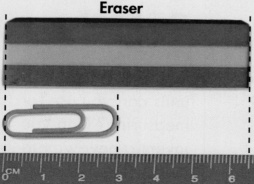

The paper clip is 3 centimeters long.

e Tools Take It to the Net
pearsonsuccessnet.com

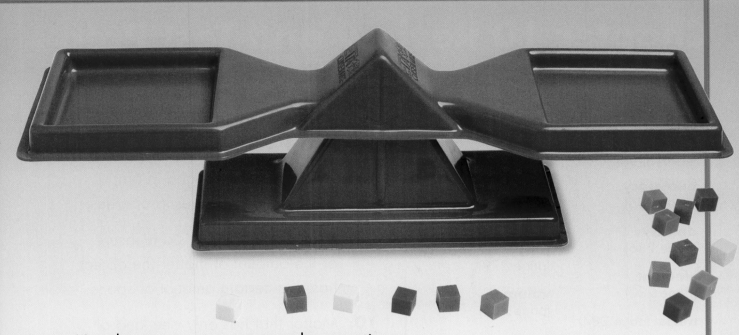

Use the pictures to answer the questions.

1 The eraser is more than 6 cm but less than 7 cm long. What is its length in millimeters?

A. 6 mm

B. 65 mm

C. 650 mm

D. 6000 mm

2 Which tool would you use to find the mass of a marble?

F. graduated cylinder

G. metric ruler

H. pan balance

I. measuring cup

3 Which has the greatest volume?

A. 1 liter of milk

B. 500 milliliters of milk

C. 50 milliliters of milk

D. 5 milliliters of milk

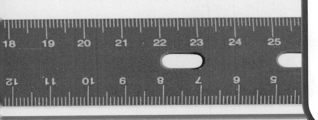

Lab zone **Take-Home Activity**

Use a metric measuring cup and a metric ruler to measure properties of liquids and objects around your home. Compare the volumes of liquids and the lengths of objects.

Chapter 10 Review and Test Prep

Use Vocabulary

atom (page 282)	**periodic table** (page 283)
buoyancy (page 286)	**pressure** (page 281)
density (page 286)	**property** (page 279)
element (page 282)	**volume** (page 285)
mass (page 284)	
matter (page 279)	

Use the vocabulary word from the list above that best completes each sentence.

1. An object's _____ is the amount of matter it has.

2. When you see that a ball is red, you are observing a(n) _____ of the ball.

3. Each of the tiny particles that make up an element is called a(n) _____ .

4. A measuring cup is used to find a liquid's _____.

5. A balloon gets larger when air is blown into it because of air _____.

6. An object that floats in water has _____ in water.

7. Anything that takes up space and has weight is _____.

8. Elements are arranged in a(n) _____ based on their properties.

9. An object's _____ is a measure of the amount of matter the object has in a certain amount of space.

10. Matter that has only one kind of atom is a(n) _____.

Explain Concepts

11. List the two properties of matter that are needed to measure density and explain why you need to measure both.

12. List the following metric units from the smallest to the largest: meter, millimeter, kilometer, centimeter.

Process Skills

13. **Predict** You pour juice from a tall, narrow glass into a short, wide glass. What happens to the volume of the juice?

14. **Infer** An object falls into a pond and sinks. What do you know about the density of the object?

MindPoint *Quiz Show*

Cause and Effect

15. Carrie and her friends wanted to play soccer. Their ball was too soft, so they needed to use a pump. Explain how the pump changed the ball so they could play with it. Use a graphic organizer to show all the causes and their effects.

Causes	Effects

 # Test Prep

Choose the letter that best completes the statement or answers the question.

16. How many states of matter can we observe?

Ⓐ 1   Ⓑ 2
Ⓒ 3   Ⓓ 5

17. Which tool is used to observe the visible properties of a tiny object?

Ⓕ balance
Ⓖ metric ruler
Ⓗ graduated cylinder
Ⓘ hand lens

18. If you weigh an object and then break it into two pieces, the sum of the weights of its pieces will be

Ⓐ less than the weight of the object.
Ⓑ equal to the weight of the object.
Ⓒ greater than the weight of the object.
Ⓓ half the weight of the object.

19. About how many different elements are there?

Ⓕ 3   Ⓖ 5
Ⓗ 100   Ⓘ 500

20. Writing in Science

Expository Make a chart that shows what tools and metric units are used for measuring mass, volume, and length.

Measurement	Tool	Unit
mass		
volume		
length		

Write a paragraph that tells what the chart shows.

Chemist

Do you like to cook? When you cook you use chemistry. Chemistry is the study of substances and how they change. You might not want to eat all the ingredients separately. After they are mixed and baked, however, they change. Then they taste just right.

Chemists also study the properties of substances. Some materials mix together easily. Sugar dissolves in water quickly. Other substances do not mix together well. Dr. John Pojman is a chemist. He directs experiments that are done in space where gravity won't interfere.

Dr. Pojman and other scientists are developing experiments to find out more about the ways that liquids mix together.

Chemists earn a degree in chemistry. Then they work for companies that make food, plastics, and medicine. Many chemists work for NASA.

Dr. John Pojman does experiments with fluids in low-gravity conditions.

Lab zone Take-Home Activity

Plastics are made from different substances. Each type of plastic has different properties. Find objects around your home that are made of plastic and list their properties.

EC CRU 10 9 8 7 6 5 4 3 2 1

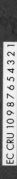

Chapter 11
Changes in Matter

You Will Discover

- how physical changes affect matter.
- different ways to mix materials together.
- how we use chemical changes every day.

online
Student Edition
pearsonsuccessnet.com

Discovery Channel School
Student DVD

physical change

mixture

solution

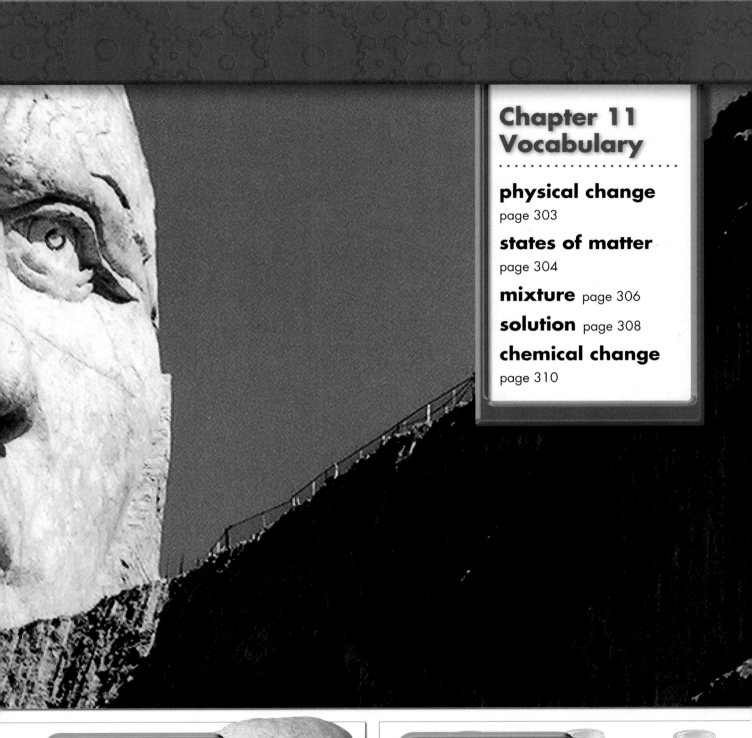

Chapter 11 Vocabulary

chemical change

states of matter

Explore How can matter change?

Materials

safety goggles

3 cups

ice cube

spoon

water, vinegar, graduated cylinder

salt and baking soda

masking tape

Process Skills

Using knowledge obtained by reading the activity and **observations** made during the activity, you were able to make an **inference**.

What to Do

1 Put 100 mL of water and 1 spoonful of salt in cup A. Stir.

2 Put an ice cube in cup B.

3 Pour 50 mL of vinegar in cup C. Add 1 spoonful of baking soda. **Observe** the contents of each cup right away and after 10 minutes.

Be careful!

Wear safety goggles!

Label the cups A, B, and C.

A — 100 mL water, 1 spoonful salt

B — 1 ice cube

C — 50 mL vinegar, 1 spoonful baking soda

Explain Your Results

Infer Think about the changes you **observed**. In which cup do you think a different kind of matter formed?

How to Read Science

Cause and Effect

- A **cause** makes something change. An **effect** is a change you **observe.** Science writers use clue words and phrases such as *because, so, since,* and *as a result* to signal cause and effect.

- A cause may have more than one effect. An effect may have more than one cause.

Science Article

Chemical Properties and Changes

Nothing shines quite like a bright new penny. But over the years, the copper on the outside of the penny changes. It becomes dull brown. Then it becomes dull light green. The copper changes into a new kind of matter. That's a chemical change. The new matter forms because copper reacts with air. The ability to react with air is a chemical property of copper.

Apply It!

Make a graphic organizer like the one shown below. Fill it in to show the **inferred cause** and each **effect** from the article.

Cause → **Effect**

301

🔊 You Are There!

You stand at the base of the great mountain. The noise of heavy equipment fills your ears. Dust sticks in your nose and throat. You look up at the top of the mountain— and can hardly believe your eyes! A huge face of stone stares out over the distant land. Amazing! What kinds of changes are happening to that mountain?

🔊 AudioText 🔊

What are physical changes in matter?

Physical properties such as size, weight, color, and position can change. Materials can also change state.

Making a Physical Change

The people in the picture are carving a statue of the Native American leader Crazy Horse out of this mountain. They are chiseling, hammering, and even blasting rock to bits. The bits of rock look different than the mountain. But each bit is still the same kind of rock as the whole mountain. The people are making a physical change to the mountain.

Matter goes through a **physical change** when it changes the way it looks without becoming a new kind of matter.

Cutting fruit into pieces causes a physical change. The pieces are made of the same kind of matter as the whole fruit.

1. **✔ Checkpoint** Describe a physical change in matter and explain why it is a physical change.

2. **Technology** in Science Use the Internet to find out more about the Crazy Horse Memorial project. Who started it? When did it begin? How long will it take to finish?

Some Ways to Cause Physical Change

There are lots of ways to cause physical change in matter. The pictures show some of them.

States of matter are the forms that matter can take—solid, liquid, and gas. Matter can change from one state to another. But if the state changes, it remains the same kind of matter. For example, when liquid water freezes, it becomes ice. Ice is a solid. However, when ice melts, you can see that it is still water. Ice and water are the same kind of matter.

A change in temperature can cause matter to change state. For example, water evaporates quickly when heated to 100°C (212°F). That means the water changes from a liquid into a gas. Even though you cannot see the gas, a physical change has happened. The water particles are still water. But the particles are so far apart in the air that you cannot see them. Even though the water has changed state, it has not become a new kind of matter.

Water also changes state when it is cooled. Above 0°C (32°F), the particles of liquid water slide past one another. At 0°C, liquid water changes to solid ice. Each water particle slows down and vibrates very fast in place.

You make a physical change when you fold clothes.

When you cut paper you are making a physical change.

And what happens when you hold an ice cube in your hand? The heat from your hand makes the water particles move faster. They no longer vibrate in place. They move freely, flowing as liquid water. You feel it dripping through your fingers. But no matter how many physical changes you make, the amount and kind of matter remain the same.

You can make a sculpture of water only when it's in a solid state.

States of Water

In ice, water particles vibrate in place.

In liquid water, the water particles slide past one another.

Some water has evaporated. The water particles in the gas called water vapor are far apart.

✓ Lesson Checkpoint

1. List ways that you can make physical changes in matter.

2. What physical changes happen to water as it freezes?

3. **Cause and Effect** Make a graphic organizer like the one on page 301. Fill it with ways to cause physical changes to a piece of paper. Describe the effects each change would have on the paper.

What are some ways to combine matter?

The different coins in this mixture can easily be separated.

Many kinds of matter can be combined. Sometimes you can separate substances from the combination.

Mixtures

Each single coin on this page is made up of matter. So what happens when you put all these different pieces of matter together? You get a mixture. A **mixture** is made of two or more kinds of matter that are placed together. The amounts of each kind of matter do not have to be the same. For example, there may be more quarters than pennies in the coin mixture. But it's still a mixture. In fact, each coin is a mixture. Two or more metals are melted together to form each type of coin.

What parts make up this mixture?

What is important about a mixture is that each kind of matter in it does not change into another substance. Each kind of matter can also be separated from every other kind in the mixture.

Some mixtures are very easy to separate. For example, you can separate sand grains and marbles because of their size. You could put the mixture into a strainer with fairly small holes. The marbles are too big to go through the holes of the strainer, but the sand pours right through.

You can also separate sand and iron pieces if you use a magnet. The magnet pulls the iron out of the mixture. The sand remains behind.

How does a magnet help separate the parts of this sand-iron mixture?

1. ✅ **Checkpoint** Give three reasons why a bowl of different kinds of beans is a mixture.

2. **Social Studies** in Science
Find out what metals are melted together to make a penny, a nickel, a dime, and a quarter.

A strainer helps separate the parts of this marble-sand mixture.

Solutions

Have you ever mixed lemonade powder into water to make lemonade? After you stir the powder into the water, the powder seems to disappear. But it doesn't go away. It dissolves. This means the particles of powder become so tiny that you cannot see them. The particles spread out in the water.

When a substance dissolves in another substance, a **solution** forms. A solution is a kind of mixture. But you may not be able to see the particles in a solution. You can't see the particles of powder in the lemonade. But you know the powder is there if you taste the solution.

You use all kinds of solutions. Soda is a solution of carbon dioxide gas and other substances dissolved in water. Shake a can of soda and the gas separates quickly from the water. In a closed can, the separated gas has no place to go. Pressure builds. When you open the can, the gas escapes.

Has this ever happened to you? Why does the gas explode from the can?

Straining doesn't separate the salt from salt water. But if you boil away the water, the salt is left behind.

Separating Parts of Solutions

Since a solution is a kind of mixture, you can separate its parts. Think about a pitcher of salt water. How can you separate the salt from the water? You can try pouring the salt water through a strainer. That helped separate the marble-sand mixture. But the salt particles in salt water are too tiny to be trapped by a strainer. If you taste the water that runs through the strainer, it's still salty.

What if you heat the salt water? The water evaporates quickly. The salt is left behind. The same thing happens with lemonade. If the water evaporates, the substances in the powder stay behind.

These "disappearing acts" are physical changes. The changes may make the substance look different. But each is still the same substance in the same amount.

Some substances, like lemonade mix, will dissolve in water.

Some substances, like these small stones, will not dissolve in water.

✓ Lesson Checkpoint

1. What makes ocean water a mixture?

2. What makes ocean water a solution?

3. **Writing in Science** **Descriptive** In your **science journal,** describe some things for a mixture. What do you think will happen when you mix them? Be sure to name the parts of your mixture.

Lesson 3

What are chemical changes in matter?

Some changes in matter can produce new kinds of matter. We use these changes all the time.

Forming Different Materials

Mmmmm . . . there's nothing like the smell of fresh, warm bread. It tastes so good right out of the oven. But you wouldn't want to eat it before it was baked. A bowl of flour, baking powder, and eggs wouldn't taste very good.

In a **chemical change,** one kind of matter changes into a different kind of matter. A chemical change happens when bread is baked. The batter is a mixture of ingredients. But the heat of the oven causes chemical changes to happen. Then a new substance, bread, is formed.

A chemical change happens when eggs cook. They can never change back into the same form as raw eggs.

Baking bread produces a chemical change. You cannot get the ingredients back because a new substance is formed.

Remember that after water freezes into ice, the ice can melt back to water. Each change is a physical change. The water and ice are the same material. But what about the materials that make up the bread? Can you ever separate them from the bread? Probably not. Materials that have gone through a chemical change usually cannot be changed back to the original kind of matter.

Rusting is a slow chemical change.

Sometimes a chemical change can happen quickly. For example, fire can burn wood in minutes. Other times, a chemical change happens slowly. Think about an iron chain that's left outside. Aided by water, the iron slowly combines with oxygen gas from the air. Then the iron and oxygen change to rust. The rust is now a different kind of matter, and it will not change back into iron and oxygen gas.

Burning is a fast chemical change. When the sticks burn, the wood changes to gases and ashes. Some of the gases and ashes make up smoke.

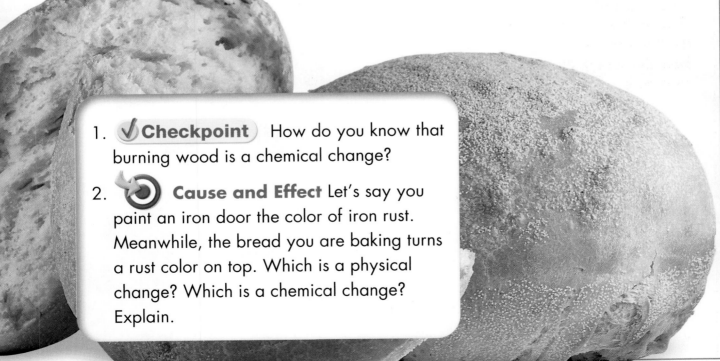

1. ✔Checkpoint How do you know that burning wood is a chemical change?

2. 🎯 Cause and Effect Let's say you paint an iron door the color of iron rust. Meanwhile, the bread you are baking turns a rust color on top. Which is a physical change? Which is a chemical change? Explain.

Using Chemical Changes

We use chemical changes every day. From eating pizza to watching a fireworks show, chemical changes are part of our lives.

Chemical changes start in your mouth the moment you begin to chew a piece of food. Then more changes happen as the food goes through your body. It's a good thing too. Chemical changes give your body the material it needs for energy and growth.

Chemical changes also help move us from place to place. Gasoline burning is a chemical change that releases the energy that the car's engine uses.

Chemical changes make many things in life easier to do. For example, laundry soap often has additives that cause chemical changes which break down stains. Without these changes, clothes might keep getting dirtier and dirtier.

Many soaps cause chemical changes that break down dirt and grime.

Burning gasoline in cars is a chemical change.

Chemical changes in batteries release electricity that appliances use.

You rely on the ability of many kinds of material to undergo chemical changes. When you turn the switch on your CD player, for example, chemicals will combine inside batteries. New substances will form. The chemical change will make a small amount of electricity to help you hear your favorite music.

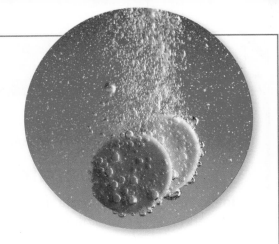

A chemical change between the water and the tablets causes the bubbles.

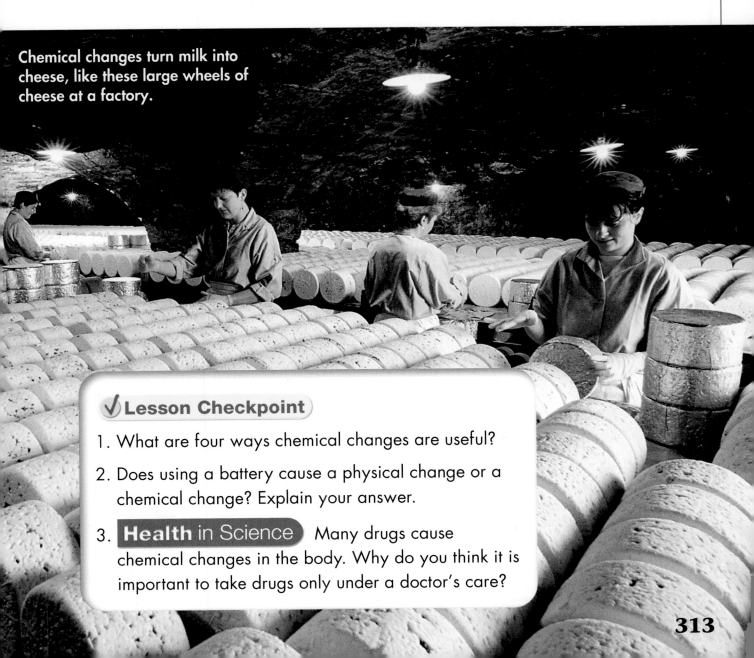

Chemical changes turn milk into cheese, like these large wheels of cheese at a factory.

✓ **Lesson Checkpoint**

1. What are four ways chemical changes are useful?

2. Does using a battery cause a physical change or a chemical change? Explain your answer.

3. **Health in Science** Many drugs cause chemical changes in the body. Why do you think it is important to take drugs only under a doctor's care?

Investigate How can properties help you separate a mixture?

In this activity you separate a mixture of particles using 2 physical properties—the size of the particles and their ability to dissolve in water.

Materials

safety goggles

spoon

4 foam cups

salt, sand, 3 marbles

warm water and graduated cylinder

pencil

coffee filter and rubber band

foil

Process Skills

You used what you knew about the physical properties of sugar and salt to make a **prediction**.

What to Do

1. Label the 4 cups A, B, C, and D. Put 1 spoonful of salt, 2 spoonfuls of sand, 3 marbles, and 100 mL of water in cup A. Stir the mixture for about 1 minute.

2. Make 4 holes in the bottom of cup B by pushing a pencil through the bottom of the cup from the inside.

3. Hold cup B over cup C. All at once, pour the mixture from cup A into cup B. Move cup B around to clean the marbles. Record the part of the mixture that was removed by straining.

Tap cup A as you pour. Less sand will stick in the cup.

Be careful!

Wear safety goggles!

4 Put a coffee filter in cup D. Fasten with a rubber band. Slowly pour the mixture from cup C into cup D. Record the part of the mixture that was removed by filtering.

5 Take off the filter. Dip the spoon in cup D. Let 2 drops of the liquid drip on a piece of foil. Let the liquid evaporate. Record the part of the mixture that was removed by evaporation.

You may need to leave the foil overnight.

rubber band

coffee filter

D

Separating Method	Results of Separation	
	Part Removed	Part Not Removed
Straining		
Filtering		
Evaporation		

Explain Your Results

1. Which physical properties did you use to separate the mixture?

2. **Predict** Both sugar and salt dissolve in water. If you used sugar instead of salt, would your results change? Explain.

Go Further

How could you separate a mixture of iron filings, sand, and water? Make and carry out a plan to find out.

A Closer Look at Mixtures

Think about mixtures you have seen: a handful of sand and shells at the beach; a bowl of sweet, cold fruit salad; even all the stuff in your junk drawer. You can separate the parts of each mixture.

A can of mixed nuts contains the following:

15	cashews
6	pecans
12	walnuts
25	almonds
38	peanuts

This mixture is made of 5 different parts, or 5 kinds of nuts. All the nuts stay the same even when mixed. You can separate the nuts to learn more about the mixture. This mixture has a total of 96 nuts. Only 6 out of 96 nuts are pecans. There are fewer pecans than any other kind of nut. There are more peanuts than any other kind. Out of 96 nuts, 38 of them are peanuts.

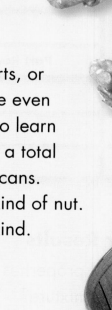

Listed below are parts of a mixture of cereal.
The mass of each part is given.

    35   grams of raisins

    12   grams of almonds

  133   grams of corn flakes

    21   grams of dried cranberries

Use the information above to answer the questions.

1 What is the total mass of the cereal?

    A. 220 grams   B. 212 grams

    C. 200 grams   D. 201 grams

2 What is the order of parts in this mixture from greatest mass to least mass?

    F. raisins, almonds, corn flakes, cranberries

    G. cranberries, corn flakes, almonds, raisins

    H. corn flakes, cranberries, almonds, raisins

    I. corn flakes, raisins, cranberries, almonds

3 The amount of corn flakes is how much greater than that of all the other parts combined?

    A. 65 grams   B. 54 grams

    C. 100 grams   D. 133 grams

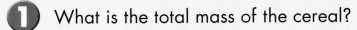

Lab zone Take-Home Activity

Find a mixture at home, such as rocks and shells like the ones shown. Separate the mixture into its parts. Make a chart listing the parts in order from greatest amount to least amount.

Chapter 11 Review and Test Prep

Use Vocabulary

chemical change (page 310)	**solution** (page 308)
mixture (page 306)	**states of matter** (page 304)
physical change (page 303)	

Use the vocabulary term from the list above that best completes each sentence.

1. A change in which the matter does not turn into a new kind of matter is called a _____.

2. Salt water is a _____ because one substance dissolves in another.

3. A _____ is two or more substances combined without changing any kind of matter.

4. A change in which one kind of matter is changed into another kind of matter is called a _____.

5. Solids, liquids, and gases are _____.

Explain Concepts

6. Explain why chopping wood is a physical change but burning wood is a chemical change.

7. Describe three different ways to cause a physical change.

Process Skills

8. **Infer** why a puddle of water can be on the sidewalk one day and be gone the next.

9. **Predict** what kind of a mixture you would have if you mix sugar and water.

10. **Predict** A dog dish of water is left outside during the night. The temperature will be –3°C during the night. What will happen to the water?

11. **Infer** Think of an egg frying in a pan. Does the frying produce a physical change or a chemical change? Give a reason for your answer.

12. **Draw Conclusions** When sugar is heated for a long time, it forms a solid black substance. What kind of change takes place? Explain your answer.

13. **Sequence** Put these steps in the correct order: ashes, paper, burning paper.

Cause and Effect

14. Make graphic organizers like the ones shown below. Fill in the correct cause and effect.

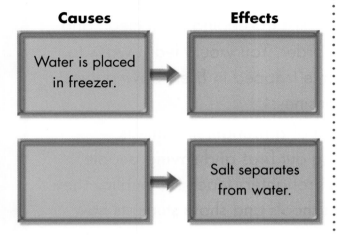

Causes   **Effects**

Water is placed in freezer. →

→ Salt separates from water.

🦉 Test Prep

Choose the letter that best completes the statement or answers the question.

15. Which of the following is a chemical change?

- Ⓐ Water freezes.
- Ⓑ Wire bends.
- Ⓒ Paper is cut.
- Ⓓ Wood burns.

16. A fruit salad is an example of a

- Ⓕ change in state.
- Ⓖ mixture.
- Ⓗ solution.
- Ⓘ chemical change.

17. What happens in a physical change?

- Ⓐ The kind of matter remains the same.
- Ⓑ The kind of matter changes to another kind.
- Ⓒ Some of the matter changes to another kind.
- Ⓓ The amount of matter changes.

18. In salt water

- Ⓕ the parts become new kinds of matter.
- Ⓖ the amount of each part is the same.
- Ⓗ the parts cannot be separated.
- Ⓘ the parts are mixed together in a solution.

19. Explain why the answer you chose for Question 18 is best. For each of the answers you did not choose, give a reason.

20. Writing in Science

Descriptive Write a paragraph describing what you see when you arrive at a forest fire. Include a description of chemical changes taking place.

Firefighter

This firefighter is teaching students about safety.

Each year fires kill people and destroy property. As a firefighter, you would work to prevent and control these disasters. You would drive and operate special trucks. You would assist in keeping them clean and in working order. You would learn ways to rescue people trapped in fires. Saving lives is serious business!

But not all of a firefighter's time is spent putting out fires and saving people. Sometimes firefighters teach the public. They might visit schools and show students how to be safe from fire at home. They also must train a lot and keep in good health.

You have to graduate from high school to become a firefighter. Then, if you can pass a physical and written test, you can go to firefighter training. Some firefighters go to college and study fire science. They learn a lot about how fires get started and how they spread.

Lab zone Take-Home Activity

On a piece of paper, design escape routes from each area of your house. Record the time it takes to move from each area through the proper exit.

Chapter 12

Forces and Motion

You Will Discover

- different ways to describe position and motion.
- how force affects motion.
- how simple machines work.

online
Student Edition
pearsonsuccessnet.com

How do forces cause motion and get work done?

position

motion

speed

relative position

gravity

Chapter 12 Vocabulary

force

friction

magnetism

work

323

Explore How can you describe motion?

Materials

2 balls

metric ruler

books or wooden blocks

2 long books

If you wish, you can use cardboard or wood to build your ramps.

What to Do

1 Make 2 ramps. Let go of a ball from the top of each ramp at the same time.

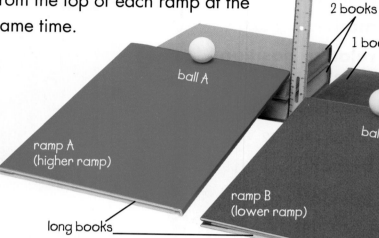

2 books

1 book

ball A

ball B

ramp A (higher ramp)

ramp B (lower ramp)

long books

2 **Observe** how each ball moves down the ramp. Does its speed increase or decrease? Which reaches the bottom first?

3 **Communicate** After each ball reaches the bottom, does its speed increase or decrease?

Explain Your Results

1. Which ball moved faster? Describe the location of each ball when it stops moving. Which was farther from the ramp?

2. **Communicate** Compare how a ball's speed changes before and after reaching the bottom of a ramp. Describe the 2 types of motion that you **observed**.

Process Skills

After the activity, you were able to **communicate** the 2 types of motion you **observed**.

How to Read Science

TARGET SKILL

Summarize

When you **summarize** an article, you **communicate** all the information in just one or two sentences. Summarizing helps you remember what you read.

- Sometimes the summary is a sentence at the beginning or at the end of an article.
- Sometimes there is no written summary. Then you think about the pieces of information and summarize them.

Science Article

A World of Motion

Look around. Do you see anything moving? What about the second hand on the clock? Cars may be rolling by outside. Is anyone walking along the sidewalk? No doubt, we live in a world of motion.

Apply It!

Study the graphic organizer below.

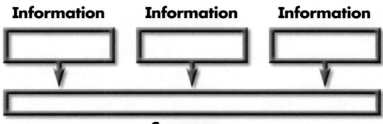

Make a graphic organizer like the one above. Write three details and the **summary** of the science article.

You Are There!

Here it comes—the wave you have been waiting for. You paddle quickly to get going. Then you stand up on your surfboard just as the monster wave arrives. Suddenly—whoosh! You're riding the wave. You're moving fast. The water crashes all around, but you keep your balance as you slice through the water. What a ride! Can you explain where you've been, where you've ended up, and how you got there?

AudioText

Lesson 1

What happens when things change position?

An object is in motion when its position changes. The speed and direction of an object's motion can also change. An object's position and motion depend on what you compare it with.

A spinning top has circular motion. What else moves like a top?

When Things Move

Can you tell when something is moving? Think about dropping a spinning top onto a hilly sidewalk. You can tell it has moved because its location has changed. It was in your hand. Now it's on the sidewalk spinning. If an object is in a different location, its **position** has changed.

Watch the top move down the sloping sidewalk in a certain direction. It is in **motion** as its position changes. It also moves in circles around a central point. The spin has given the top circular motion. You have made your top move down, then forward, and round and round as well.

1.  **Checkpoint** How can you tell something is in motion?

2. **Writing in Science** **Descriptive** Write a paragraph in your **science journal** describing different kinds of motion you have observed.

327

Ways of Looking at an Object's Position

Have you ever gotten lost trying to get somewhere? Finding your way can be confusing. As you change position, things around you stay in place. For example, as you walk along, the water fountain is in front of you. Then you walk past. The water fountain is behind you. The fountain seems to be moving away. The position, direction, and movement of an object often depend on how a person looks at it.

Sometimes a map can help. A map is a drawing of a place. Objects marked on a map are not real, of course. They are models of things. A map models the position of objects in relation to each other. Maps work because the objects on the map are fixed in place.

Suppose you visit the school shown in the map below. Can you describe a trip to the lunch room using position terms? Position terms include words like *forward, left, right,* and *behind.*

The arrows on the school map show a path from a classroom to the lunch room.

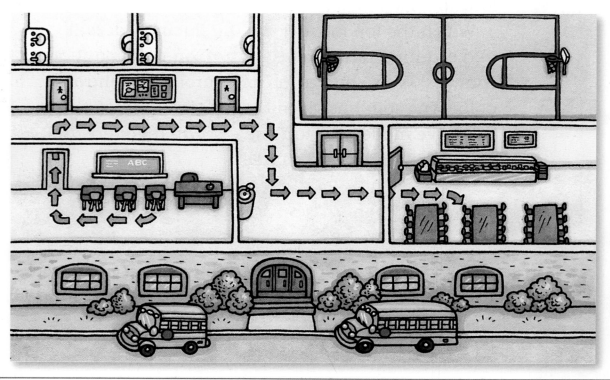

Positions of Moving Objects

The position of each object on a map is relative to other objects. *Relative* can mean that one thing depends on another thing for its meaning.

What is the position of car 64 in the picture? You would say its relative position is in front of the other cars. **Relative position** is the position of one object compared with the position of other objects.

Will car 64 win the race? Only if its relative position when it crosses the finish line is in front of the other cars.

But what about cars that aren't in the picture? Some might be in front of car 64. You would say car 64 is behind those cars. So the position of car 64 depends on the position of the other cars. The relative position of car 64 changes depending on the position of cars around it.

Look at the train moving down the track. The locomotive is in front of the cars it is pulling. Could the train cars move in front of the locomotive? They could if the train started moving backward. The direction of their motion changes the relative position of objects.

1. ✓**Checkpoint** In what ways can the relative position of an object change?

2. **Social Studies** in Science
Describe a trip to the lunch room of your school. Use position words.

When the locomotive is pulling the train cars, it is in front of them. When it's pushing the train cars, the locomotive is behind them.

How Fast Things Move

How fast does a jet plane fly? How fast does a caterpillar move? **Speed** is the rate, or how fast, an object changes its position. When things change position, they do so at a certain rate of speed.

Speed can be very fast. A jet plane moves fast. The two arms of the tuning fork are moving back and forth so fast they are just a blur. Did you ever see a meteor flash across the sky? It moves so fast that if you blink, you might miss it.

Speed can also be very slow. Some things have such a slow speed that you can't even see them move. The flowers in the picture have moved to face the light. If you turn the plant around, the flowers will slowly move back to face the light. The thick, syrupy honey is another slow mover. It moves slowly from the scoop down into the jar.

The arms of the tuning fork move back and forth very fast as they vibrate.

Constant Speed

Sometimes moving objects do not change how fast or slow they move. They are moving at a constant speed. Objects that move at a constant speed change position at the same rate. For example, suppose a car is moving steadily on a road at 35 miles an hour. It is moving at constant speed. Its speed, or rate, stays the same.

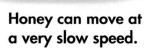

Honey can move at a very slow speed.

These flowers slowly change position as they grow toward the light. This motion is too slow to see.

Variable Speed

If you were in one of the bumper cars, you could change the direction of the car's motion. You could move forward, backward, to the side, or in a circle. You could also change the speed of the bumper car. You might try to bump into another car. You can cover the distance between you and the other car in less time by going faster. Maybe you can get away before the other car can bump into you!

The bumper cars move at a variable speed. Variable means that it changes. An object moving at a variable speed changes speed as it moves.

The bumper cars can move in different directions. They also can move at different speeds.

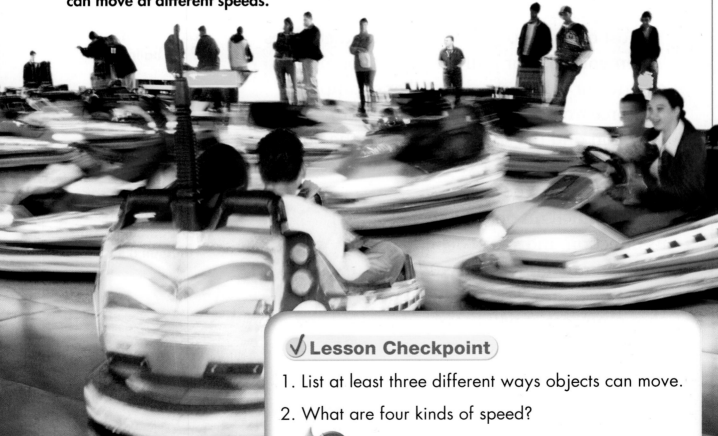

✓**Lesson Checkpoint**

1. List at least three different ways objects can move.

2. What are four kinds of speed?

3. **Summarize** Write a sentence that summarizes what relative position is.

Lesson 2

How does force affect motion?

Forces act on objects to change their motion. A force can involve two or more objects that contact each other. Other kinds of forces can act on an object without touching it.

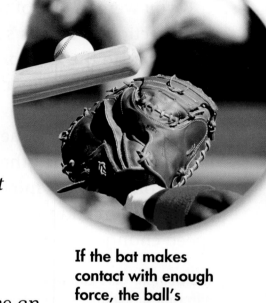

The Causes of Motion

Did you push or pull on a door today? A **force** is any push or pull. A force can change an object's position or the direction of its motion.

Most of the forces you use are contact forces. When you push or pull an object, you must contact, or touch, the object. For example, the force from a baseball bat, can change the direction and the speed of a ball. If the bat doesn't make contact with the ball, these changes cannot occur.

How much an object changes its direction and speed depends on how much force is used. If you push harder on a moving shopping cart, it will move faster. If a larger force acts on an object, the object will have a greater change in motion.

If the bat makes contact with enough force, the ball's change in speed and direction could take it out of the ballpark.

This shopping cart needs little force to start it moving, but wait until it's full!

Effects of Mass and Friction

How an object moves also depends on how much mass it has. When you start shopping, your cart is empty. You don't need to use much force to push it. As you fill the cart with groceries, it gains mass. You have to use more force to make it move.

As you push your cart along, its wheels rub against the floor. This causes friction. **Friction** is a contact force that goes against motion. Friction can cause a moving object to slow down or stop.

The amount of friction between two objects depends on their surfaces. Pushing a cart over smooth tiles is pretty easy. You need more force to push the cart across a bumpy parking lot. The smooth tile produces less friction on the wheels than the parking lot.

Sometimes friction is a helpful force. Think about a time you were skating or sledding and wanted to slow down or stop. What did you do? If you dragged your foot on the ground, you used friction to slow you down.

1. **√Checkpoint** What is a force?

2. **Writing** in Science

   Narrative Make a two-column chart in your **science journal**. Head the first column, *Forces*. Head the second column, *Change*. Fill in the chart with different forces that you have used today. Include how the forces changed the position or speed of objects.

The greater mass of more carts causes you to use more force to get them going.

333

Motion and Combined Forces

You have learned that pushes, pulls, and friction change the motion of objects. Now, think about pulling on a rope in a game of tug-of-war. Your team's pull is a force in one direction. The pull of the other team is a force in the opposite direction. If the forces are equal, the rope does not move.

How can you win the game? If more people join your team, you can pull with greater force. The pulls of everyone on your team combine to move the rope in your direction. But what if even more people join the other team? Their pulls combine to move the rope in their direction. The rope will move in the direction of the stronger force.

The pulls of the two teams oppose each other. The team pulling with the greater force moves the rope in their direction.

The forces the cyclists are applying to their bikes overcome friction. These forces keep the bikes moving forward.

By shifting his weight, the rider can make the turn without losing speed.

Many forces can cause a bicycle to change its motion. What forces do you use when you ride a bike? Your legs push on the pedals. You shift your weight and push the handlebars to turn. Friction between the bicycle tires and the ground slows your motion. When you go uphill, you have to pedal with more force. Going downhill, you speed up. You use the brakes to slow down. As you move, wind pushes against you. You keep pedaling to keep moving forward.

Each force has its own amount and acts in its own direction. All the forces combine to keep the bicycle going forward safely.

What a workout!

The road produces less friction than the dirt path.

1. **✓ Checkpoint** What two things about forces are important when forces are combined?

2. **Math in Science** If two pulling forces applied to an object are in the same direction, would the forces be added together or subtracted?

Gravity and Magnetism

The forces you have learned about so far need objects to be touching or in contact. Another kind of force is a non-contact force. A non-contact force is a push or pull that can affect an object without touching it. **Gravity** is a non-contact force that pulls objects toward each other. These skydivers, for instance, are being pulled toward Earth by gravity. Without the force of gravity, they would all float away. Gravity pulls you and everything else on Earth toward Earth's center.

Gravity pulls the skydivers toward the ground.

Gravity pulls the bobsled down the hill. The sled speeds up quickly because the slippery ice surface causes little friction.

SciLinks **Take It to the Net** pearsonsuccessnet.com · keyword: gravity code: g3p336

The amount that gravity pulls on an object is its weight. An object's weight depends on where it is. Since the Moon has less gravity than Earth, for instance, you weigh less on the Moon. The pull of gravity is also less the farther you are from the center of Earth. So you weigh a little less on a mountaintop than you do at the base of the mountain.

The pull of gravity on an object depends on how much matter is in it. Objects with more matter have more mass. So the pull of gravity is greater if the object it is pulling has more mass. Even if the pull of gravity on an object changes, the object's mass remains the same.

Magnetism is another non-contact force. Magnets pull on, or attract, certain kinds of metal such as iron. For example, a strongly magnetic bar might pull a steel paper clip from halfway across your desk. Steel is a metal that has iron in it. Magnets do not attract wood, plastic, paper, or other objects that do not contain these metals.

A magnet does not affect a crayon because the crayon lacks metal that the magnet can attract.

✓ Lesson Checkpoint

1. What are three contact forces?

2. What are two non-contact forces?

3. **Math** in Science Denver, Colorado, is more than 1 kilometer above sea level. How would your weight in Denver compare to your weight on an ocean beach? How would your mass compare in both places?

Magnetism attracts these paperclips because they contain iron.

The soccer player applies force to change the direction of the soccer ball. Is work being done?

The snowball appears stuck, despite all the pushing. Is work being done?

How do simple machines affect work?

Work is done when a force moves an object. Simple machines help you do work more easily.

Work

Have you done any work today? In science *work* has a special meaning. You do **work** when you use a force to move an object. You do work when you move a shopping cart, rake leaves, or carry out the trash. But work can be fun too. You do work when you pedal a bike or kick a soccer ball. The amount of work you do depends on how far you move an object and the mass of the object you move.

Work is NOT done when the position of an object does not change. Imagine pushing a big ball of snow with all the force you can. If the snowball does not move, no work is done. The football players are pushing against each other with as much force as they can. But the players are not moving in the direction they are pushing. No work is being done because none of the players moved.

How much work can you do in one day? To answer this, you would need to add up the amount of pushing and pulling you do. You would also need to measure the distance those pushes and pulls moved things. And you must measure the mass of the objects you moved.

Suppose you put a library book back on its shelf. That would be a certain amount of work. What if you put the book on a shelf that is twice as high? You do twice as much work. What if you move two books to the first shelf? Again you did twice as much work as you did the first time.

When Work Is Done	
Activity	**Work**
Thinking about a math problem	No
Turning a jump rope	Yes
Holding a puppy	No
Lifting a puppy	Yes
Pulling on a locked door	No
Opening an unlocked door	Yes
Trying to scoop rock-hard ice cream	No

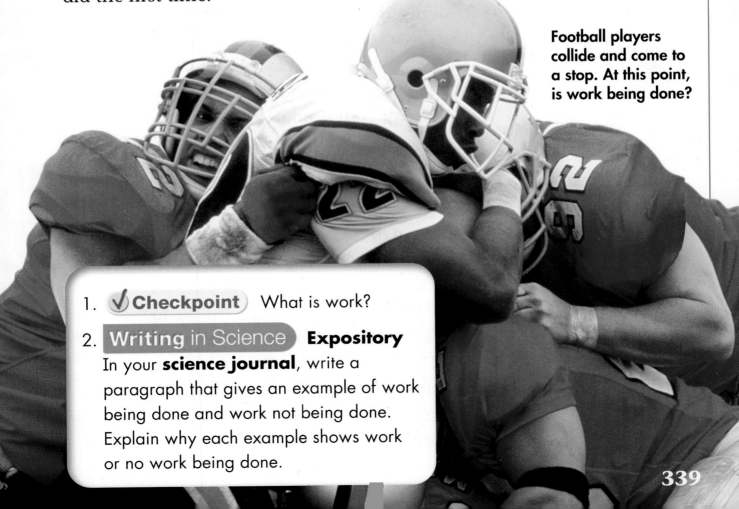

Football players collide and come to a stop. At this point, is work being done?

1. ✓**Checkpoint** What is work?

2. **Writing in Science** **Expository** In your **science journal**, write a paragraph that gives an example of work being done and work not being done. Explain why each example shows work or no work being done.

339

Instead of lifting the cart, the mover pushes the cart up a ramp.

The axe head is a wedge that separates the wood of the log.

Some Simple Machines

Making work easier is the reason for many inventions. Machines don't actually lessen the amount of work that is done. Machines help make work easier. Six kinds of simple machines help you do just that.

Inclined Plane

Look at the man pushing a cart up the ramp. Without the ramp, he would have to lift the cart straight up off the ground high enough to place it in the truck. That would take a great deal of effort. He is using a simple machine called an inclined plane. An inclined plane, or a ramp, is a slanting surface that connects a lower level to a higher level. The mover pushes the cart with less force over a longer distance. He still has the same amount of work to do, but it takes less effort to do it.

Wedge

Wedges are used to split, cut, or fasten things. A wedge is a simple machine made up of two slanted sides that end in a sharp edge. They act as a pair of inclined planes working together. When work is done with a wedge, the wedge moves through the material being worked on. The material separates as it slides up the sides of the wedge. A knife cutting through a pie, and a nail moving through a piece of wood are wedges.

A screw is an inclined plane wrapped around a center post.

This slide is an inclined plane wrapped around a center post. It is a kind of screw!

Screw

A screw is an inclined plane wrapped around a center post. A good example of how a screw looks is the spiral slide in the picture. Do you see how the slide wraps around the center post?

The slide is similar to a screw you use with a screwdriver. Screws can be used to hold things together, and to raise and lower things. When you open a jar, the lid raises if you turn it one way and lowers if you turn it the other way. The jar lid is a screw.

Lever

A seesaw is an example of a simple machine known as a lever. A lever is a stiff bar that rests on a support. A lever is used to lift and move things. If you push down on one side of the bar, you can raise an object on the other side.

A seesaw is a lever that rests on a support.

support

1. ✓**Checkpoint** What is an inclined plane?

2. **Summarize** State briefly how using an inclined plane makes work easier.

More Simple Machines
Wheel and Axle

When you turn a doorknob to open a door, you are using a simple machine called a wheel and axle. The knob is a wheel and the post that attaches to its center is an axle. You would use less force to turn the doorknob a far distance than to turn the axle attached to the knob a shorter distance. This makes opening the door easier, although the work is the same.

A Ferris wheel and merry-go-round use a huge wheel and axle too. Instead of turning the wheel, however, the motor in these rides turns the axle. The distance over which the motor turns the axle is small. But the distance the axle turns the wheel is great. The force applied to the axle to do this must be great. The people on the ride are having fun. They probably are not thinking about the simple machine at work.

What kind of simple machine are the Ferris wheel and merry-go-round?

Pulley

Sailors pull sails to where the sails can fill with wind and push the sailing ship. But the sailors have to move the sails in directions that are uncomfortable for them. Simple machines called pulleys can help them. A pulley changes the direction of motion of an object to which a force is applied. The sail is attached to a pulley. The pulley has a grooved wheel that turns on an axle. The sailors can pull on the rope to turn the grooved wheel. As they pull the rope toward them, the sail is pulled in the proper direction. Now they are ready to hit the high seas!

Pulleys, like those on the boat above, help workers reposition heavy sails.

✓ Lesson Checkpoint

1. How do you know when a simple machine has done work?

2. What simple machine has a grooved wheel, an axle, and a rope?

3. **Summarize** Write a sentence that summarizes how simple machines are useful.

343

An overpass is an inclined plane.

Investigate How much force will you use?

Materials

string and paperback book

long book

2 books

meter ruler

spring scale

What to Do

1 Tie string around the paperback book.

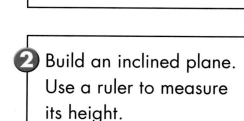

2 Build an inclined plane. Use a ruler to measure its height.

3 Hook a spring scale under the string. Hold the spring scale and lift the book straight up to the height of the inclined plane.

Pull straight up.

The force of gravity pulls the book down. The scale measures the force you used to overcome gravity.

4 **Observe** the reading on the scale. Record.

5 **Predict** what the scale will read when you pull the book up the inclined plane. Record.

6 Holding the scale, pull the book up the inclined plane. Observe the reading on the scale.

If you wish you can construct your ramp out of cardboard or wood.

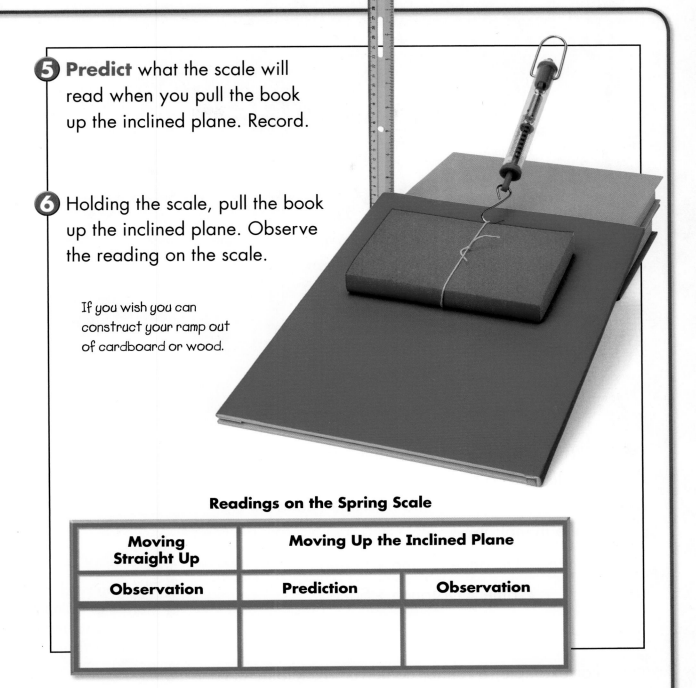

Readings on the Spring Scale

Moving Straight Up	Moving Up the Inclined Plane	
Observation	Prediction	Observation

Explain Your Results

1. What information did you use to make your **prediction**?

2. Compare your **observations**.

3. **Infer** How do you think the steepness of the ramp affected the amount of force needed to pull the book up the ramp.

Go Further

Use your data to predict what would happen to the force if you changed the steepness of the ramp. Make a plan to test your prediction.

Math in Science

Relating Speed, Distance, and Time

In a race, the winner is the one who covers the total distance in the least amount of time. To win, you must have the highest average speed.

The following rules can help you find the distance a racer moved, the length of time in motion, or the average speed while in motion.

Distance = Time × Speed

Time = Distance ÷ Speed

Speed = Distance ÷ Time

This stopwatch can be started and stopped at any instant, and is thus useful for timing races.

For example, a runner could run 40 kilometers in 4 hours at an average speed of 10 kilometers per hour.

Distance	Time	Speed
40 = 4 × 10	4 = 40 ÷ 10	10 = 40 ÷ 4

Use the rules on page 346 to answer each question.

1 How far could you run in 3 hours at an average speed of 12 kilometers per hour?

2 If you walked a half-marathon (about 21 kilometers) in 3 hours, what was your average walking speed?

3 How long would it take a race-walker to finish a marathon (about 42 kilometers) at an average speed of 7 kilometers per hour?

How can you find the avevage speed of this racer?

Lab zone **Take-Home Activity**

Plan a 2-hour trip to take with your friends, riding your bikes or walking. Choose a reasonable average speed and find out how far you could ride or walk each way, in order to be back home in 2 hours. Include time for rest stops.

Chapter 12 Review and Test Prep

Use Vocabulary

force (page 332)	**motion** (page 327)
friction (page 333)	**position** (page 327)
gravity (page 336)	**relative position** (page 329)
magnetism (page 337)	**speed** (page 330)
	work (page 338)

Use the vocabulary term from the list above that best matches each statement.

1. If an object is in a different location, it has changed _____.

2. An object is in _____ if its position is changing.

3. A force that slows down a moving object is _____.

4. A push or a pull is a _____.

5. How fast an object changes position is its _____.

6. A change in position of one object compared to another object is its _____.

7. The non-contact force of _____ pulls any two objects toward each other.

8. The non-contact force of _____ pulls objects that contain iron.

9. If you use force to move an object, you have done _____.

Explain Concepts

10. Explain how you can tell that an object is in motion.

11. A train is moving 435 kilometers (270 miles) per hour. A plane is flying 965 kilometers (600 miles) per hour. How much faster is the plane moving than the train?

12. Write a paragraph about a simple machine you have used and how it helped you do work.

Process Skills

13. **Infer** what would happen to a thrown baseball if gravity and air friction did not affect it.

14. **Predict** how much more work you would do lifting two identical books compared to lifting just one.

Summarize

15. Make a graphic organizer like the one below. Fill in the summary.

Work is the force it takes to move an object a certain distance.	The amount of force it takes to move an object is called effort.	Machines change the amount of effort it takes to move an object.

Test Prep

Choose the letter that best completes the statement or answers the question.

16. Friction is a

Ⓐ moving object.

Ⓑ contact force.

Ⓒ gravitational force.

Ⓓ magnetic force.

17. What machine is an inclined plane wrapped around a center post?

Ⓕ lever

Ⓖ pulley

Ⓗ wedge

Ⓘ screw

18. Which of the following describes a constant speed?

Ⓐ fast, slow, fast

Ⓑ slow, slower, slowest

Ⓒ fast, faster, fastest

Ⓓ fast, fast, fast

19. Explain why the answer you chose for Question 18 is best. For each of the answers you did not choose, give a reason why it is not the best choice.

20. **Writing** in Science

Descriptive Choose one of the skydivers on page 336 and describe the position of that person. Hint: You can use position words such as *to the left of, across from,* and *to the right of.*

Exercising in Space

Do you like to exercise? Running, playing ball, and bicycling are exercises that have motion, speed, and force. But you don't have to be moving to exercise your muscles. Pushing against a wall may not do any work, but the pushing force you use exercises your muscles.

On Earth, the force of gravity helps you exercise. That's because every time you lift your legs or arms, you have to lift them against the force of gravity. So, you have to give your arms and legs force, and that's good exercise. Suppose you are an astronaut aboard the Space Shuttle or the International Space Station. You do not feel the tug of gravity. The very high speed it takes to stay in orbit around the Earth is the reason. It reduces the effect of gravity to zero. You float around the cabin. This makes exercising in space harder than on Earth. Imagine trying to push against a wall on the shuttle. It just sends you off in another direction!

In space, elastic straps keep the astronaut on the treadmill.

The cycle machine exercises the heart, legs, and arms.

Without exercise, your muscles and bones get weaker. Astronauts in space must exercise every day to keep their muscles and bones healthy.

Special exercise machines had to be built for space. One kind of machine is like an exercise bicycle. Another machine is like a treadmill. The third kind of machine is like a rowing machine that pushes and pulls on muscles. Astronauts have to be strapped to the machines so they don't float away. Then they put on weights so they can exercise their muscles.

Information learned about muscles and bones in space has helped people on Earth know more about keeping healthy. Many gyms on Earth have exercise machines based on those designed for space. This is just another example of how things developed for use in space can help us here on Earth.

Muscles and bones are made stronger by using the resistance machine.

Lab zone Take-Home Activity

On a piece of paper, design a machine, using pulleys and levers, that allows you to exercise one or more parts of your body.

The Wright Brothers

Orville and Wilbur Wright were inventors who changed the world. They had been making and selling bicycles. Stories of flying machines, however, got their attention.

The Wright brothers studied forces that affect the motion of aircraft. They knew about the forces that keep a craft in the air and pull the craft down. They also knew about the forces that move the craft forward and slow the craft's motion.

In 1902 they used their skills to build a successful glider. The Wright brothers became the first people to design, build, and fly a craft that could be successfully controlled by a pilot in the air.

Orville and Wilbur's next step was to design and build an aircraft that could fly using an engine. They had to build a gasoline engine that didn't weigh too much. Yet it had to provide enough force to move the craft in the air. In 1903, the brothers made the first controlled flight in an aircraft with an engine.

Lab zone Take-Home Activity

Ask each family member to design and build a paper plane. Have a contest to see which plane flies the farthest and the longest.

You Will Discover

- different forms of energy.
- how energy changes from one form to another.
- how energy travels.

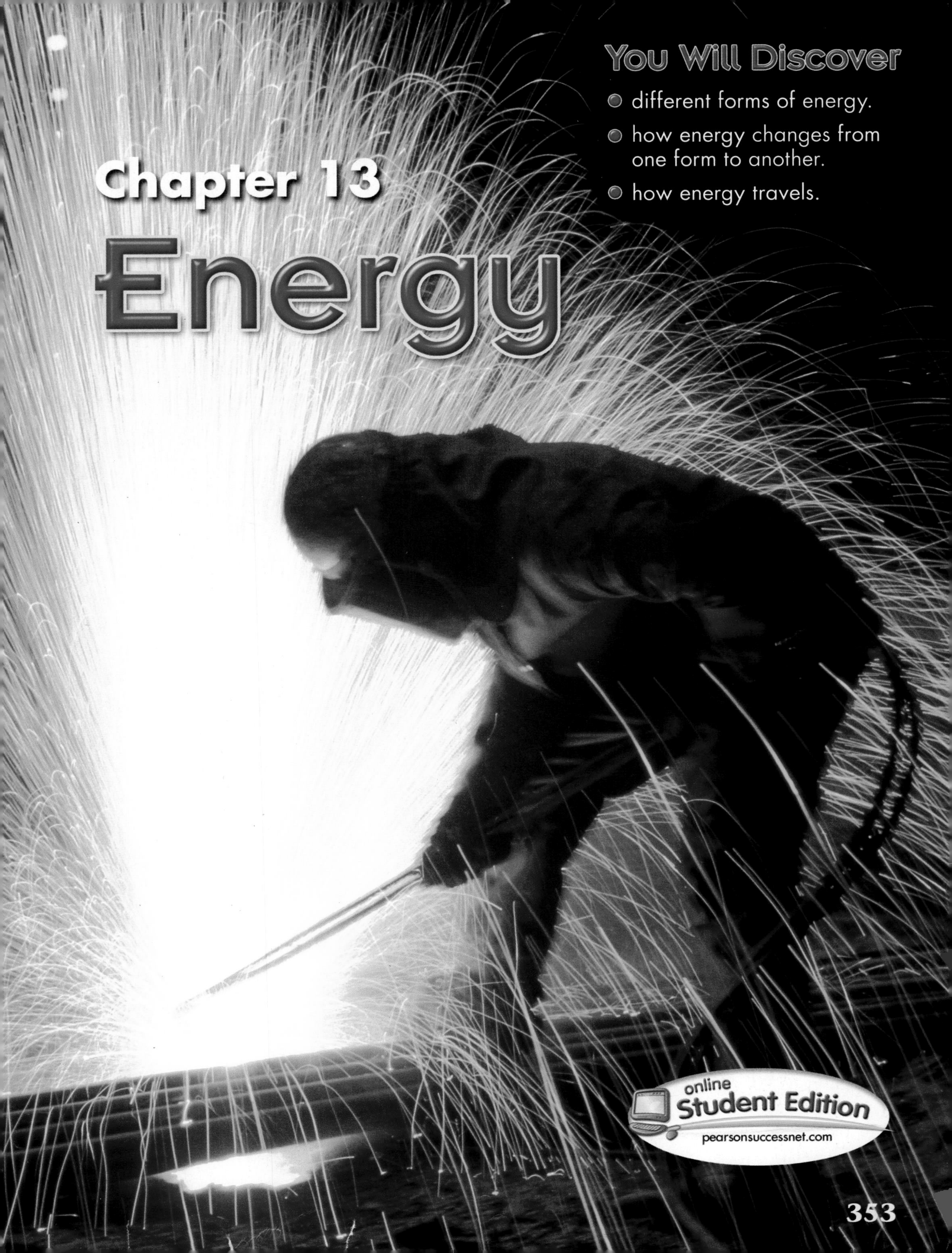

Chapter 13
Energy

online
Student Edition
pearsonsuccessnet.com

reflect

kinetic energy

potential energy

absorb

354

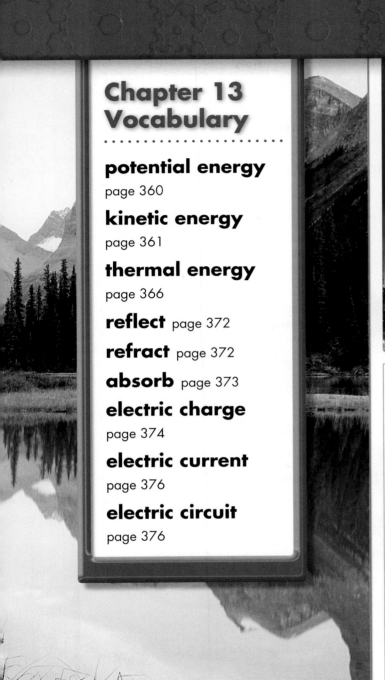

electric charge

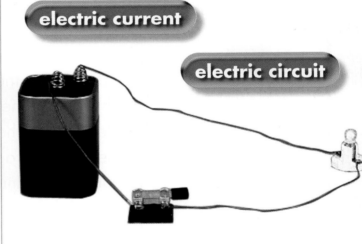

electric current

electric circuit

refract

thermal energy

Explore Can electricity produce light and heat?

Materials

safety goggles

2 pieces of wire

flashlight bulb and holder

battery and battery holder

thermometer

What to Do

Wear safety goggles. **Be careful!**

1 Make an electric circuit.

2 **Observe** the light.

3 Use a thermometer to observe heat. First, record the temperature you observe on the thermometer. Next, place the bulb of the thermometer against the light bulb for 1 minute. Then, record the temperature.

The bulb of the thermometer should touch the light bulb.

Explain Your Results

Explain the procedure. Name 2 forms of energy you **observed**. Describe where each was used or produced. Draw and label a diagram or sketch to help **communicate** your ideas.

Is every part of the circuit needed? Use your drawing to help predict, investigate, and describe what would happen if one part of your circuit were missing.

Process Skills

To help **communicate** clearly, scientists use sketches, diagrams, and drawings.

How to Read Science

 Main Idea and Details

- To find the topic of a paragraph, ask who or what the paragraph is about.
- To find the **main idea** in a paragraph, ask "What is the one important idea that all the sentences tell about?"
- To find supporting **details** in a paragraph, ask "Which sentences give information that supports the main idea?"

Science Article

Heating Homes

Energy heats your home. The energy comes from fuel that is burned. Some people heat their homes with natural gas. Some people burn wood to heat their homes. Other people use electricity. The electric company burns coal to make electricity. Gas, coal, and wood are natural resources. They come from Earth.

Apply It!

You can use a graphic organizer to **communicate** the **main idea and details.** Use one like this to show supporting details from the Science Article.

Main Idea

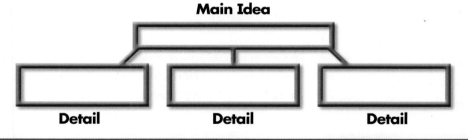

Detail   Detail   Detail

🔊 You Are There!

The Sun is shining brightly, but the air outside is cold. You stomp your feet and rub your hands together to warm them. You're looking forward to going inside and warming up. Maybe you'll listen to some music or play a DVD. How many different forms of energy will you use by the end of the day?

Lesson 1

What is energy?

The main source of energy on Earth is the Sun. Energy takes many forms. Energy can be stored and can change form.

Energy

Energy is the ability to do work or to cause change. Remember that work is done when a force makes an object move. You already know about the effects of the Sun's energy. Its warmth makes Earth a place in which we can live. The Sun's light energy makes plants grow. The Sun's energy also causes winds to blow and water to move through the water cycle.

We use many forms of energy in addition to the forms that come directly from the Sun. Electrical energy runs just about everything in this kitchen. Sound energy comes out of your CD player. Chemical energy in fuel runs the engine of a car. The energy of the car's motion gets you to the store. How do all these forms of energy come about?

How many things in this kitchen use energy?

1. **✔ Checkpoint** What are two forms of energy that Earth gets from the Sun?

2. **Writing in Science** **Descriptive** Write a paragraph in your **science journal** about the forms of energy you observe or use on your way to school.

Stored Energy

As you stand ready to jump, run, or ski, your body has stored energy that makes movement possible. Stored energy is **potential energy.** Potential energy changes into another kind of energy if you use it to do work or cause a change.

Oil, coal, natural gas, and gasoline, also have potential energy. The energy stored in these fuels started as sunlight. Long ago, plants used energy from sunlight to make food. After the plants died, they changed into a fossil fuel. When we burn a fuel, we release its potential energy. We use the energy to do work.

Every time you use batteries, you also release potential energy. The stored energy in food, fuels, and batteries is chemical energy.

Position or height stores another kind of potential energy. This energy is gained from gravity. A skier standing at the top of a hill has potential energy of position.

The standing skier has potential energy.

Gasoline contains the stored energy of living things that died long ago.

Batteries store energy as chemical energy.

Energy of Motion

Potential energy can change to kinetic energy. **Kinetic energy** is the energy of motion. A car can move when the potential energy stored in gasoline changes to kinetic energy. Look at the picture of the standing skier. When he pushes off, he goes down the hill. He's in motion. Potential energy the skier had at the top of the hill changes to kinetic energy. The force of gravity pulls him down the hill.

Many sources of energy are renewable. After a day of skiing, the skier can replace the energy he used by eating food. The skier can climb the hill again. You have learned that some sources of energy are not renewable. We cannot easily replace gasoline, natural gas, and other fossil fuels.

WHOOSH!

As the skier slides down the hill, potential energy changes to kinetic energy.

✓ Lesson Checkpoint

1. What are two kinds of potential energy?

2. Give two examples of potential energy and kinetic energy that you see every day.

3. **Main Idea and Details** Use a graphic organizer. What is the main idea of the paragraph at the top of this page? What details support it?

Lesson 2

How does energy change form?

Energy comes in different forms. Energy can change from one form to another. When energy changes form, some energy is given off as heat. People change energy into forms they can easily use, such as electricity.

Living things, such as this tarsier, change chemical energy stored in food to energy of motion and heat.

Changing Forms of Energy

Energy changes into more useful forms all the time. For example, your body stores potential energy as chemical energy. The chemical energy stored in your body changes to kinetic energy as you move.

Using Energy

You can't use the kinetic energy of your moving arm to make a light bulb burn bright. But you can use this kinetic energy to flip a light switch. This, in turn, helps change electrical energy to light energy. Most light bulbs also get hot. Some of the electrical energy changes to a kind of energy felt as heat. Energy cannot change completely from one form to another. Some energy is always given off in the form of heat.

Electrical energy changes to kinetic energy as the cable car moves along the track.

Forms of Energy

Chemical	Motion	Electrical	Light	Thermal

This energy holds the particles of matter together, such as in food. Eating food is the way we get energy.	This is the energy of moving objects. The moving parts in our machines and playground equipment have this form of energy.	This energy can pass through wires. This form of energy can change into forms that run appliances in our homes.	We see the Sun's energy in this form. Plants make food with light energy. We also change other forms of energy into light so we can see.	This form of energy makes particles of matter move faster. We feel this energy as heat.

People also use machines to change forms of energy. The cable car in the picture changes electrical energy to energy of motion. The electric toothbrush in the picture stays in a base that has an electric cord that plugs into an outlet. The electrical energy is stored as chemical energy in the toothbrush's battery. The chemical energy changes back to electrical energy and then to energy of motion when the toothbrush is turned on.

Chemical energy changes to electrical energy, which changes to energy of motion as the toothbrush moves.

1. ✔ **Checkpoint** What form of energy do living things change into mechanical energy and thermal energy?

2. **Math in Science** Food energy is measured in Calories. John eats 2,000 Calories in food in a day. How many Calories does he eat in a week?

Ways That Energy Travels

Energy can travel from one place to another. A moving object, such as a baseball, carries energy. You feel the energy when you try to catch the ball. You can tell how much energy the ball has by how hard it hits your hand.

Energy can also travel as waves. Have you ever seen waves of water? These waves carry energy as the baseball does. These waves of energy have the same shape as the waves of a moving rope. Look at the rope on the next page. How would you describe it? Notice that parts of the rope take turns going from side to side. Energy causes this effect as it travels from one end of the rope to the other. The rope itself does not travel forward. Light and certain other forms of kinetic energy move as waves.

Waves in water can be as small as the ripples in the bucket below. Waves caused by hurricanes can be huge. How big the wave is depends on how much energy it carries.

Ocean waves carry energy.

PLOP!

The energy from the falling drop moves in waves across the water. As the waves move away from the source, they lose strength.

Parts of a Wave

You can measure the amount of energy that a wave carries. Look again at the waving rope. One way to measure a wave's energy is by measuring the distance from the midpoint of the wave. The bottom of the wave is called a *trough*. The top of the wave is called a *crest*. Waves with greater distance from the midpoint have more energy. Waves with lesser distance have less energy.

Another way to measure a wave's energy is by measuring the length of the wave. The length of a wave can be the distance from the top of one crest to the top of the next crest. Shorter waves have more energy. Longer waves have less energy.

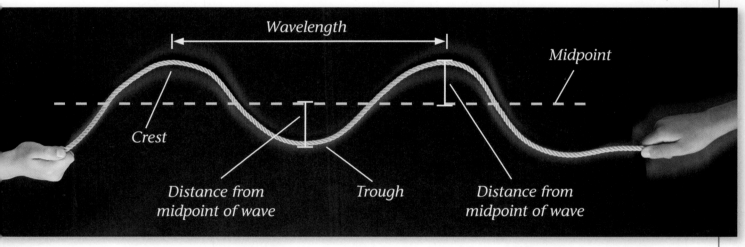

Wavelength

Midpoint

Crest

Distance from midpoint of wave

Trough

Distance from midpoint of wave

✔ Lesson Checkpoint

1. Name two types of energy that travel in waves.

2. What happens to energy as it travels away from the source?

3. **Main Idea and Details** Read the paragraph at the top of this page. Use a graphic organizer. What is the main idea? What are the supporting details?

Moving a loose rope from side-to-side on a table makes energy move forward along the rope in the form of waves. The rope itself does not travel forward.

Lesson 3

What is heat energy?

Matter contains thermal energy. Thermal energy travels through objects and space as heat. Heat travels from warm objects to cool ones until they are both at the same temperature.

Heat Energy

Matter is made of very small, moving particles. Each particle of matter is moving because it has energy. The sun's rays feel warm on your skin, for instance. The sun's rays warm matter by making its particles move faster. The energy of moving particles is called **thermal energy.** Thermal energy is the total energy of all the particles in matter.

Thermal energy moves as heat from a warmer object to a cooler object. Put a spoon into a hot drink. Heat travels from the drink through the cooler spoon. In a short time, the top of the spoon will feel warm. Once the drink and the spoon reach the same temperature, the flow of energy stops.

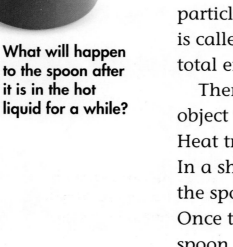

What will happen to the spoon after it is in the hot liquid for a while?

The fish is in a bag of water at room temperature. It waits for the clean, cold tank water to warm up. Why will the temperature of both soon be the same?

366

Sources of Heat

When energy is changed from one form to another, at least some heat is given off. The burner coils below the pot change electrical energy to heat. Burning matches, wood, and natural gas are examples of chemical changes that give off heat. You notice friction when you rub your hands together to warm them. The friction caused by rubbing gives off heat. Every time energy moves, there is heat.

OUCH!
Be careful! The chemical change that happens when a match is lit is a source of heat.

1. ✓**Checkpoint** What are four different kinds of heat sources?

2. **Writing in Science** **Expository** Write a paragraph in your **science journal** to explain how energy travels to the vegetables in the pot.

The heat in the water spreads through the frozen vegetables. The temperature is becoming the same throughout the pot.

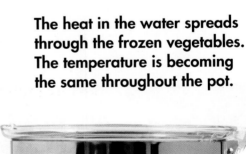

Effects of Heat on Matter

Heat energy affects matter. Think about a cup of liquid water. At 0°C (32°F) water has too little thermal energy to stay in its liquid state. At 0°C, water is a solid called ice.

What happens when you add heat to ice? When the temperature of the air is above 0°C, ice melts. It becomes a liquid.

You can measure the effect of heat on matter. For example, you could record the time ice takes to melt. Look at the stack of ice cubes in the pictures. At 9 A.M. you put the ice cubes in a warm place. At 9:15 A.M. what do you observe? Heat has moved from the air into the ice. You can measure the amount of ice that has melted. At 9:30 A.M. what do you observe? Record the time when all the ice is melted. Measure the volume of melted ice. Calculate the amount of time it takes for a certain amount of ice to melt at a certain temperature. The time is a rough measure of the change caused by heat energy.

This thermometer shows that the temperature inside and outside is about the same.

The change from ice to liquid water is related to a change in temperature.

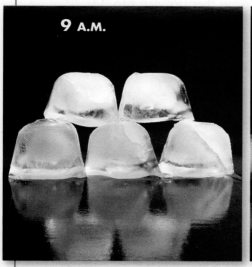

9 A.M.

9:15 A.M.

9:30 A.M.

If heat is added to liquid water, it evaporates. It becomes the invisible gas called water vapor. At a temperature of 100°C (212°F), heat makes liquid water boil. Look at the bubbling water. Heat at the bottom of the container makes water expand. Expand means to get bigger. The liquid water expands enough to evaporate. It becomes a hot gas. Bubbles of this gas float to the water's surface. These bubbles break open and release a cloud of hot water droplets.

At 100°C (212°F) heat makes liquid water boil.

Toast Time!
How has heat energy changed this piece of bread?

✓ Lesson Checkpoint

1. What is the main source of heat on Earth?

2. What causes matter to be in a solid, liquid, or gas state?

3. **Writing in Science**
   Descriptive In your **science journal,** write a paragraph that describes how a campfire keeps campers warm on a cold night.

Burning fuels, such as the gas in this gas lamp, can produce light as well as heat.

Electricity in heat lamps makes heat and light. A heat lamp is keeping this meerkat warm.

What is light energy?

Light is a form of energy. We can see some of the ways that light behaves. Light affects some of the properties of matter.

Sources of Light

The Sun is our main source of energy. The Sun's energy travels from the Sun to Earth as waves. The waves have different amounts of energy. We can see or feel the effects of only some of these waves. Light is energy that we can see.

Chemical changes are another source of light. Burning is a chemical change. Candles, campfires, and matches, for instance, give off light as they burn. The lamp in the picture gives off light as the gas burns. The anglerfish's tentacle gives off light too. Chemical changes in the fish's body produce light.

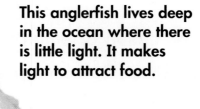

This anglerfish lives deep in the ocean where there is little light. It makes light to attract food.

370

Electricity is also a source of light. It makes the wire in a light bulb get so hot that it glows and gives off light. Most sources of light are also sources of heat. Heat lamps are used to keep things warm.

The Path of Light

Light travels from its source in straight lines in all directions. Light will continue to travel in this way until it is stopped by an object. Light will not bend or turn corners in order to get around objects. That is why objects that block light's path cause shadows. Shadows are areas behind the objects that are not getting direct light. The length of the shadow depends on the angle of the light. The shadows you have cast may have been taller than you really are!

1. **Checkpoint** Name three sources of light energy.

2. **Writing in Science** **Narrative** Write a paragraph in your **science journal** telling about the light sources you have seen today. Include what caused the light.

Why do these tables and chairs make shadows in the sunlight?

How Light Changes

You can see through a window and a clear glass of water. These objects do not block all of the light. Most light can pass through objects like these.

If you can see an object, it **reflects** light. This means light bounces in a different direction. Some objects reflect light better than others. A flat, smooth surface reflects light evenly. For example, a mirror reflects light evenly. The light bounces back to your eyes. A smooth lake also reflects light evenly.

What is happening to light in the water droplets in the picture? The droplets **refract,** or bend, the light. Refracted light changes direction. The droplets refract light that bounced off the flowers. The refracted light forms tiny images of the flower. The lens in a telescope refracts light to make big images of objects that looked small. The lenses in your eyes refract light to form images too.

The trees are reflected in the smooth water of the lake.

Each water droplet refracts light. A tiny image of the flower forms.

Light refracts because it passes through different materials at different speeds. Light passing through air slows down when it enters water. This causes the straw in the picture to look broken.

Sometimes refraction causes light to separate into its many colors. Then you see a rainbow. Water droplets in the air over a sprinkler refract light this way.

How We See Color

Light is made up of different colors. An object **absorbs,** or takes in, some of the light that hits it. It reflects the rest. Different objects absorb and reflect different colors of light. If an object looks red, it is reflecting red light and absorbing other colors of light. If an object looks white, it is reflecting all the colors of light. If an object looks black, it is absorbing all the colors of light. Dark objects get warmer in sunlight. The light energy they absorb turns to heat.

Water causes light to refract, so the straw looks broken.

✓ Lesson Checkpoint

1. What is the main source of light on Earth?

2. How does a shadow form?

3. **Writing in Science** **Narrative** Write a story about light in your **science journal.** Use examples of light being absorbed, reflected, and refracted. Brainstorm with others what your story might include.

Effects of Light

Objects can change light. They can reflect, refract, or absorb it. For instance, in sunlight, this chicken looks mostly white. In turn, light can change objects. How is this green light changing the white chicken?

What is electrical energy?

Matter is made of particles that have electric charges. Electric charges can move as electrical energy through a closed circuit.

Electric Charges

All matter is made up of small particles that have electric charges. An **electric charge** is a tiny amount of energy. Particles have both positive and negative charges. When particles have an equal number of positive and negative charges, they balance each other. The matter has no overall charge. Matter with more negative charges than positive charges has an overall negative charge. Matter with more positive charges than negative charges has an overall positive charge.

A balloon with a balanced charge does not attract the paper pieces.

Lightning is a result of moving electric charges.

How Charged Matter Acts

What happens when matter with a negative charge is near matter with a positive charge? The positive and negative charges attract. A negative charge moves toward the positive charge. If you get a shock when you touch someone, negative charges have jumped between you and that person. Lightning is the result of a much bigger jump of charges. Lightning happens when negative electric charges travel within clouds or between clouds and the ground.

The attraction between positive and negative charges can cause objects to stick together. Rubbing a balloon on your hair, for instance, causes the balloon to pick up negative charges. The extra negative charge on the balloon pushes aside the negative charges on one side of a piece of paper. This leaves the side of paper closest to the balloon with a positive charge. The balloon then attracts the positive side of the paper. The paper sticks to the balloon.

Charges that are the same can cause objects to push away from each other. Rubbing two balloons on your hair gives both balloons the same charge. The balloons then push apart.

Rubbing the balloon gives it an electric charge. It attracts objects with the opposite charge. It pushes away objects with the same charge.

1. ✓ **Checkpoint** What causes lightning?

2. **Art** in Science Draw a picture of two balloons that shows what happens when one balloon has a positive charge and the other balloon has a negative charge.

Electric Currents and Circuits

Electric current is the movement of electrical energy or electric charge from one place to another. Lightning is an uncontrolled electric current. Lightning can travel in any direction. To be useful, an electric current must travel in a planned way through wires or other materials. This way, electric current can turn on lights or make a CD player work.

Batteries or an outlet that you can plug a cord into are good sources of electrical energy. The path that a controlled electric current flows through is an **electric circuit.** The path must be unbroken for the energy to flow through it. Find the switch in the picture. The switch is on, or closed, so the circuit is unbroken. Electrical energy can flow through the wires of the circuit. If the switch was off, or open, the current could not flow through the circuit.

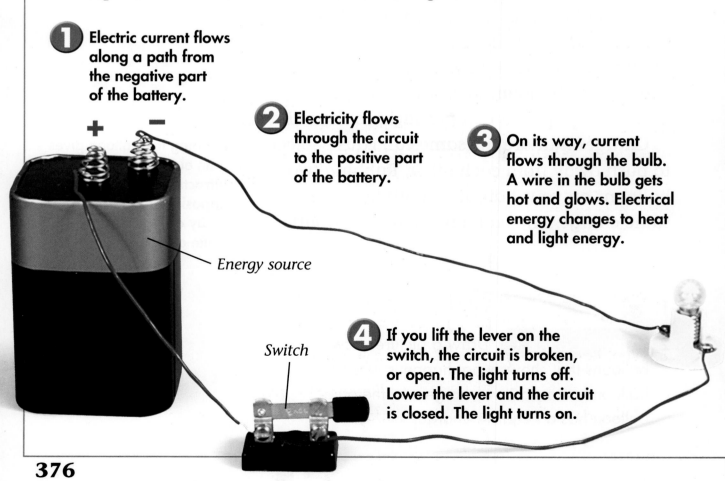

1 Electric current flows along a path from the negative part of the battery.

2 Electricity flows through the circuit to the positive part of the battery.

3 On its way, current flows through the bulb. A wire in the bulb gets hot and glows. Electrical energy changes to heat and light energy.

Energy source

Switch

4 If you lift the lever on the switch, the circuit is broken, or open. The light turns off. Lower the lever and the circuit is closed. The light turns on.

How Electrical Energy Changes Form

	Light	Electricity passes through bulbs of all kinds. Bulbs change electrical energy to light so we can see at night. Some heat is given off.
	Heat	Electricity passes through coils in heaters. Coils change electrical energy to heat so we can be warm in winter, or cook our food.
	Sound	Electricity passes around a magnet. The magnet changes electrical energy to vibrations of plastic discs in headphone speakers. Then we can hear music.
	Magnetic Force	Electricity passes around a huge magnet. The moving electricity makes a magnetic field that attracts metal containing iron to the magnet. The magnet can be used to lift heavy cars.

We rely on electricity for most of our everyday needs. We therefore spend a great deal of effort changing sources of energy into electricity. We change the power of moving water into electricity. We turn the heat of burning coal into electricity. We even turn sunlight into electricity. What happens to electricity once it gets to our homes? Study the table above. Can you imagine not having electricity?

✔ Lesson Checkpoint

1. What is the difference between a controlled and an uncontrolled electric current? Give an example of each.

2. What happens when an electric circuit is open?

3. **Main Idea and Details** Describe the path of electricity through a simple electric circuit.

Investigate Do freshwater ice and saltwater ice melt the same way?

Materials

2 cups and masking tape

water and graduated cylinder (or measuring cup)

spoon and salt

2 thermometers

tub with very warm water (for Day 2)

timer or stopwatch (or clock with a second hand)

Process Skills

By making careful **observations** of ice melting and by **collecting data** and organizing it into a chart, you learned how salt affects the melting of ice.

What to Do

1 Label one cup *fresh water*. Add 100 mL of water.

2 Label the other cup *salt water*. Add 100 mL of water and 1 spoonful of salt. Stir.

3 Place a thermometer in each cup. Your teacher will put the cups in a freezer overnight.

4 After the water is frozen, record the temperature in each cup.

5 Put both cups in a tub of very warm water. **Observe** the temperature in each cup until all the ice in the cup melts. Record the temperature every minute.

salt water   fresh water

6 Construct a chart or table to help you **collect** your **data**.

Melting Time of Ice

Time (minutes)	Temperature of Salt Water (°C)	Temperature of Fresh Water (°C)
0 (start)		
1		
2		
3		

Make a graph if you think it will better help you interpret the data.

Explain Your Results

1. You put the cups of ice in warm water. This added energy to the frozen water. Heat moved from the warm water to the ice. How did the temperature in each cup change? Look at your chart. Describe the pattern of change.

2. Based on your **observations**, in which cup did the ice finish melting first?

Go Further

How would adding more salt to the water affect how fast the ice would melt? Investigate to find out.

Measuring Temperature

Recording temperature is one way to measure thermal energy. You can use different scales to measure temperature.

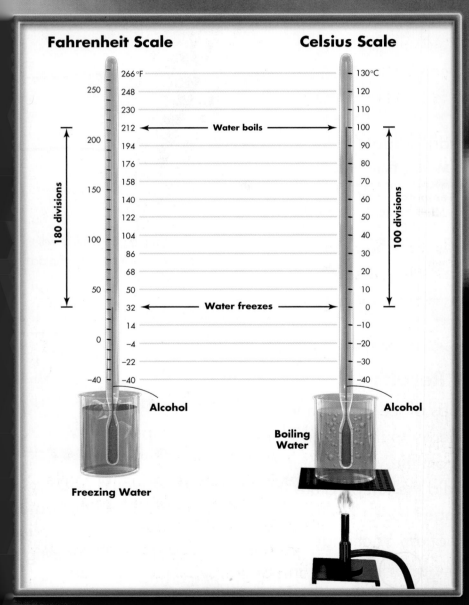

Fahrenheit Scale

Celsius Scale

180 divisions

100 divisions

266°F   130°C

250   248   120

230   110

212   Water boils   100

200   194   90

176   80

158   70

150   140   60

122   50

104   40

100   86   30

68   20

50   50   10

32   Water freezes   0

14   −10

0   −4   −20

−22   −30

−40   −40   −40

Alcohol

Alcohol

Boiling Water

Freezing Water

The Celsius scale is often used in science. The Fahrenheit scale is often used in everyday life, such as reading the temperature outdoors. Sometimes both scales are used.

Degrees Celsius is written °C. So 40°C is read "forty degrees Celsius."

Degrees Fahrenheit is written °F. So 40°F is read "forty degrees Fahrenheit."

1. What is the boiling point of water on the Celsius scale? What is the boiling point on the Fahrenheit scale?

2. What is the freezing point of water on the Celsius scale? What is the freezing point of water on the Fahrenheit scale?

3. About what is the temperature in degrees Fahrenheit when it is 30°C?

Lab zone Take-Home Activity

Watch the weather report on TV. Are temperatures given in degrees Fahrenheit, Celsius, or both? Make a list of three cities talked about in the report. Write down their temperatures in degrees Fahrenheit and in degrees Celsius. You can use the thermometers shown here.

Use Vocabulary

absorb (page 373)	**potential energy** (page 360)
electric charge (page 374)	**reflect** (page 372)
electric circuit (page 376)	**refract** (page 372)
electric current (page 376)	**thermal energy** (page 366)
kinetic energy (page 361)	

Use the term from the list above that best completes each sentence.

1. Energy that has the ability to cause a change is _____.

2. A lens causes light to bend or _____.

3. The energy of motion is _____.

4. Objects _____ light that they take in.

5. The path that a controlled electric current flows through is a(n) _____.

6. Two balloons will push away from each other if they have the same _____.

7. Mirrors work because they _____ light.

8. A(n) _____ is the movement of electrical energy from one place to another.

9. The total energy of all the particles in an object is the amount of _____ the object has.

Explain Concepts

10. Explain how to measure the energy in a wave.

11. Describe how light energy travels.

12. If an object has a temperature of 10°C and the air around it is 20°C, will the object gain or lose heat energy? Explain your answer.

Process Skills

13. **Infer** What would happen to the electric current if the part of the light bulb that glows breaks?

14. **Predict** You are having hot soup for lunch. You put a metal spoon in your soup and leave it for a minute. Predict what will happen to the spoon.

⟳ Main Idea and Details

15. Make a graphic organizer like the one shown below. Fill in details that support the main idea.

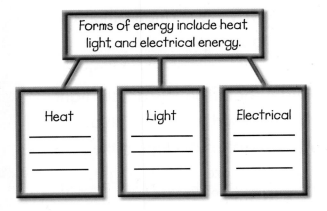

Forms of energy include heat, light, and electrical energy.

Heat	Light	Electrical
___	___	___
___	___	___

Test Prep

Choose the letter that best completes the statement or answers the question.

16. What kind of energy is stored in a battery?
- (A) kinetic
- (B) light
- (C) chemical
- (D) thermal

17. What color is an object if it reflects blue?
- (F) red
- (G) blue
- (H) yellow
- (I) orange

18. A dark towel that is placed in the sunlight feels warm because it
- (A) reflects the Sun's rays.
- (B) refracts the Sun's rays.
- (C) absorbs the Sun's rays.
- (D) allows the Sun's rays to pass through.

19. Explain why the answer you chose for Question 18 is best. For each of the answers you did not choose, give a reason why it is not the best choice.

20. Writing in Science

Descriptive Write a paragraph that describes different forms of energy.

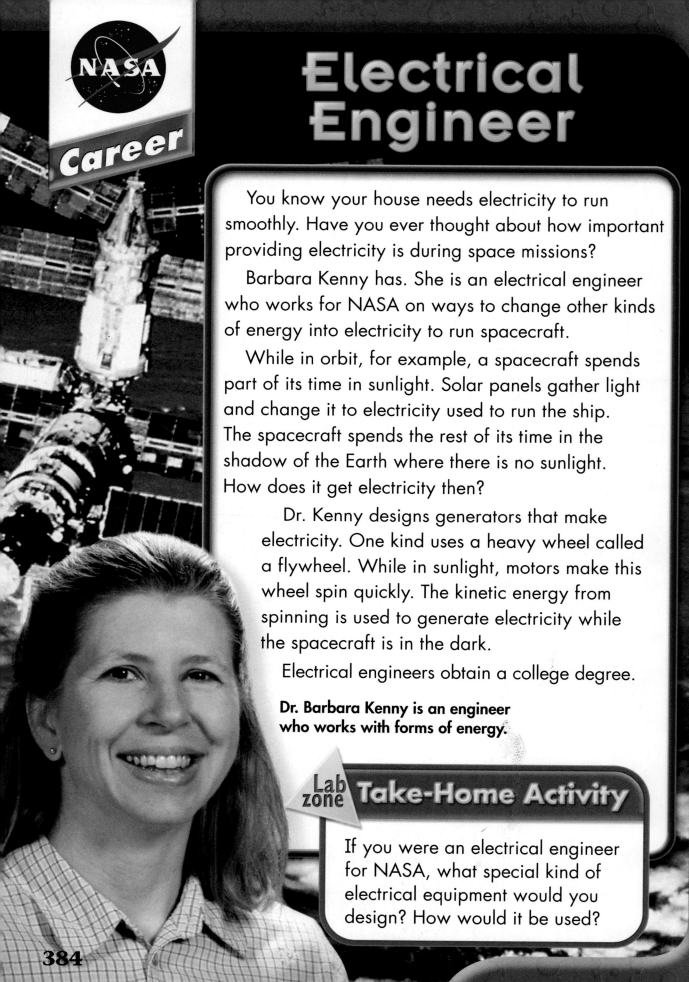

Electrical Engineer

You know your house needs electricity to run smoothly. Have you ever thought about how important providing electricity is during space missions?

Barbara Kenny has. She is an electrical engineer who works for NASA on ways to change other kinds of energy into electricity to run spacecraft.

While in orbit, for example, a spacecraft spends part of its time in sunlight. Solar panels gather light and change it to electricity used to run the ship. The spacecraft spends the rest of its time in the shadow of the Earth where there is no sunlight. How does it get electricity then?

Dr. Kenny designs generators that make electricity. One kind uses a heavy wheel called a flywheel. While in sunlight, motors make this wheel spin quickly. The kinetic energy from spinning is used to generate electricity while the spacecraft is in the dark.

Electrical engineers obtain a college degree.

Dr. Barbara Kenny is an engineer who works with forms of energy.

Lab zone Take-Home Activity

If you were an electrical engineer for NASA, what special kind of electrical equipment would you design? How would it be used?

EC CRU 10 9 8 7 6 5 4 3 2 1

Chapter 14
Sound

You Will Discover

- how different kinds of sound are produced.
- how sound energy and matter interact.
- how sound travels through different materials.

online
Student Edition
pearsonsuccessnet.com

How does energy produce the sounds we hear?

vibration

pitch

compression wave

Explore How can you see sound vibrations?

Hold your fingers on your throat. Speak. When you speak, air from your lungs moves past your vocal cords. Feel the vibrations caused by your vocal cords.

Materials

safety goggles

cup

plastic wrap

rubber band

salt

metric ruler

What to Do

1 Make a vibration viewer.

Be careful!

Wear safety goggles.

Sprinkle a little salt on top.

Tightly cover a cup with plastic wrap. Hold it on with a rubber band.

2 Look down at the cup from 3 cm away. Talk softly and loudly. Use a high pitch and a low pitch. Observe how loudness and pitch affect what the salt does.

Optional: If musical instruments are available, observe the vibrations made as you blow, pluck, or tap a musical instrument. Discuss and compare the ways you change pitch and the ways the vibrations change.

Explain Your Results

Collect Data Make a chart to show what you **observed**.

Process Skills

When you make **observations** and show them in a chart, you are **collecting data**.

Reading Skills

Compare and Contrast

When you **compare** things, you tell how they are alike.
When you **contrast** things, you tell how they are different.

- Writers sometimes use clue words such as *similar*, *alike*, *all*, *both*, or *in the same way* when they compare things.
- Writers sometimes use clue words such as *different*, *unlike*, or *in a different way* when they contrast things.

You can use what you have already **observed** about how instruments sound to help you compare and contrast.

Advertisement

Sound Machines

All our instruments are alike in one way. Vibrate them and you'll get music! But the sounds and how they are made are very different. How are the sounds alike and different? Come try them out!

Apply It!

The advertisement above asks you to **compare and contrast.** Tell how the sounds of the instruments are alike and different. Use a graphic organizer to compare and contrast.

Different **Alike** **Different**

◄)) You Are There!

You are in the middle of a huge celebration. Everyone is watching the parade and listening to the marching bands. Thousands of people are in the crowd. Horns are honking. People are cheering. You know that later, after it's dark, the fireworks will make different sounds. What's the reason for all this sound? It's the Fourth of July!

◄)) AudioText ◄))

Lesson 1

What causes sounds?

Sounds are all around you. You enjoy some sounds, like music. But other sounds hurt your ears. All sounds are made when matter moves.

Suppose you are taking a walk in a city. You might hear the loud sounds of car horns and garbage trucks. You might hear the soft sound of your friend's voice. If you are taking a walk in the country, you might hear the loud sounds of farm tractors. You might also hear cows mooing. In a forest, you might hear the soft sounds of water trickling in a creek and the sounds of birds chirping.

Some of these sounds might be pleasant to you. Others might bother you. Some noises, like the sound of a jet plane taking off, might even hurt your ears. The sounds we hear every day are different. Yet all sounds are alike in some ways.

Noisemakers like these are sometimes used on New Year's Eve. What kind of sounds do they make?

1. **✓Checkpoint** Describe some ways that sounds are alike and different.

2. **Writing in Science** **Descriptive** In your **science journal,** write two paragraphs about the sounds you hear every day. Tell why you think the sounds are pleasant or unpleasant.

The Causes of Sound

Sounds happen when matter moves back and forth very quickly. A back-and-forth movement is called a **vibration.** Sounds happen only when something vibrates.

Suppose you are listening to these instruments being played. You would hear high sounds and low sounds. **Pitch** describes how high or low a sound is. Objects that vibrate slowly make sounds with a low pitch. Objects that vibrate more quickly make sounds with a higher pitch.

A tambourine makes sounds when you hit it with your hand or shake it.

When a drum or cymbal is struck, it vibrates and makes a sound. Different sizes and shapes of drums produce sounds with different pitches.

Hitting or Plucking to Make Sound

Percussion instruments make sound when they are hit. Steel drums are played by tapping them with a rubber hammer. Other drums are played with wooden sticks, metal brushes, or the hands.

If you lightly tapped a drum, you would hear a soft sound. If you hit the drum harder, you would hear a louder sound. The harder you hit the drum, the farther the drumhead moves back and forth. The vibrations become stronger. The loudness of the sound depends on the strength of the vibrations.

Stringed instruments make sound when the strings are plucked or when a bow is rubbed across the strings. The pitch of the sound each string makes depends on how long, thick, and tightly stretched it is. The short, thin, and tight strings make faster vibrations. So the sounds they make have higher pitches.

When a musician plucks the harp strings, they vibrate. The vibrations make sound.

This instrument makes sounds when it is hit with a rubber hammer. The vibrations of the blocks make sounds.

1. ✓ Checkpoint How is sound made?

2. Compare and Contrast
How are the sounds produced by different strings of a harp alike and different?

Using Air to Make Sound

The sound of your voice also comes from vibrations. You are able to speak and sing because your vocal cords vibrate. When you speak, your vocal cords tighten. They vibrate as air passes between them. The tighter your vocal cords get, the higher the pitch of your voice becomes.

Wind instruments make sounds when air inside them vibrates. You make sounds with a trumpet by blowing into it and vibrating your lips. This makes the air inside the trumpet vibrate also.

You can change the pitch of a trumpet's sound in two ways. One way is to change how your lips vibrate. The other way is to press on the valves of the trumpet. This changes the length of the vibrating air column inside the trumpet.

Place your fingers lightly across your throat. Then hum. Can you feel your vocal cords vibrate?

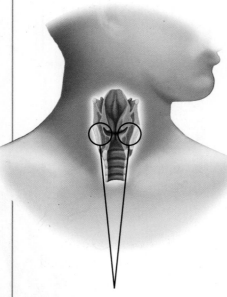

Vocal cords are two pairs of thin tissue in the windpipe.

The trumpet makes sounds when the player blows air into it. The player's lips vibrate against the mouthpiece of the trumpet.

An oboe is also a wind instrument. It has a double reed at the top. A reed is a thin piece of wood. The player blows on the reeds, making them vibrate. This vibration makes the air inside the oboe vibrate and make a sound. Pressing keys on the oboe changes the pitch of the sound.

A harmonica has several metal reeds that vibrate when a person blows air across them.

A saxophone has a longer air column than a clarinet. So the sounds it makes have lower pitches than the sounds a clarinet can make.

A clarinet uses a single wooden reed like this one. The reed presses on the player's lower lip and vibrates when the player blows air across it.

This clarinet produces its lowest note when all the holes are covered. Uncovering the last hole makes the air column shorter. Then the pitch of the sound is higher.

✓ Lesson Checkpoint

1. What makes the vocal cords vibrate?

2. What are two ways that sounds can be different?

3. **Writing** in Science **Descriptive** Write a paragraph in your **science journal** describing how guitar strings with different lengths make music with different sounds.

Lesson 2

How does sound travel?

Sound travels through matter. You can hear the sound of a fire engine several blocks away. But if you were on the Moon, you would not be able to hear anything. The Moon has no atmosphere, and sound can travel only through matter.

Sound waves from a megaphone spread out in all directions. They travel through the air.

What Are Sound Waves?

The energy of back-and-forth vibrations makes sound. Think about the sound of a bell that startles you, for example. As the bell rings, its vibrations result in spaces where air particles are squeezed together and spaces where air particles are spread apart. This movement of particles makes a kind of wave called a **compression wave.** Sound waves are compression waves.

Sound waves travel through matter like energy travels through a coiled spring. Particles that make up matter along the way take turns being squeezed together and spread apart. The length of a sound wave is its wavelength. It is measured from the center of one compression to the center of the next compression.

These bells make sounds only when they vibrate.

Wavelength

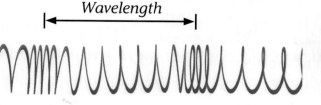

Find the places where the coils in the spring are squeezed together. Find the places where the coils are spread apart. Sound waves carry energy from one place to another in this way.

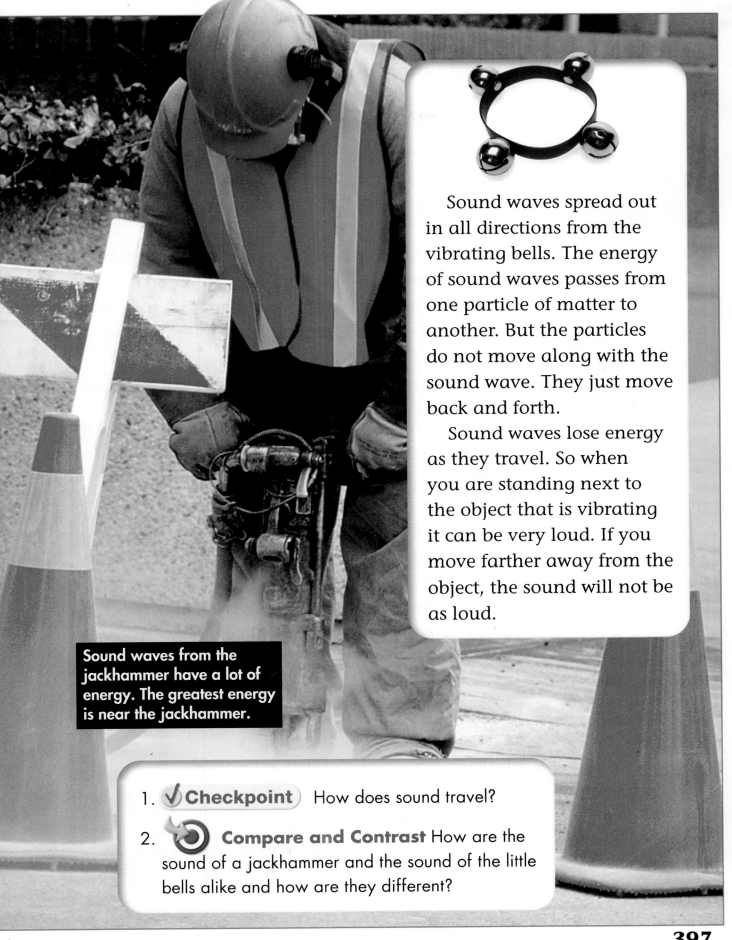

Sound waves spread out in all directions from the vibrating bells. The energy of sound waves passes from one particle of matter to another. But the particles do not move along with the sound wave. They just move back and forth.

Sound waves lose energy as they travel. So when you are standing next to the object that is vibrating it can be very loud. If you move farther away from the object, the sound will not be as loud.

Sound waves from the jackhammer have a lot of energy. The greatest energy is near the jackhammer.

1. ✓Checkpoint How does sound travel?

2. **Compare and Contrast** How are the sound of a jackhammer and the sound of the little bells alike and how are they different?

The speed of sound through air is about 340 meters per second. You would hear the sound of this bell in less than $\frac{1}{100}$ second if you were 3 m away.

Sound and Matter

Sound travels only through matter. There is no matter between stars and planets in outer space. So there is no sound in space. Sound moves through solids, liquids, and gases. The speed of sound depends on what kind of matter it is traveling through.

Air is made of gases. The particles in gases are farther apart than in liquids and solids. So it takes longer for one gas particle to hit another and move the sound energy along. Particles in liquids are closer together. Water is a liquid. So sound travels more quickly in water than it does in air. Particles in solids are even closer together. Sound travels quickest through a solid.

Echoes

You hear an echo when sound waves strike an object and then bounce back. Ships with sonar equipment send sound waves to the ocean bottom. Equipment measures how long it takes the sound to bounce back. Sound waves travel about 1,530 meters per second in seawater. Scientists can use this to find the depth of the ocean.

The particles in a solid are close together. So sound waves travel quickest in solids. When you use a tin-can telephone, sound waves travel quickly through the string from one can to the other.

Speed of Sound	
Material	**Speed (meters per second)**
Solid—Steel	5,200
Liquid—Seawater	1,530
Gas—Air	340

If you watch fireworks from far away, you see the flash before you hear the sound. That is because light travels much faster than sound.

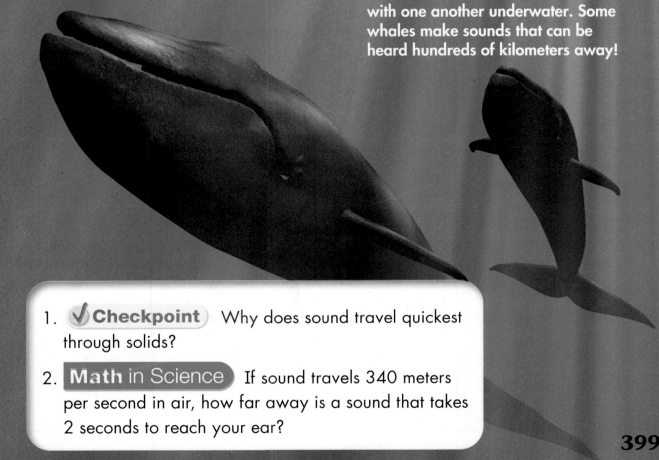

Whales use sounds to communicate with one another underwater. Some whales make sounds that can be heard hundreds of kilometers away!

1. ✓**Checkpoint** Why does sound travel quickest through solids?

2. **Math** in Science If sound travels 340 meters per second in air, how far away is a sound that takes 2 seconds to reach your ear?

399

The Ear

We hear sounds because of our ears. Our ears receive sound waves. The waves travel along a path toward our brain. The brain receives signals that we recognize as sounds.

Eardrum
Inside the ear, the sound waves hit the eardrum. The eardrum is a thin, skin-like layer stretched across the inside of the ear. When sound hits the eardrum, it begins to vibrate.

Little Bones
Three tiny bones touch the eardrum. When the eardrum vibrates, it makes these bones vibrate. These bones are part of the middle part of the ear.

Outer Ear
The part of the ear that you can see collects sound waves traveling in air.

Humans cannot hear some of the sounds that other animals can hear.

Inner Ear
The inner ear has a part that is shaped like a shell. It is filled with liquid. The movement of the tiny bones makes tiny hairs in the liquid vibrate. The hairs are attached to nerves that carry signals to the brain. This is how we hear.

Zebras make sounds by vibrating their vocal cords, lips, and nostrils.

Many kinds of insects make sounds by rubbing body parts together. This katydid makes chirping sounds by rubbing its wings together.

Most people know the sounds made when animals vibrate their vocal cords. Most have heard a dog's bark or a cow's moo. But not all animals make sounds by using only vocal cords. Woodpeckers use their beaks to tap out sounds on tree trunks. The vibrating wings of bees and mosquitoes make buzzing sounds.

Some bats send out high-pitched clicking sounds that people cannot hear. These sounds bounce off insects and return to the bats' ears. This is how bats find their food.

A male seal can roar loudly at other males. Seals use sound to defend their resources.

✔ **Lesson Checkpoint**

1. What path do sound waves follow through the ear?

2. How do some insects make sounds?

3. **Art in Science** Draw a picture of a musical instrument or an animal making a sound. Label your drawing to tell how the sound is made and how it travels.

Chimpanzees make many different sounds. They grunt, bark, squeak, scream, and even laugh.

Investigate How well does sound travel through different materials?

Materials

resealable plastic bags

block of wood

water

unsharpened pencil

What to Do

1 Prepare the bags.

Fill a bag with air by blowing into it. Seal tightly.

Fill another bag $\frac{1}{2}$ full with water. Squeeze out any air. Seal tightly.

Put the block of wood into a third bag. Squeeze out any air. Seal tightly.

Process Skills

You **infer** when you use your **observations** to put materials in order from best to poorest carrier of sound.

2 If necessary, roll down the top of the bag to make it puff up. Hold it against your ear. Cover your other ear with your hand. Listen as your partner taps the bag gently with the pencil eraser. Then repeat the test using the bag with water and the bag with wood.

What part of your body is the receiver of sound vibrations?

3 Compare the sounds you heard. Record your **observations**. Which was loudest? Which was softest?

How Well Sound Travels Through Different Materials

Material	Observations (soft, louder, loudest)
air (gas)	
water (liquid)	
wood (solid)	

Explain Your Results

1. Did the tapping seem loudest through air (gas), water (liquid), or wood (solid)?

2. **Infer** Compare how well sound travels through different materials. Arrange the materials in order from the best carrier of sound to the poorest carrier of sound.

Go Further

How can you use a sound recorder to help collect data about the way sound travels through different materials? Make a plan to investigate.

403

Math in Science

Comparing Speeds of Sound

You know that sound waves travel at different speeds through different types of matter. Sound travels most slowly through gases and most quickly through solids. But what about the same kind of matter? Does sound travel through plastic and through steel at different speeds, even though they are both solids?

The table below shows that sound waves travel at different speeds through different solids. For example, sound travels at 2,680 meters per second through silver. Sound travels almost twice that speed through steel. Out of all the solids in the table, sound travels most slowly through plastic.

Speed of Sound through Solids	
Material	**Speed** (meters per second)
Plastic	1,800
Silver	2,680
Gold	3,240
Copper	3,560
Brick	3,650
Oak wood	3,850
Glass	4,540
Iron	5,130
Steel	5,200

e Tools Take It to the Net pearsonsuccessnet.com

Sound also travels at different speeds through the same material at different temperatures. The table below shows the speed of sound through air at different temperatures. Use the table to answer the questions.

Speed of Sound through Air

Air Temperature (°C)	Speed (meters per second)
0	332
10	338
20	343
30	349

1 At which temperature do sound waves travel most slowly through air?

A. 0°C   B. 10°C   C. 20°C   D. 30°C

2 How much more quickly do sound waves travel through air at 20°C than at 0°C?

F. $8 \frac{m}{s}$ G. $11 \frac{m}{s}$ H. $13 \frac{m}{s}$ I. $14 \frac{m}{s}$

3 During which season do you think sound travels most quickly in air?

A. spring   B. summer   C. fall   D. winter

Lab zone Take-Home Activity

Find a very thick book. Hold the book against one ear while someone taps the other side of the book. Do you hear the sound with your ear touching the book before you hear it with your other ear? Explain the difference.

Chapter 14 Review and Test Prep

Use Vocabulary

compression wave (page 396)	pitch (page 392)
	vibration (page 392)

Use the term from the list above that best completes each sentence.

1. _____ describes how high or low a sound is.

2. A back-and-forth movement that causes sound is called a _____.

3. A sound wave is a kind of _____.

Explaining Concepts

4. How can harp strings with different lengths make music that has different sounds?

5. Explain how covering your ears can keep you from hearing a sound.

6. Why does sound travel more slowly through air than it does through water?

7. Explain how people make sounds when they talk.

8. Explain how an oboe makes musical sounds.

Process Skills

9. **Infer** what happens if you sprinkle confetti on a drumhead and then hit the drum with a drumstick.

10. Suppose you place a rubber band around a book. You place two pencils under the rubber band to hold it up. Then you pluck the rubber band between the pencils. **Predict** how the pitch of the sound will change when the pencils are moved closer together and then farther apart.

11. The loudness of sounds is measured in units called decibels. Sounds with levels between 60 and 84 decibels can be annoying. Sounds above 85 decibels can harm your hearing. Look at the chart below. **Classify** each sound as annoying or harmful.

Sound	Loudness (in decibels)
Jet plane	150
Lawn mower	80
Rock band	110
Vacuum cleaner	70

MindPoint Quiz Show

12. Infer how sonar might be used to protect a ship from going into water that is too shallow.

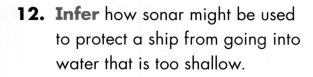

Compare and Contrast

13. Use a graphic organizer to show how the sounds made by a car horn and a song bird are alike and different.

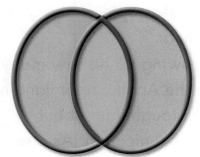

Test Prep

Choose the letter that best completes the statement or answers the question.

14. Which part of the ear collects sound waves?

Ⓐ eardrum   Ⓑ outer ear
Ⓒ nerve   Ⓓ bones

15. Hitting a drum harder will make the sound

Ⓕ louder.
Ⓖ the same.
Ⓗ softer.
Ⓘ lower in pitch.

16. Sound waves travel fastest through

Ⓐ solids.   Ⓑ liquids.
Ⓒ air.   Ⓓ gases.

17. A special nerve inside the head carries messages from the ear to the

Ⓕ eardrum.
Ⓖ brain.
Ⓗ tiny bones.
Ⓘ outer ear.

18. If a guitar string vibrates slowly it will have a pitch that is

Ⓐ high.
Ⓑ soft.
Ⓒ low.
Ⓓ loud.

19. Which instrument is a percussion instrument?

Ⓕ harp
Ⓖ clarinet
Ⓗ trumpet
Ⓘ cymbal

20. Writing in Science

Narrative Suppose that you are a sound wave. Write a story describing how you were produced, how you traveled, and how you were heard.

Dr. Clifton Horne

If you have been in an airport, you know that planes can make a lot of noise. Some scientists are working on ways to make planes quieter. Clifton Horne, NASA Aerospace Engineer, is doing just that.

Dr. Horne uses many microphones and computers to find the direction to the noise source in a jet plane engine and to find out how to make it quieter. Clifton Horne said, "...in the next 10 years we should be able to ... fly on airplanes that people on the ground can see but hardly hear."

While Clifton was growing up he saw many exciting things, such as the Apollo moon landings. He enjoyed hobbies that taught him about astronomy and radio communication. As a result, Clifton decided to become an aerospace engineer.

Dr. Horne says that his English classes, as well as math and science classes, have been very useful in his career. Scientists, including Dr. Horne, spend much time writing and working together in groups. So, the communication skills that Dr. Horne learned in his English classes are very important to him.

Dr. Clifton Horne uses test engines like the one above in the wind tunnel at NASA's Ames Research Center.

Lab zone Take-Home Activity

People use sound to communicate, to entertain, and to warn of danger. Research a career in industries where sound is important.

Unit C Test Talk

Use Information from Text and Graphics

Information in text, pictures, and diagrams can help you answer test questions. Read the text and study the graphics. Then answer the questions.

The diagrams show how the particles in solids, liquids, and gases are connected. The captions explain how the particles in solids, liquids, and gases are connected and how they move.

The particles of a solid are firmly connected. They jiggle in place.

The particles of a liquid are loosely connected. They flow past one another.

Gas particles are not connected. They bounce off one another and move freely.

Use What You Know

To answer the questions, find the information in the captions and the graphics. Read each question and decide which answer choice is best.

1. A solid has particles that are
  (A) loosely connected.   (C) firmly connected.
  (B) not connected.   (D) connected in pairs.

2. A liquid has particles that
  (F) stay in place.   (H) move freely.
  (G) flow past one another.   (I) move in pairs.

3. Which statement describes gas particles?
  (A) They are packed closer together than liquid particles.
  (B) They are firmly connected.
  (C) They are connected in groups.
  (D) They are farther apart than solid or liquid particles.

Unit C Wrap-Up

Chapter 10

What are the properties of matter?

- Matter takes up space, has mass, and has other properties that can be observed.
- Mass, volume, density, and length are some properties of matter that can be measured.

Chapter 11

What are physical and chemical changes in matter?

- Matter can change in its size, shape, or state during a physical change.
- During a chemical change, matter changes into new kinds of matter.

Chapter 12

How do forces cause motion and get work done?

- Forces cause a change in motion and work to be done by changing an object's speed or direction.
- Contact forces change motion only by touching objects. The forces of gravity and magnetism can change an object's motion without touching it.

Chapter 13

How does energy change form?

- Potential energy can change to kinetic energy and kinetic energy can change to potential energy.
- Energy can transfer between the forms of light, electrical, thermal, sound, chemical, mechanical, and magnetic energy.

Chapter 14

How does energy produce the sounds we hear?

- Sound is produced by the energy of vibrating matter traveling as compression waves.
- The pitch of a sound depends on how fast an object vibrates.

Performance Assessment
Identify Electric Charges

Use a wool cloth and balloons to show what happens when objects have different charges. What happens when you move two balloons with no charge toward each other? How can you make a balloon negatively charged? What happens when you move a negatively charged balloon toward a balloon with no charge?

Read More About Physical Science!

Look for books like these in the library.

Experiment How does energy affect the distance a toy car travels?

When you pull back a pullback car, you wind it up. You give it potential energy. When you let it go, the potential energy changes to kinetic energy as the car begins to move. In this activity, you will find out how a car's potential energy affects the distance the car can travel.

Materials

meterstick

pullback toy car

masking tape

Process Skills

The basis of an **experiment** is a **hypothesis**, a testable **prediction** that helps guide the experiment.

Ask a question.

How does a car's potential energy affect the distance it can travel?

State a hypothesis.

If a pullback car's potential energy is greater, then will the distance it travels increase, decrease, or remain about the same? Write your **hypothesis**.

Identify and control variables.

You will change the potential energy your toy car has just before it begins to move. You do this by changing the distance you pull the car back. You will measure the distance the car travels. Everything else must stay the same.

Test your hypothesis.

1 Make a starting line with masking tape.

2 Put down another piece of tape and mark it at 0, 5, 10, 15, 20, 25, and 30 cm.

3 Put the front of the car at the 5 cm line.

4 Pull the car back until the front of the car is at the starting line and let the car go.

5 **Measure** the distance the car travels. Record the distance.

6 Repeat steps 3 to 5, but use the 10, 15, 20, 25, and 30 cm lines. Record your data each time.

What happens to the car's potential energy when you let go? What happens to its speed as it travels? What causes the car to stop?

Measure from the starting line to the front of the car.

Pull back the car and let it go.

Collect and record your data.

Distance Moved by Pullback Car	
Distance Pulled Back (cm)	**Distance Traveled** (cm)
0	0
5	
10	
15	
20	
25	
30	

Find a pattern in your chart or graph. Make a prediction based on the evidence. How far would your car go if you pulled it back 35 cm? You might wish to test your prediction.

Interpret your data.

Use your data to make a bar graph. Look at your graph closely. Did the number of centimeters you pulled the car back affect the distance it traveled? Explain. Describe the evidence for your explanation.

How does evidence differ from opinion?

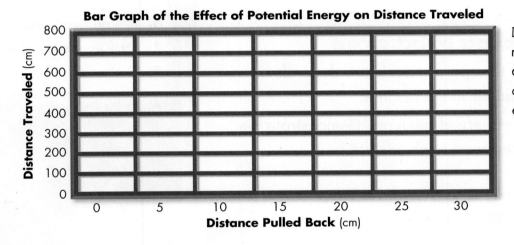

Bar Graph of the Effect of Potential Energy on Distance Traveled

Discuss your results with others and consider their explanations.

State your conclusion.

How does increasing a car's potential energy affect the distance it travels? Compare your hypothesis with your results. **Communicate** your conclusion.

Go Further

Suppose you add more mass to the car. How would this affect the distances it travels? Make a prediction. Make and carry out a plan to answer this or another question you may have.

Science Fair Projects

Full Inquiry

Using Scientific Methods

1. Ask a question.
2. State a hypothesis.
3. Identify/control variables.
4. Test your hypothesis.
5. Collect and record your data.
6. Interpret your data.
7. State your conclusion.
8. Go further.

Comparing Density

Matter that has less density than water has buoyancy—it will float in water.

Idea: Compare the density of objects with that of water. Use a container of water and a variety of objects.

Separating Mixtures

The best way to separate a mixture depends on the kinds of matter in the mixture.

Idea: Use a variety of mixtures. Demonstrate the best way to separate each mixture.

Changing Potential to Kinetic Energy

Energy can be stored as potential energy and released as kinetic energy.

Idea: Use a wind-up toy to show how the amount of potential energy affects the distance the toy can travel.

Making Sounds

Sounds vary depending on the way matter vibrates.

Idea: Show how sound changes. Stretch rubber bands of varied sizes across the opening of a box.

Unit D

Space and Technology

Chapter 15
Patterns in the Sky

You Will Discover

- what causes day, night, shadows, and seasons.
- why the Moon's shape seems to change.
- what tools help people study stars.

online
Student Edition
pearsonsuccessnet.com

What patterns do the Earth, Sun, Moon, and stars show?

star

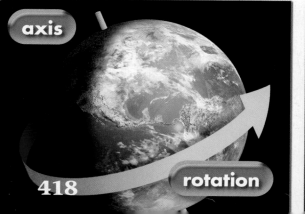

axis

418 rotation

revolution

Chapter 15 Vocabulary

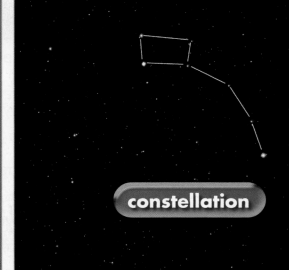

constellation

phase

lunar eclipse

telescope

Explore How can shadows change over time?

Materials

tape

construction paper circle

large paper (optional)

What to Do

1. Tape a circle of construction paper onto a sunny window.

2. Find the shadow of the circle. Think of a way to keep track of the shadow's position.

3. Record the shadow's position every 15 minutes for 2 hours. **Observe** how the shadow's position changes.

Process Skills

Observing carefully can help you **predict** accurately. Further observations can help you test your predictions.

Explain Your Results

1. What do you think caused the changes you **observed**?

2. **Predict** the shadow's position 3 hours after you began.

How to Read Science

Sequence

The diagrams below show the **sequence** of a pattern.

- A *pattern* happens over and over again. A *sequence* is the order in which things happen.

- **Observing** diagrams and noticing what is different about each one can help you find the sequence of a pattern.

Diagram

By studying diagrams that show a pattern, you can **predict** or tell what will happen next.

Apply It!

Use the diagrams on the right to **predict** what will happen next. Make a diagram that shows which city will have daylight and which city will have darkness.

You Are There!

You are floating in space outside the Space Shuttle. The Sun has just risen above the curve of the Earth. Look how bright the Sun is in the blackness all around! Sunlight shimmers on the ocean far below. It's another amazing sunrise. What are these patterns of movement, light, and darkness that you have seen on your space journey?

AudioText

What are some patterns that repeat every day?

Every day there is light during the day followed by darkness at night. If the day is sunny, you might notice shadows. Day, night, and shadows are caused by light from the Sun and the movement of Earth.

The Sun

You see the Sun in the sky on a sunny day. The Sun is in the sky on cloudy days too. The Sun is a **star**—a giant ball of hot, glowing gases. If you think of a plate that is almost round, the Sun would be in its center. Earth would be between the center and the plate's edge. The Sun is the main source of light and energy for Earth.

Earth is very small compared to the Sun. Like the Sun, Earth is shaped like a ball. Unlike the Sun, Earth does not glow or make its own light. The half of Earth's curved surface facing the Sun is lit by sunlight. The half of Earth's surface facing away from the Sun is not lit by sunlight and is dark.

1. ✔**Checkpoint** What star is the source of light on Earth?

2. **Sequence** Describe a pattern on Earth that happens every day.

Earth Spins

If you stand outside, you do not feel as if you are moving. But you are. Earth is always moving. One way it moves is that it spins around an imaginary line. The ends of the line would stick out of Earth at the North Pole and at the South Pole. This imaginary line around which Earth spins is its **axis.** Find Earth's axis in the drawing below. If you could look down at the North Pole, you would see the Earth turns in a counterclockwise direction. This is the opposite direction to the way the hands of a clock move. We could also say that Earth turns from west to east.

Daytime begins when the Sun first appears over the horizon. Although the Sun looks like it rises, it actually stays in the same place. As Earth rotates, this part of Earth is just beginning to face the Sun.

Half of Earth faces the Sun and receives sunlight as Earth spins on its axis.

Day and Night

Earth makes one complete spin, or **rotation,** on its axis every 24 hours. During this time, half of Earth faces the Sun. That half of Earth has day. The half of Earth that is not facing the Sun has night. As Earth spins, or rotates, a different part of Earth faces the Sun.

Earth rotates at the same speed every day of the year. You may have noticed that the number of hours of sunlight and darkness changes during the year. But if you add the hours of sunlight and darkness for one day together, you will find they equal 24 hours.

Things are not always as they seem. For instance, the Sun appears to rise in the east. It seems to move across the sky and set in the west. You might think that the Sun moves around Earth. But the Sun only appears to move across the sky. Actually Earth is moving.

The path that the Sun appears to take across the sky is predictable. We can tell ahead of time when the Sun will rise and set.

1. ✓ **Checkpoint** What is Earth's axis?

2. **Writing in Science** **Expository** Write a paragraph in your **science journal** that explains how spinning on the Earth's axis causes day and night.

As Earth rotates on its axis, the half of Earth that was in darkness begins to receive sunlight.

Around noon the Sun is at its highest point in the sky.

As Earth continues to rotate, the Sun appears to set in the west. Daytime ends when the Sun disappears below the horizon.

Shadows

On a hot summer day, you might escape the heat by standing in the shade of a tree. Did you know you are standing in a shadow? As you look out from your spot, you see shadows in other places. Yet other places have no shadows.

You might notice that a shadow forms when light, like sunlight, hits an object. The object stops the light that hits it. You also need a surface on which to see the shadow. The shadow is an area that is not getting direct light. The shadow has about the same shape as the object that blocks the light.

The Sun has just risen in the east. In what direction do the shadows stretch?

West

Morning

Midday

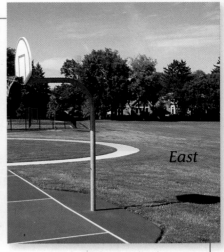
East

Afternoon

The length and direction of shadows change during the day. Find the shadows made by the basketball hoop in the pictures. Notice that the morning shadow is long and is in the opposite direction from the Sun in the eastern sky.

As the Sun appears to move higher in the sky, the shadow becomes shorter. Around midday the Sun is at its highest point in the sky. The shadow is very short as seen in the second picture.

As the Sun continues moving across the sky, the shadow becomes longer. Notice the length of the shadow in the third picture. The afternoon shadow stretches in a different direction than the morning shadow did. As the Sun moves toward the horizon in the west, the shadow stretches toward the east. After the Sun sets, there is no sunlight to make shadows.

How do the length and direction of the shadow cast by this basketball hoop change during the day?

√ Lesson Checkpoint

1. Explain how each place on Earth has a beginning and an end to daytime.

2. What three things are needed to have a shadow?

3. **Sequence** Describe the pattern of shadows from sunrise to sunset. Include the length and direction of the shadows.

Lesson 2

What patterns repeat every year?

Earth's tilt and movement around the Sun cause the seasons. The amount of light and heat Earth receives during different seasons causes seasonal patterns.

Earth Moves Around the Sun

You know that Earth rotates on its axis. Earth also moves, or revolves, around the Sun. Find Earth's axis in each part of the diagram. Earth's axis is not straight up and down. It is tilted.

Earth makes one **revolution** when it makes one complete trip around the Sun. One revolution takes one year. As Earth revolves around the Sun, Earth's tilted axis always points in the same direction in space.

Earth's Position During the Year
The part of Earth pointed toward the Sun receives the most direct sunlight and has warmer temperatures.

In this diagram sizes are not true to scale.

June
The northern half of Earth tilts more toward the Sun. The northern half gets more direct sunlight than the southern half. It is summer in the northern half and winter in the southern half of Earth.

In some places on its path around the Sun, the northern half of Earth is tilted toward the Sun. In other places along its path, the southern half of Earth tilts toward the Sun. The part of Earth that is tilted toward the Sun receives the most direct rays of the Sun and is heated the most. That part of Earth also spends more hours in daylight than in darkness during each 24 hours.

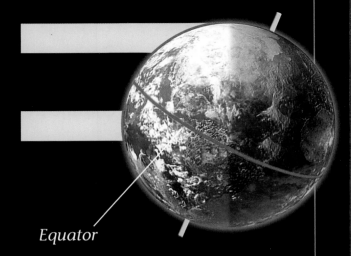

March
The northern and southern halves of Earth get about the same amounts of sunlight. Neither pole points toward the Sun or away from it. The northern half is getting warmer, but the southern half is getting cooler.

Equator

Direct rays near the equator cover less area. The equator is the imaginary line that separates the north and south halves of the Earth. The rays here are more concentrated. They heat Earth more than rays that strike at an angle.

December
The northern half of Earth tilts away from the Sun. This tilt causes the northern half of Earth to receive less sunlight and have colder temperatures than the southern half. It is winter in the north, but summer in the south.

September
As in March, neither end of the axis points toward the Sun or away from the Sun. The northern half of Earth is getting cooler, but the southern half is getting warmer.

1. ✓**Checkpoint** What does Earth revolve around?

2. **Sequence** Describe the pattern of temperature changes during the year in the northern half of Earth. Why does this happen?

Seasons

What's your favorite season—spring, summer, fall, or winter? The amount of sunlight and the temperatures change in patterns with the changing seasons.

Look at the position of Earth in the December part of the picture on page 429. The northern axis is tilted away from the Sun. Because of the tilt, the northern half of Earth gets less sunlight in December. It has more hours of darkness than daylight in each 24 hours. Less sunlight means colder temperatures. As spring approaches, the number of hours of daylight increases.

In the spring and fall, Earth's axis does not point directly toward the Sun or away from the Sun. Temperatures are usually warmer than in winter. The hours of daylight are about the same as the hours of darkness in each 24 hours. As winter approaches, the daylight hours become fewer. The chart shows the hours of daylight in the northern part of the United States.

Another effect of Earth's tilt is that we see the Sun at different places in the sky in different seasons. In the northern half of Earth, the Sun is higher in the sky in summer. The Sun is lower in the sky in winter.

June

When the Sun is higher in the sky, there are more hours of daylight.

Hours of Daylight in Northern United States	
Month	**Hours of Daylight Per Day**
December	9
March	12
June	15
September	12

East

West

December

The picture and chart show the effects of Earth's tilted axis on the Sun's position and hours of daylight.

The way the Sun appears to cross the sky changes with the seasons.

✓Lesson Checkpoint

1. How does Earth's position and movement cause seasons?

2. What causes summer to be warmer than winter?

3. **Writing** in Science **Descriptive** Write a paragraph in your **science journal** that describes your favorite season. Tell about the patterns in nature during that season.

431

Lesson 3

Why does the Moon's shape change?

The Moon revolves around Earth while Earth revolves around the Sun. These movements and light from the Sun cause the Moon to appear different throughout a month.

The Moon and Earth

Did you ever see a full moon rise above the horizon or a half-moon set below it?

Like Earth, the Moon rotates and revolves. It rotates on its axis and revolves around Earth. Unlike Earth, the Moon takes about 27 Earth days to complete one rotation. The Moon completes one revolution of Earth in almost the same time.

Can you describe how the Earth and Moon move in space?

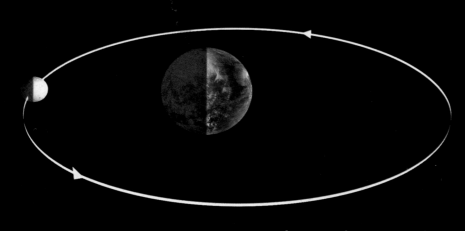

The time the Moon takes to rotate and revolve once is about the same.

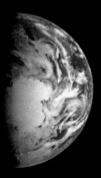

This photo taken from space shows that the Moon is small compared to Earth.

The Moon is the closest natural object to Earth. It is 384,000 kilometers (239,000 miles) away. The Moon also is the brightest object in the night sky, but it does not make light. The light you see from the Moon is light from the Sun that shines on the Moon and bounces off.

Notice the sunlight hitting half of Earth and half of the Moon in the picture. Sometimes you can even see the Moon during the day. It does not look as bright as it does at night. Sunlight that reflects off the Moon is only a little brighter than sunlight that passes through the daytime atmosphere. Sometimes you cannot see the Moon at night.

Did you know that we always see the same side of the Moon? We never see the other side from Earth. A spacecraft took the first pictures of the Moon's far side in 1959.

1. ✓**Checkpoint** What are two ways the moon moves? How do these movements affect the appearance of the Moon?

2. **Math** in Science About how many days does it take for the Moon to revolve around the Earth 4 times?

The Moon and the Sun

On some nights, the Moon looks like a circle of bright light in the night sky. Other nights, you cannot see any part of the Moon, even if the sky is clear. In between these two times, you can see different amounts of the Moon. How the Moon looks in the sky changes a little each day. The pattern of changes is predictable. And the entire pattern repeats itself about every four weeks or 29 1/2 days.

Each different way that the Moon looks is a **phase** of the Moon. Find some of these phases on the next page. Notice that you can see more and more of the Moon until you see a full Moon. Then you see less and less of the Moon. When you cannot see the Moon at all, the phase is known as a new Moon.

Lunar Eclipse

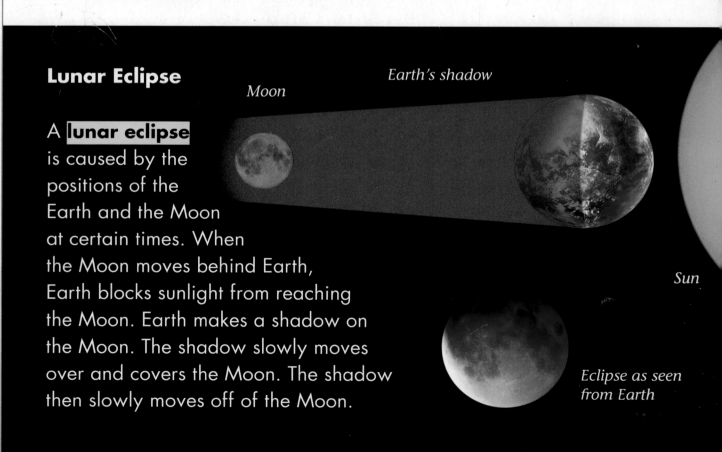

Moon

Earth's shadow

Sun

Eclipse as seen from Earth

A **lunar eclipse** is caused by the positions of the Earth and the Moon at certain times. When the Moon moves behind Earth, Earth blocks sunlight from reaching the Moon. Earth makes a shadow on the Moon. The shadow slowly moves over and covers the Moon. The shadow then slowly moves off of the Moon.

SciLinks   Take It to the Net
pearsonsuccessnet.com   keyword: lunar eclipse
code: g3p434

The Lunar Cycle

The pictures show some of the changes in the Moon's appearance along its path around Earth. Half of the Moon is always lit by sunlight. The lit half of the Moon cannot always be seen from Earth. The movements of Earth and the Moon cause different amounts of the lit half of the Moon to be seen from Earth. The amount of the Moon that can be seen from Earth is a phase of the Moon.

New Moon Phase
None of the Moon appears lit.

First Quarter Phase
About a week after the New Moon, the Moon looks like a half circle.

Full Moon Phase
About two weeks after the New Moon, you see all of the lit half of the Moon. It looks like a circle.

Third Quarter Phase
Three-fourths of the Moon's cycle is complete. In about a week, there will be a New Moon phase again.

✓ Lesson Checkpoint

1. How much of the Moon is lit by sunlight?

2. What position of Earth causes a lunar eclipse?

3.  **Sequence** Describe the pattern of the phases of the Moon starting with a New Moon.

Lesson 4

What are star patterns?

Stars appear to move in the night sky. Telescopes make studying patterns of stars easier.

Stars and the Telescope

Think about being outside on a clear, dark night. You see thousands of twinkling stars. You notice that some stars are brighter than others and are easier to see. They all look so small in the sky because they are trillions of miles away. But some of the stars are actually larger than the Sun. Other stars are smaller. The stars that are the farthest away are the dimmest and the hardest to see. You cannot see many stars at all without certain tools to help you.

The camper in the picture is using binoculars to see the stars more clearly. Binoculars and the **telescope** are tools that magnify objects that are far away. They make objects look larger and easier to see. If you use a telescope, you can see many more stars than with your eyes alone.

Find the huge mirror inside the Keck telescope in Hawaii. Telescopes help people see stars that they cannot see with their eyes alone.

436

Scientists use different kinds of telescopes. The telescope on page 436 and telescopes you might use are similar. These telescopes use tubes, mirrors that make light reflect, and lenses that bend light or refract it. All these parts help bring as much light as possible into the telescope. The result is a larger and clearer view of objects in the sky. Other kinds of telescopes do not collect light. They collect other kinds of waves, such as radio waves.

Binoculars make far-away objects appear larger, brighter, and easier to see.

1. ✔Checkpoint   What are two tools that can help you see stars?

2. **Art** in Science   Draw a picture of some star patterns that you have seen.

Patterns of Stars

Have you ever spent time looking at stars? You might notice that some groups of stars seem to make patterns or shapes. A group of stars that makes a pattern is a **constellation.** You can imagine lines drawn between stars. Find the lines drawn in the pictures of the stars on page 439. Many people see two cups with handles. These patterns are the Big Dipper and the Little Dipper. The Big Dipper is a part of the constellation Ursa Major (the Big Bear). The stars of the Little Dipper make up the constellation Ursa Minor (the Little Bear).

People living in ancient times saw the shapes of animals, people, and objects in star patterns. They made up stories about the constellations and gave them names. Some of these names are still used today. You might have heard of the constellation Orion. When people living in ancient Greece saw the stars of Orion, they saw a hunter.

The stars that make up a constellation look like they are close together in space. They really are very far apart. Some of the stars are much farther from Earth than others. If you looked at the same stars from far away in space, they would not make the same pattern.

How Stars Seem to Move

The picture on the right shows how stars appear to move across the sky at night. Like the Sun, stars really do not move this way. They look like they move across the sky because Earth rotates on its axis. The stars look like they revolve around the North Star. The patterns of stars also change with Earth's seasons. As Earth revolves around the Sun, constellations are in different parts of the night sky. Notice that the Big Dipper and the Little Dipper are in different positions in the sky.

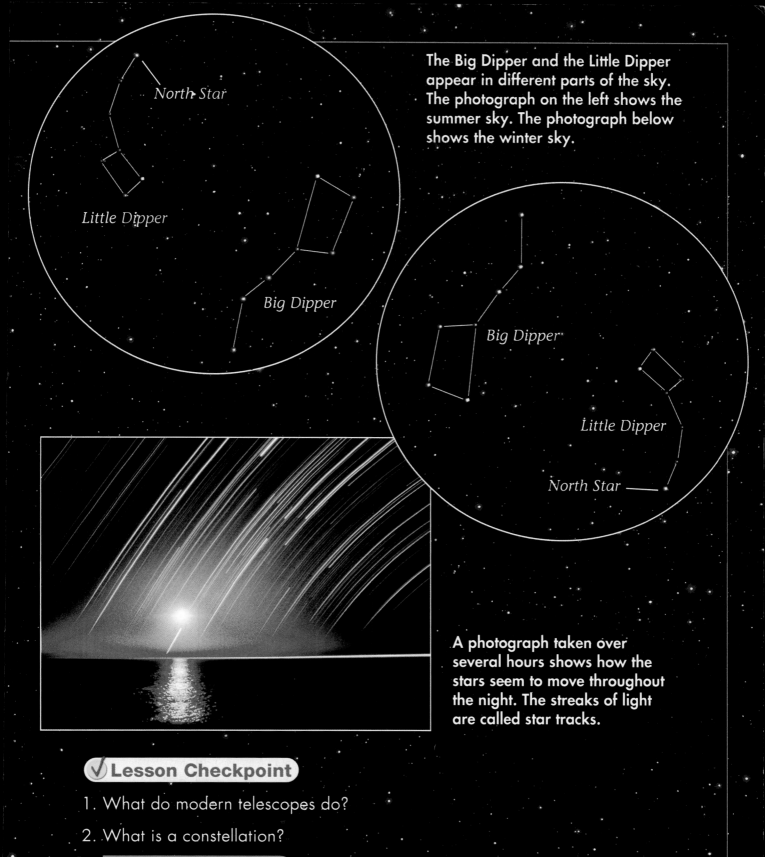

North Star

Little Dipper

Big Dipper

The Big Dipper and the Little Dipper appear in different parts of the sky. The photograph on the left shows the summer sky. The photograph below shows the winter sky.

Big Dipper

Little Dipper

North Star ———

A photograph taken over several hours shows how the stars seem to move throughout the night. The streaks of light are called star tracks.

✓ Lesson Checkpoint

1. What do modern telescopes do?

2. What is a constellation?

3. **Writing** in Science **Narrative** Choose any constellation and write a story in your **science journal** about the constellation.

Investigate When is the Big Dipper not the Big Dipper?

A constellation is a pattern of stars people see from Earth. Viewed from a faraway part of the universe, the same pattern might not be seen.

Materials

Pattern for a Big Dipper Model and Drawing of the Big Dipper

7 straws and 7 pieces of foil

metric ruler

scissors, tape, and clay

What to Do

1 Use the Pattern for a Big Dipper Model. Label the straws from A to F. Cut each to the correct length.

2 Make a foil ball around one end of each straw.

3 Put each straw on top of its letter on the Pattern for a Big Dipper Model. Use a small ball of clay to make each straw stand up.

4 Observe from the front, 2 steps back. Identify the pattern you see.

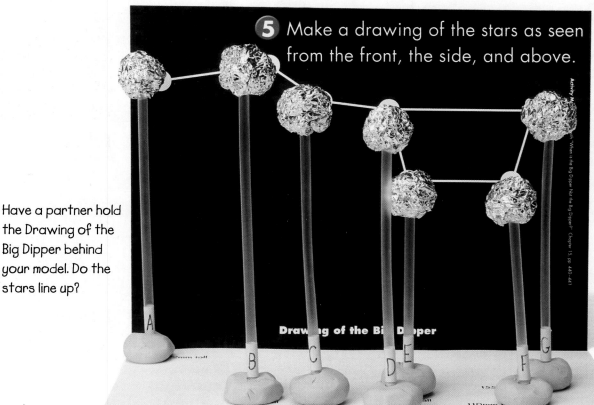

5 Make a drawing of the stars as seen from the front, the side, and above.

Have a partner hold the Drawing of the Big Dipper behind your model. Do the stars line up?

Drawing of the Big Dipper

Pattern for the Big Dipper Model

Sketches or Drawings of Big Dipper Model		
View from Front	**View from Side**	**View from Above**

Explain Your Results

1. **Observe** Does your Big Dipper **model** look like the Big Dipper from all directions? Explain.

2. **Infer** If you were a space traveler, could you see all the familiar constellations? Explain.

Go Further

Do constellations change as they "move" across the night sky? Can different ones be seen in different seasons? Find out.

Comparing Times of Sunrises and Sunsets

As Earth revolves around the Sun, the amount of sunlight hitting different parts of Earth changes each day. The Sun looks like it rises above the horizon and sets below the horizon at different times. In the northern half of Earth, the Sun rises a little earlier and sets a little later each day from January to late June. The days slowly have more daylight hours and fewer hours of darkness. The pattern is reversed in the southern half of Earth.

The chart below shows the pattern in the times of sunrise and sunset for four days during the year.

Sunrise and Sunset Standard Times for a City in the Northern Half of Earth		
Date	Sunrise	Sunset
March 21	5:52 A.M.	6:05 P.M.
June 21	5:16 A.M.	8:29 P.M.
September 21	6:38 A.M.	6:49 P.M.
December 21	7:15 A.M.	4:23 P.M.

Comparing Times

Use the chart to answer the following questions.

1 How many hours and minutes of daylight are there on March 21?

2 Which day has the most hours of daylight?

3 Which day has the fewest hours of daylight?

4 During which month would the southern half of the Earth have its longest day? Explain.

Lab zone Take-Home Activity

Find the times of sunrise and sunset in your area daily for the next week. Compare the times and decide if the days are getting longer or shorter.

Chapter 15 Review and Test Prep

Use Vocabulary

axis (page 424)	**revolution** (page 428)
constellation (page 438)	**rotation** (page 424)
lunar eclipse (page 434)	**star** (page 423)
phase (page 434)	**telescope** (page 436)

Use the vocabulary word from the list above that best completes each sentence.

1. A(n) _____ is a giant ball of hot, glowing gases.

2. Earth spins on its _____.

3. Earth makes one complete _____ every 24 hours.

4. Earth makes one complete _____ around the Sun every year.

5. A(n) _____ of the Moon is the way the moon looks in the sky.

6. A(n) _____ happens when Earth's shadow moves across the Moon.

7. A(n) _____ magnifies objects that are far away.

8. The Big Dipper is part of a(n) _____.

Explain Concepts

9. Explain what causes the phases of the Moon.

10. Explain what causes constellations to move across the sky at night.

11. On March 1, sunrise is at 6:25 A.M. and sunset is at 5:42 P.M. On March 30, sunrise is at 5:36 A.M. and sunset is at 6:15 P.M. Which day has the most daylight?

Process Skills

12. **Infer** What would happen to daytime and nighttime if Earth did not spin on its axis?

13. **Infer** You notice that the shadow made by a pole outside your window has been getting longer. What does this tell you about the time of day? Explain your answer.

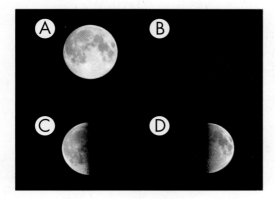

14. Draw the images of the Moon phases in the boxes below in the order that they would appear in the sky. Start with picture B.

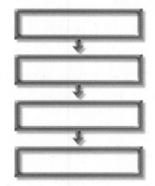

Test Prep

Choose the letter that best completes the statement or answers the question.

15. A Full Moon can be seen about once every
   (A) night.
   (B) month.
   (C) season.
   (D) year.

16. You can see many more stars if you use a
   (F) calendar.
   (G) microscope.
   (H) telescope.
   (I) hand lens.

17. What season does the southern half of Earth have if Earth's north axis is tilted toward the Sun?
   (A) spring
   (B) summer
   (C) fall
   (D) winter

18. Which of the following is closest to Earth?
   (F) Moon
   (G) Sun
   (H) stars
   (I) constellations

19. Explain why the answer you chose for Question 18 is best. For each of the answers you did not choose, give a reason why it is not the best choice.

20. **Writing** in Science

Expository Write a paragraph that describes the patterns of light and temperatures in different seasons.

445

The Hubble Space Telescope

You can use a telescope to make stars and other objects in space easier to see. Imagine how many stars you could see with a telescope 13.2 meters (43.5 feet) long and 4.2 meters (14 feet) wide. Imagine it weighing 11,000 kilograms (24,000 pounds)—about the size of a school bus. You would not be taking it over to a friend's house to look at stars. A telescope this size would not fit in a car, but it did fit in a Space Shuttle.

In 1990, NASA launched the Hubble Space Telescope. The Hubble stays in space about 600 kilometers (375 miles) above Earth. It revolves around Earth every 97 minutes.

The Hubble collects information from space and sends it to scientists on Earth every day. It provides detailed images of Mars and Pluto. It helps scientists understand more about Uranus and Neptune. The Hubble also has helped scientists learn about objects outside our solar system. It provides information about black holes, quasars, and the birth and death of stars.

An astronaut works on the Hubble Space Telescope.

The Hubble Telescope was made in a way that makes it easy to repair and update. Since it has been launched, astronauts have made missions to the Hubble to keep it working well. During space walks, astronauts have replaced parts that have worn out. Astronauts also have added parts so that the Hubble always has the newest technology. Each servicing mission adds four to five years to the working life of the Hubble.

This image of the ant nebula, a dying star, was taken by the Hubble Space Telescope.

The solar panels provide power to the telescope.

Lab zone

Take-Home Activity

If you have Internet access at home or at the library, go to the NASA Web site (http://hubblesite.org) and look at images from the Hubble.

Galileo
1564–1642

Galileo was born in Italy in 1564. He studied medicine and mathematics at a university in Italy. He later became the head of the math department at another university.

Galileo became known for inventing science tools and experimenting. One of the tools he is most famous for is a better telescope. When he heard that someone had invented a tool that could magnify objects, he went to work to improve the telescope. Galileo soon had a telescope that could magnify objects twenty times.

Galileo pointed his telescope toward space and made many discoveries. He found that the Moon has craters. Galileo saw four moons revolving around Jupiter and different phases of Venus.

Galileo used his observations to show that Earth revolves around the Sun. Most people during that time believed that the Sun revolved around Earth. Galileo's experiments and observations challenged beliefs of the time and added to the knowledge of science.

Lab zone Take-Home Activity

Look up the work of Galileo. Describe other observations he made. Tell what his experiments led him to say about patterns in the sky.

448

Chapter 16
The Solar System

You Will Discover

- how the Sun makes heat and light.
- how the planets move in space.
- what is special about each planet.

online
Student Edition
pearsonsuccessnet.com

Web Games
Take It to the Net
pearsonsuccessnet.com

How are the planets in the solar system alike and different?

solar system

planet

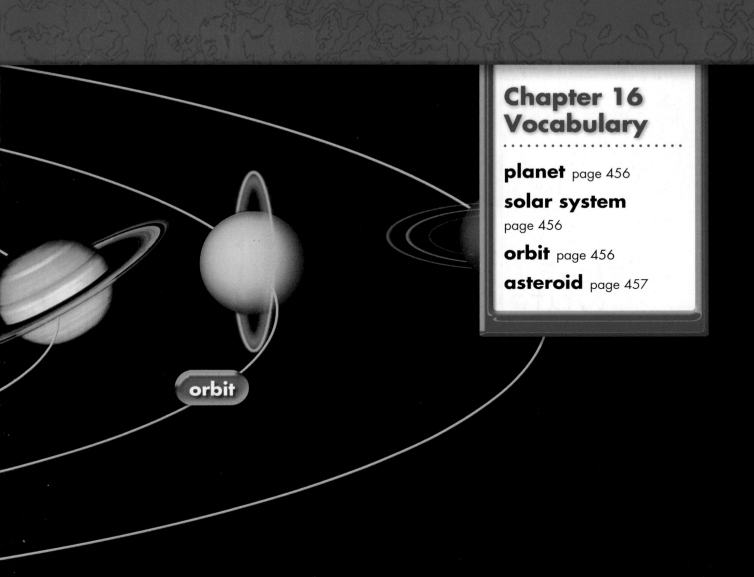

orbit

asteroid

Explore How can you make a distance model of the solar system?

Materials

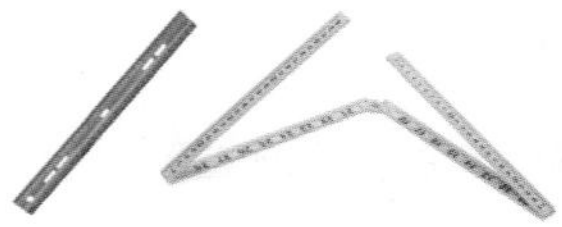

metric ruler
and meterstick

adding machine tape

scissors

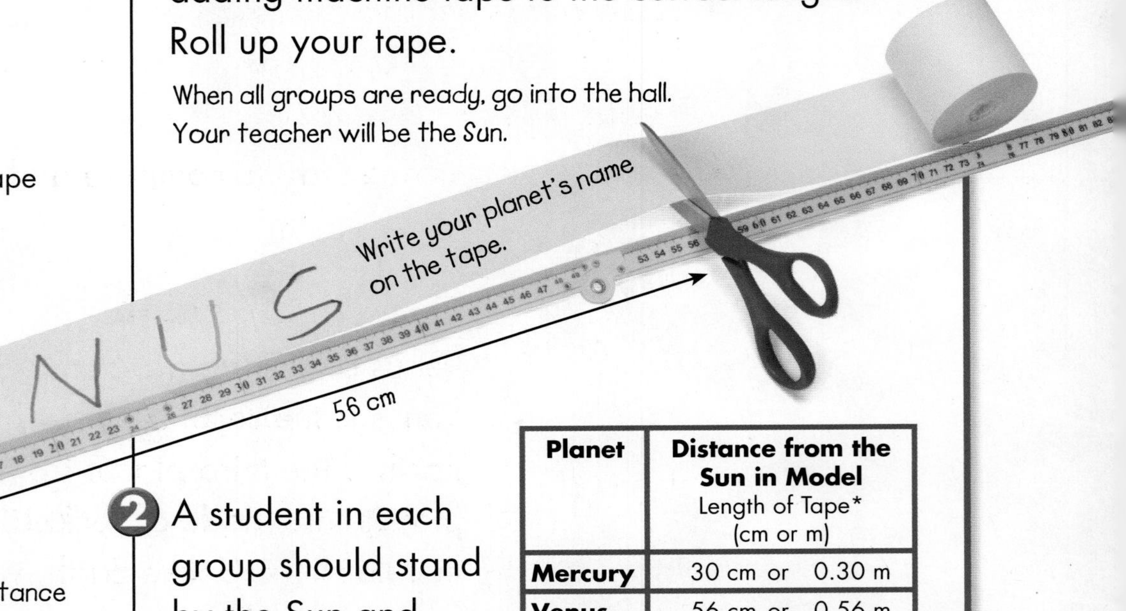

The chart shows distance in cm and m. Select the easier one to use. Select a ruler or a meterstick for your measuring tool.

Process Skills

Your class **measured** the adding machine tape using two standard units, centimeters and meters.

What to Do

Your teacher will help you select a planet.

① The chart shows the distance your planet is from the sun in the model. **Measure** and cut adding machine tape to the correct length. Roll up your tape.

When all groups are ready, go into the hall. Your teacher will be the Sun.

Write your planet's name on the tape.

VENUS

56 cm

② A student in each group should stand by the Sun and hold the free end of the tape. Another student should walk down the hall, unrolling the tape.

Planet	Distance from the Sun in Model Length of Tape* (cm or m)
Mercury	30 cm or 0.30 m
Venus	56 cm or 0.56 m
Earth	77 cm or 0.77 m
Mars	120 cm or 1.2 m
Jupiter	400 cm or 4 m
Saturn	740 cm or 7.4 m
Uranus	1500 cm or 15 m
Neptune	2300 cm or 23 m

*Scale: 1 cm = about 1,940,000 km

③ Compare the distances to the planets.

Explain Your Results

Based on your **model**, would it be harder to travel to Mars or Neptune? Explain.

How to Read Science

Compare and Contrast

When you **compare** things, you tell how they are alike.
When you **contrast** things, you tell how they are different.

- Clue words and phrases such as *similar, like, both, all, unlike, in the same way* or *in a different way* may signal *comparing* or *contrasting*.
- **Measuring** is one way to compare and contrast objects.

Science Article

Venus

Earth

Venus and Earth

Venus and Earth are both inner planets. Venus is the second planet from the Sun. Earth is the third planet from the Sun. Both planets are made of rock. Like Earth, Venus has no rings. Unlike Earth, which has one moon, Venus has no moons. Earth is the only planet known to have living things.

Apply It!

Use a graphic organizer to **compare and contrast** Venus and Earth.

Different	Alike	Different
How is Venus different?	How are Earth and Venus alike?	How is Earth different?

You Are There!

Don't look at it! The Sun has a great amount of energy. You should never look directly at it. The Sun is the fiery center of our solar system. This huge ball of energy holds our solar system together. But what's going on underneath its surface?

AudioText

What are the parts of the solar system?

The solar system includes the Sun and other objects that travel around it. The Sun gives off energy that moves out in all directions through space.

The Sun

The Sun is a ball of hot, glowing gases called plasma. It is a star. The Sun looks larger and brighter than stars you see at night because it is a lot closer to Earth. The other stars in the sky look small because they are so far away.

How big is the Sun? In a word—huge! It is 109 times as wide as Earth, or wider than the length of 15,000,000 football fields! In fact, the Sun is large enough to hold one million Earths inside it!

The temperature on the surface of the Sun is 5,500°C. The center is millions of degrees hot. It's so hot that gas particles that have a positive charge collide and join. This releases a lot of energy. Energy that travels from the Sun through space includes sunlight.

1. **✔Checkpoint** Why is the Sun so bright and hot?

2. **Art in Science** Draw a tiny circle to represent Earth. Then use information from this page to decide how big to draw the Sun.

The Sun is much nearer to Earth than other stars.

How Objects In the Solar System Move

You live on the planet Earth. A **planet** is a large, ball-shaped body that revolves, or travels, around the Sun. Find Earth and the seven other planets in the drawing. Many of these planets have moons. The Sun, the eight planets and their moons, and other objects that revolve around the Sun make up the **solar system.** The Sun is the center of the solar system.

The path an object takes as it revolves around the Sun is its **orbit.** Planets travel in an orbit that is a slight oval shape. The strong pull of the Sun's gravity holds the planets in their orbits.

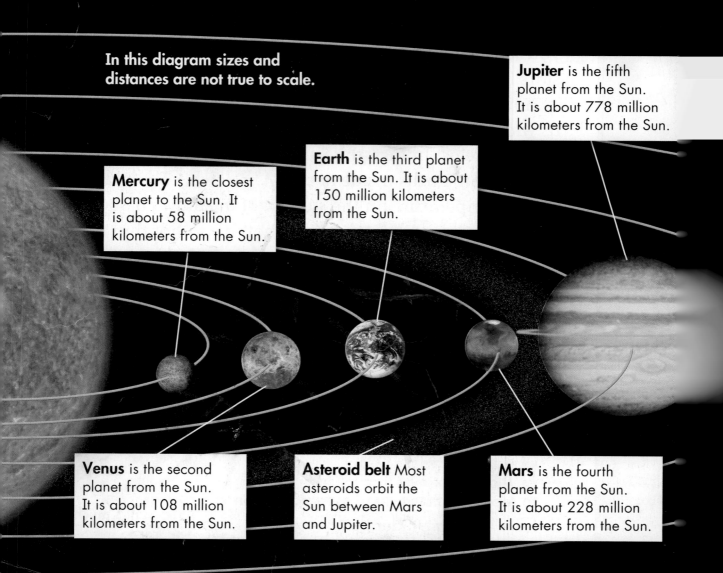

In this diagram sizes and distances are not true to scale.

Jupiter is the fifth planet from the Sun. It is about 778 million kilometers from the Sun.

Mercury is the closest planet to the Sun. It is about 58 million kilometers from the Sun.

Earth is the third planet from the Sun. It is about 150 million kilometers from the Sun.

Venus is the second planet from the Sun. It is about 108 million kilometers from the Sun.

Asteroid belt Most asteroids orbit the Sun between Mars and Jupiter.

Mars is the fourth planet from the Sun. It is about 228 million kilometers from the Sun.

The planets are divided into inner and outer planets based on their distances from the Sun. The four inner planets are Mercury, Venus, Earth, and Mars. The outer planets are Jupiter, Saturn, Uranus, and Neptune. Compare the distances of the planets from the Sun.

An **asteroid** is a small chunk of rock that orbits the Sun. Thousands of asteroids are found in the asteroid belt between Mars and Jupiter.

✓Lesson Checkpoint

1. What makes up the solar system?
2. How do objects in the solar system move?
3. **Math in Science** How much farther from the Sun is Venus compared to Mercury?

Saturn is the sixth planet from the Sun. It is about 1 billion, 400 million kilometers from the Sun.

Uranus is the seventh planet from the Sun. It is about 3 billion kilometers from the Sun.

Neptune is the eighth planet from the Sun. It is over 4 billion, 500 million kilometers from the Sun.

Lesson 2

What are the planets?

Each of the planets in our solar system has special features. They are different sizes. Some are rocky. Some are made of gases. Some have many moons. Some have no moons.

The Inner Planets

The inner planets—Mercury, Venus, Earth, and Mars—are alike in some ways. They are the planets closest to the Sun. They are rocky planets. But they have many differences too.

Look at the surface of Mercury below. It has many craters like those on our Moon. Mercury is also dry and very hot. That's because it is the closest planet to the Sun. Mercury is the smallest planet. It is less than half the size of Earth. It has no atmosphere. In 59 Earth days, Mercury rotates once. Mercury takes 88 Earth days to revolve around the Sun one time. It has no moons.

Venus, like Mercury, is a very hot, rocky planet. It has craters, mountains, and valleys. It has an atmosphere and is covered by thick clouds that trap a lot of heat. Venus takes 225 Earth days to revolve around the Sun. It takes 243 Earth days for Venus to rotate one time. Venus is larger than Mercury. It is a little smaller than Earth. Venus has no moons.

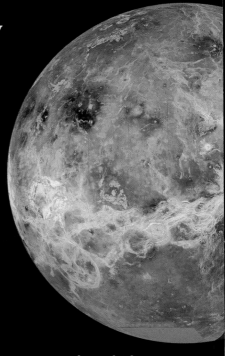

Venus

No atmosphere hides the craters of Mercury, seen below. Volcanoes and wide lava fields cover Venus, seen above without its cloud cover.

Mercury

Earth

 Mars

Oceans of liquid water make Earth the "blue planet." Rust in the soil of Mars makes it the "red planet."

Find the planet that looks like a blue, white, and brown marble. You found the third planet from the Sun—Earth. The swirling white clouds are part of its atmosphere. Our planet is slightly larger than Venus. One Earth year lasts $365\frac{1}{4}$ days. That means it takes 365 days and 6 hours for Earth to revolve around the Sun one time. Its day, or rotation, lasts 24 hours. Earth has one moon.

Mars is the next farthest planet from the Sun. Mars is called the "red planet" because it has a reddish-orange surface. Mars has a very thin atmosphere. It has volcanoes and deep canyons. Mars is about half the size of Earth. One year on Mars is equal to 687 Earth days, or almost two Earth years. One day on Mars lasts 25 Earth hours. That's very close to a day on Earth. Mars has two moons.

1. **✓Checkpoint** Which of the planets are inner planets?

2. **Compare and Contrast** How do the sizes of the four inner planets compare?

Earth Supports Life

From space you can see that Earth is very different from the other planets. Blue water covers almost three fourths of Earth's surface. You also can see white clouds in the atmosphere, the solid land of the continents and, the white ice caps.

What you cannot see from space is that Earth is the only planet in the solar system that can support a wide variety of living things. Earth has the mild temperatures, liquid water, and atmosphere that living things need. Its atmosphere contains the right amounts of oxygen and carbon dioxide. The atmosphere also absorbs most of the rays of light that can harm living things. Earth's gravity holds the atmosphere close to Earth.

Extremes on Earth	
Highest place	Mount Everest in Nepal and China 8850 meters (29, 035 feet)
Lowest place	Dead Sea between Israel and Jordan 400 meters (1, 300 feet) below sea level
Hottest place	El Azizia in Libya once measured 57.8°C (136°F)
Coldest place	Antarctica once measured −89°C (−129°F)
Driest place	Possibly Atacama Desert in Chile 0.76 mm (0.03 inches) of rain a year
Wettest place	Possibly Lloro, Colombia 13,299 mm (523.6 inches) of rain a year

The coldest place on Earth is Antarctica.

The hottest place in the United States is Death Valley, California. A very hot 57°C (134°F) has been recorded there.

The Sun is the main source of energy for Earth. Sunlight warms Earth. It also provides energy for plants to grow. However, about one half of the Sun's light that comes toward Earth does not reach Earth's surface. The atmosphere absorbs one fifth. One third more is reflected off the ground and clouds. Much of the reflected light is scattered by gases in the atmosphere. This makes the sky look blue.

Earth's rocky surface, both on land and under the oceans, is broken up into sections called plates. The plates constantly move. Earthquakes and volcanoes often happen where the plates meet. In some places the plates move apart from each other. In other places the plates collide or slide past each other. The moving plates cause the Earth's surface to keep changing.

1. ✓ **Checkpoint** What makes life on Earth possible?

2. **Writing** in Science **Descriptive**
Brainstorm with a partner why the surface of Earth keeps changing. Write your explanation in your **science journal**.

Jupiter and Saturn, Two Gas Giants

The outer planets are much farther apart than the inner planets are. Unlike the rocky inner planets, most of the outer planets are huge and made mostly of gas. They are called gas giants. Their surfaces are not solid. They have deep atmospheres with thick layers of clouds and strong winds. Gas giants also have rings around them. The two largest gas giants are Jupiter and Saturn.

Jupiter is the fifth planet from the Sun and the largest planet in the solar system. It is over 11 times the size of Earth. It takes almost 12 Earth years for Jupiter to revolve around the Sun one time. Jupiter rotates in only 10 Earth hours. Jupiter is covered with thick layers of clouds that reflect sunlight. Bands of clouds, strong winds, and storms make the planet look like it does in the picture. Jupiter has more than 60 moons, but only four are as large or larger than Earth's Moon. Jupiter's rings are hard to see.

Jupiter's Great Red Spot is actually a huge storm. This storm is always present but it changes in size.

The asteroid belt is between the orbits of Mars and Jupiter. Some asteroids are hundreds of kilometers wide. Most are less than 1 kilometer wide.

Saturn's rings are very bright and easy to see with a telescope. Gravity holds the rings in orbit around Saturn.

Saturn is the sixth planet from the Sun and the second largest planet. Saturn's most famous feature is its rings. They are made of chunks of ice and rock that circle the planet. Saturn takes 29 Earth years to make one revolution around the Sun. Saturn rotates in about 11 Earth hours. Saturn has at least 30 moons.

1. **✓ Checkpoint** In what ways are Jupiter and Saturn alike?

2. **Technology** in Science Scientists use the Hubble Telescope to learn about the planets. Use the Internet or other resources to find out more about the Hubble Telescope.

Uranus and Neptune

Like Jupiter and Saturn, Neptune and Uranus are gas giants. Uranus is the seventh planet from the Sun. It is smaller than Saturn or Jupiter but about 4 times the size of Earth. It takes Uranus 84 Earth years to revolve around the Sun just one time. However, Uranus rotates in just 17 Earth hours. Uranus is unlike other planets because it rotates on its side. It has 26 moons.

Neptune is the eighth planet from the Sun. It is only slightly smaller than Uranus. Neptune is so far away from the Sun that its orbit around the Sun takes 165 Earth years. Like the other gas giants, Neptune has strong winds and storms. Neptune looks light blue and has rings that are hard to see. Neptune takes about 16 Earth hours to rotate one time. It has at least 13 moons.

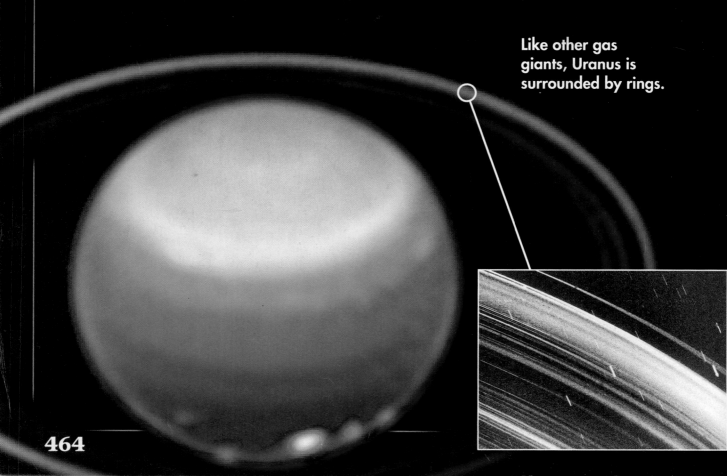

Like other gas giants, Uranus is surrounded by rings.

One of Pluto's moons (shown in the right-hand corner) is named Charon.

The weather on Neptune constantly changes. Light cloud-like bands appear and disappear. Storms are seen as dark spots.

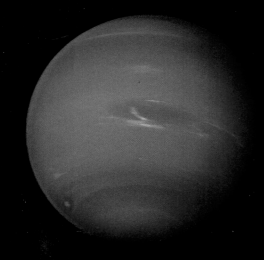

Pluto, a Dwarf Planet

A small, cold, rocky object called Pluto orbits far from the Sun. Until 2006, Pluto was described as the ninth planet in the solar system. But many scientists think that Pluto should never have been called a planet. Pluto has a very unusual orbit. Sometimes Pluto is closer to the Sun than Neptune is. Pluto's orbit is at an angle to the orbits of the eight planets. Pluto is smaller than Earth's Moon. In August of 2006, scientists decided to put Pluto into a different category. It is now called a dwarf planet.

Other objects similar to Pluto have been discovered. Some are bigger than Pluto. Scientists think there are many more objects beyond Neptune's orbit.

✓ Lesson Checkpoint

1. Which of the planets are outer planets?

2. What small, ball-shaped object orbits the Sun and is now called a dwarf planet?

3. **Compare and Contrast** On a two column chart list the ways that the inner planets and the gas giants are alike and different.

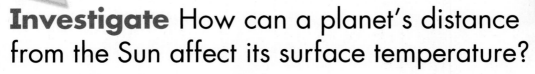

Investigate How can a planet's distance from the Sun affect its surface temperature?

A planet's temperature can be affected by its atmosphere, its surface, and other factors. How does a planet's distance from the Sun affect its surface temperature?

Materials

metric ruler

lamp and
3 thermometers

books

What to Do

1 **Make a model** of the Sun and the planets. Place a lamp, books, a metric ruler, and thermometers as shown.

Be careful!

The light bulb and parts of the lamp will get hot!

The thermometers that are different distances from the light bulb stand for planets that are different distances from the Sun.

Remove ruler before turning on the lamp!

large books

The lamp stands for the Sun.

Process Skills

You can use a **model** to help you make accurate **inferences**.

2 Turn on the lamp.

More Lab zone Activities Take It to the Net
pearsonsuccessnet.com

3 Make a data chart like this one. **Collect** the **data** you need to complete the chart.

4 Wait 15 minutes. Turn off the lamp. Parts of the lamp will be hot!

5 Record the temperature of each thermometer. Make a line graph of your data.

Effect of Distance on Temperature	
Distance from Light Bulb (cm)	**Temperature after 15 Minutes** (°C)
7 cm	
14 cm	
28 cm	

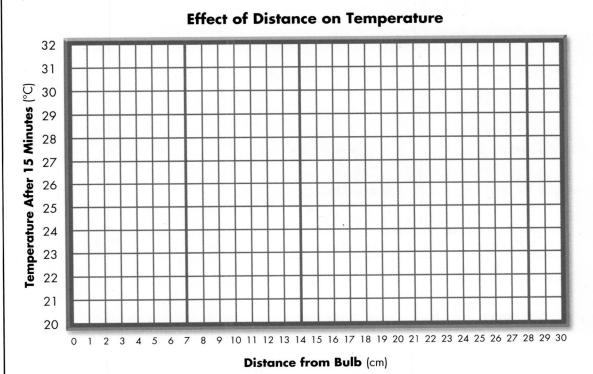

Effect of Distance on Temperature

Temperature After 15 Minutes (°C)

Distance from Bulb (cm)

Explain Your Results

1. Which thermometer showed the highest temperature? Which showed the lowest temperature?

2. **Infer** Think about your **model**. How does a planet's distance from the Sun affect its surface temperature?

Go Further

What do you think happens to the temperature on the side of the planet not facing the Sun? Make a plan using a model to help investigate.

Math in Science

Patterns in Planets

The distance of a planet from the Sun affects the time needed to revolve around the Sun.

The first column in the chart below lists the outer planets in the order of their distances from the Sun, from the nearest to farthest. The second column gives the length of time each planet takes to complete one orbit.

The Outer Planets

Planet	Revolution Time
Jupiter	12 Earth years
Saturn	29 Earth years
Uranus	84 Earth years
Neptune	165 Earth years

e Tools Take It to the Net pearsonsuccessnet.com

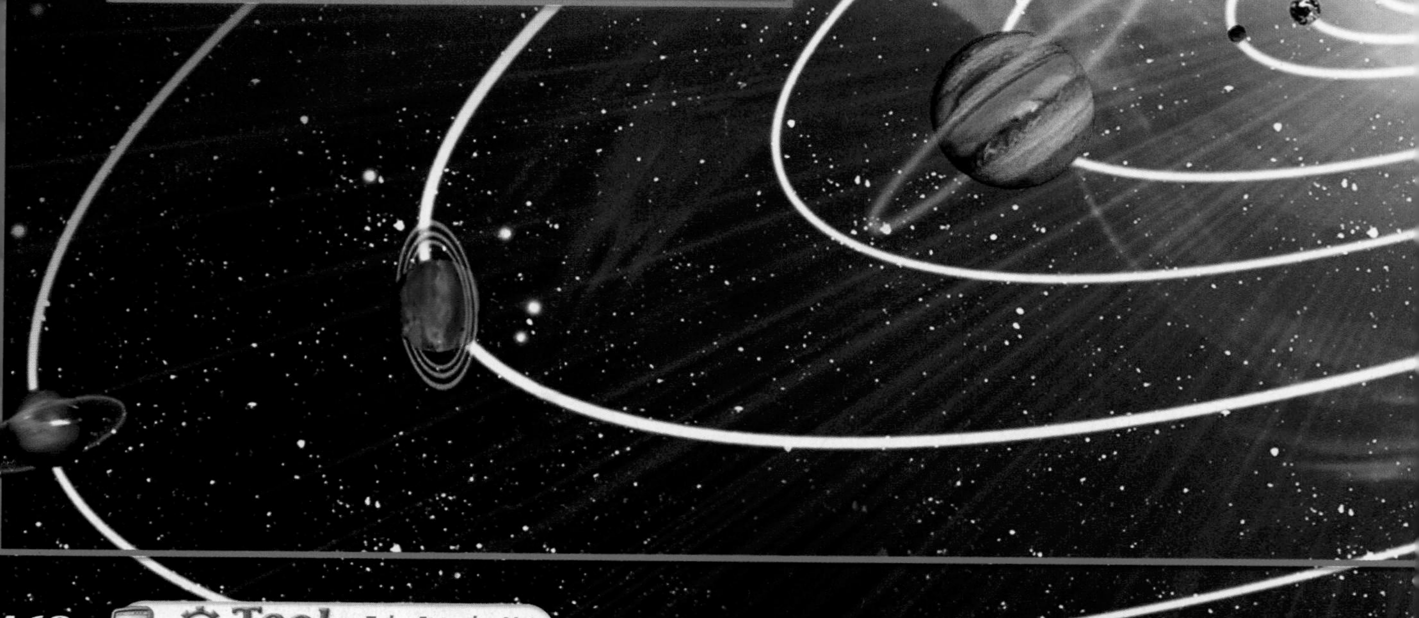

Use the chart to answer the questions.

1. Which of the outer planets takes the shortest time to revolve around the Sun?

    A. Jupiter   B. Saturn   C. Neptune   D. Uranus

2. How much longer is the revolution time of the outer planet farthest from the Sun than that of the outer planet closest to the Sun?

    F. 17 Earth years   G. 83 Earth years

    H. 81 Earth years   I. 153 Earth years

3. What pattern do you see about the distance of a planet from the Sun and the planet's revolution time?

    A. Planets closer to the Sun take longer to revolve around the Sun.

    B. Planets farther from the Sun take longer to revolve around the Sun.

    C. Planets farther from the Sun take a shorter time to revolve around the Sun.

    D. The chart shows no pattern.

Lab zone Take-Home Activity

Choose two charts of information about things in newspapers and magazines. Write down what patterns you see in the tables.

Chapter 16 Review and Test Prep

Use Vocabulary

asteroid (page 457)	**planet** (page 456)
orbit (page 456)	**solar system** (page 456)

Use the vocabulary term from the list above that best completes each sentence.

1. A(n) _____ is a large, ball-shaped body that revolves around the Sun.

2. The path a planet takes to revolve around the Sun is its _____.

3. The Sun, eight planets and their moons, and other objects that orbit the Sun make up the _____.

4. A(n) _____ is a small chunk of rock that orbits the Sun.

Explain Concepts

5. Explain why some stars seem so much brighter in the night sky than other stars.

6. Explain how energy is released from the Sun.

7. Explain why the four outer planets are called gas giants.

8. If you were traveling from the inner planet farthest from the Sun to the closest outer planet, what would you see in orbit? Explain your answer.

9. Why is Mars called the Red Planet?

10. Use the chart below to find a pattern in the number of moons and the size of the planets. How does the size of a planet seem to be related to the number of moons a planet has?

Planets and Moons

Planet	Distance Through Planet's Center	Number of Moons
Mercury	4,900 kilometers	0
Venus	12,000 kilometers	0
Earth	12,750 kilometers	1
Mars	6,800 kilometers	2
Jupiter	143,000 kilometers	more than 60
Saturn	120,000 kilometers	more than 30
Uranus	51,000 kilometers	26
Neptune	49,000 kilometers	at least 13

11. Write a paragraph explaining how Pluto is different from the eight planets.

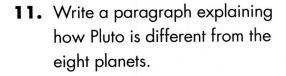

12. Predict where Earth will be in its orbit around the Sun exactly one year from now.

13. Model Make a model to show the orbits of the planets around the Sun.

Compare and Contrast

14. Reread the information about the inner and outer planets. Make a chart that compares and contrasts information about the eight planets.

Test Prep

Choose the letter that best completes the statement or answers the question.

15. Which planet is an inner planet?

(A) Uranus   (B) Venus
(C) Neptune   (D) Jupiter

16. What do all of the gas giants have?

(F) oxygen
(G) rocky surfaces
(H) liquid water
(I) rings

17. Which is the only planet that supports many living things?

(A) Earth
(B) Mars
(C) Venus
(D) Mercury

18. Which object has an unusual orbit and is called a dwarf planet?

(F) Jupiter
(G) Mercury
(H) Pluto
(I) Uranus

19. Explain why the answer you chose for Question 18 is best. For each of the answers you did not choose, give a reason why it is not the best choice.

20. Writing in Science

Persuasive Choose a planet that you would like others to visit. Then write a travel brochure that tries to persuade them that it would be a great place to spend a vacation.

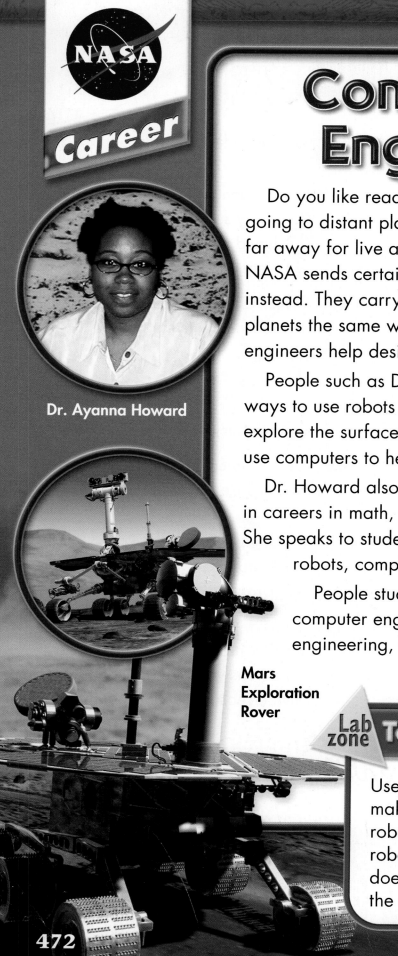

Dr. Ayanna Howard

Mars
Exploration
Rover

Computer Engineer

Do you like reading adventure stories about going to distant planets? Most planets are too far away for live astronauts to explore them. NASA sends certain spacecraft without people instead. They carry robots that can explore planets the same way astronauts can. Computer engineers help design the robots.

People such as Dr. Ayanna Howard study ways to use robots called rovers. These machines explore the surfaces of other planets. The rovers use computers to help find answers to problems.

Dr. Howard also tries to interest students in careers in math, science, and engineering. She speaks to students around the world about robots, computers, and technology.

People study in college to become computer engineers. Classes include math, engineering, and computer science.

Lab zone Take-Home Activity

Use objects from your home to make a model of a rover or other robot. Describe the parts of your robot and tell what your robot does. Compare your robot with the ones that explore other planets.

472

Chapter 17
Science in Our Lives

You Will Discover

- ways we use science and technology every day.
- ways we use technology to solve problems.

Discovery Channel School
Student DVD

online
Student Edition
pearsonsuccessnet.com

How does technology affect our lives?

technology

invention

tool

474

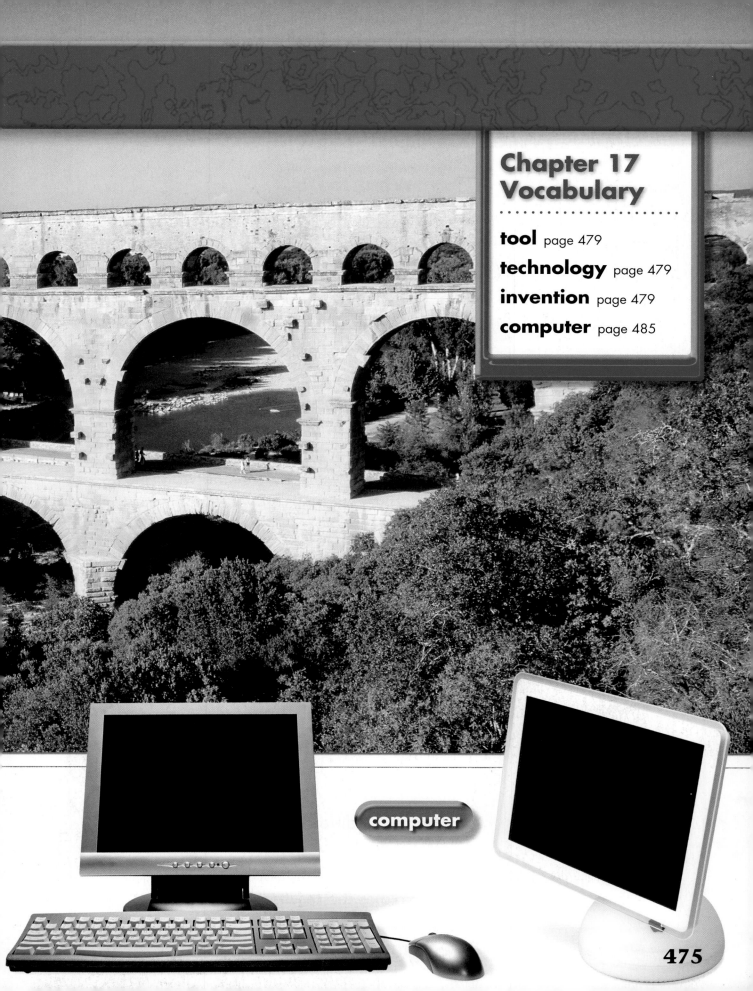

Chapter 17 Vocabulary

computer

Explore Which transport system works best?

Materials

Possible Water
Transport Systems

newspaper

plastic tube

funnel

empty cup and
cup with water

What to Do

1 Examine *Possible Water Transport Systems*. **Predict** which of these systems will always work? Which will never work? Which will trap some water?

2 Test your predictions. Set up each system.

3 For each system, pour a half cup of water in the funnel. Have a group member hold the tube in place. **Observe** how well the water flows through the system.

Put down newspaper before you begin.

Repeat each test. This will help make your results more reliable.

Explain Your Results

1. In what direction does water flow best through a system?

2. Examine the different designs, your **predictions**, and your results. Find a rule that explains the results you **observed**.

How to Read Science

Sequence

A **sequence** is a series of actions that happen in a certain order.

- Sometimes writers use clue words such as *first, then, next,* and *finally* to signal a sequence.

- When a sequence has a repeating pattern, you can **predict** what comes next.

Newspaper Article

The Wright Brothers Fly!

Kitty Hawk, North Carolina–December 17, 1903. Today, Wilbur and Orville Wright flew their powered airplane. How did they do it? At first, the Wrights watched how birds control their flight. Then they flew kites to test their ideas. Next they built gliders to find the right wing shape. Finally, they built an airplane with an engine. The flying machine, called *Flyer I*, became the world's first powered airplane.

Apply It!

Make a graphic organizer like the one shown. Fill it in to show the **sequence** of events that led to the Wright brother's historic first flight.

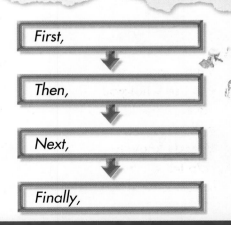

What a beautiful bridge! The arches seem perfectly lined up. It's hard to believe this structure was built by the ancient Romans over 2,000 years ago. The bottom part was used as a road. But the top part was made to carry something completely different. This bridge was part of an amazing system designed to bring water from mountain springs to Roman cities. The ancient Romans, like other people, used technology to solve problems.

AudioText 🔊

Lesson 1

How does technology affect our lives?

Science helps people understand the way the world works. Technology helps people apply this understanding to solve problems and improve their lives.

Finding New Ways

People have always asked questions about the world around them. As they learned new things, they began to use this knowledge. They used it to solve problems and form new ideas. People invented tools to help. A **tool** helps to do work more easily. Tools, in turn, helped people think of new ways of doing things. In other words, they used technology. **Technology** is the use of knowledge to design new tools and new ways to do things. A tool can be as simple as a sewing needle. A tool can be as complicated as a computer.

The invention and use of arches was important technology in ancient Rome. An **invention** is something made for the first time. The Romans needed to get water to their cities. They figured out that an arch with a central stone could support a lot of weight. They used these arches for building bridges and for carrying water to the cities.

The keystone, or central stone wedged at the top, keeps the stones of the arch in place.

1. ✓ **Checkpoint** What is technology?

2. **Art in Science** Draw a picture in your **science journal** of two kinds of technology that were not around 100 years ago.

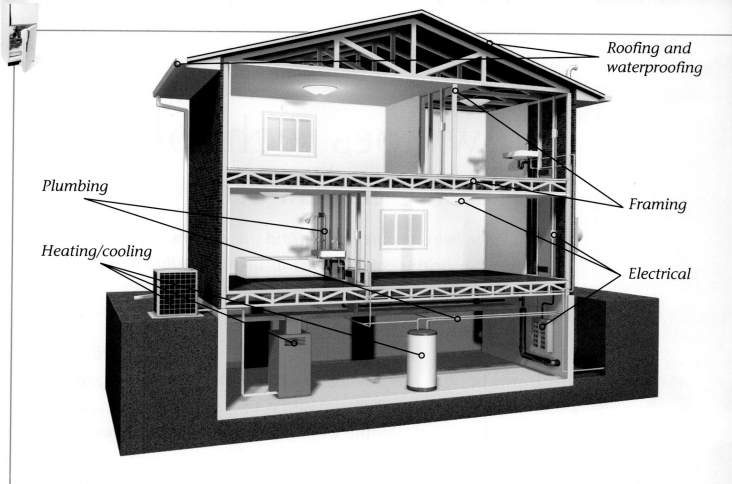

Roofing and waterproofing

Plumbing

Heating/cooling

Framing

Electrical

Technology in Your Home

Technology found in a house or apartment is more than a loose bunch of inventions. Different parts of buildings work together as systems, which interact.

For example, when you flush the toilet, you use the plumbing system. This system is made of faucets, drains, sinks, and pipes linked together. Some water in the system passes through a water heater. The electrical system is connected to it. Electricity heats the water. You wouldn't like to take a shower if these systems didn't interact, would you?

In a similar way, the heating and cooling system is made up of many parts that work together. The furnace in some systems burns fuel. Others use electricity. No matter what energy source is used, the heating system needs the electrical system to turn it on and off. In these ways, technology systems interact and work together.

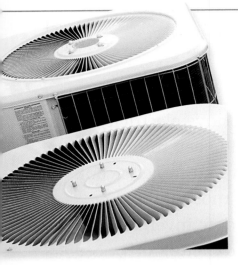

These air conditioning units are part of the cooling system. This system keeps us comfortable during hot summers.

What technology do you see in the frame of the house shown here? Boards are not placed just any old way. House designers know that placing the boards in certain patterns makes the building sturdy. To create the form of something, you need to plan it out in a skillful way.

Now look closely at the particle boards that form part of the wall. They are made of wood chips that have been pressed and glued together. Such wood chips used to be burned. That caused air pollution. New technology now turns those chips into strong boards for buildings.

Particle board is a technology that solves two problems at once. It provides a strong building material and uses waste wood chips that would otherwise be burned.

1. ✓ **Checkpoint** Explain how some technology systems work together in a house.

2. **Writing in Science**
   Expository In your **science journal** write a paragraph about two technology systems you would expect to find in a kitchen.

481

Technology Yesterday, Today, and Tomorrow

A kitchen in the early 1800s did not have electricity. So there was no refrigerator or freezer to keep things cold. People had to chop wood to burn in a stove to cook their food. Preparing meals could take most of the day.

Every few years brought more and more inventions and ideas. Ice boxes made of wood and metal, for example, held blocks of ice that kept food cold. Food could be kept longer without spoiling. Ice boxes were a fantastic technology—until electric refrigerators came along.

Technology has made today's kitchens change in many ways since the 1800s. Microwave ovens cook food in minutes. Electric dishwashers replace the chore of washing dishes by hand.

What do you do with leftovers? Plastic bowls with an airtight seal were invented in 1947.

The non-stick coating on this pan was invented in 1954. How did that make cooking easier?

To hear music not long ago, you played a record with wavy grooves scratched into it. While it spun, a metal needle was dragged along the groove. A machine read the vibrations in the needle. The machine then translated the vibrations into sound. In an audio CD player, a special beam of light now reads the computer-coded plastic discs. A computer translates the information to sound.

It's hard to imagine how technology will affect the homes of tomorrow. Some people think that computers will soon run the entire home. Perhaps computer chips in each package of food will tell the oven how to cook it. Refrigerators might be connected to the Internet. The refrigerator could order food over the Internet when food supplies are running low.

Will these and other ideas come true? Probably some of them will. One thing is for sure. As long as people continue to learn, technology will change. Who knows what exciting things are in store?

This CD player uses a light beam to read and play back the music stored on compact discs.

This DVD player uses a light beam to play back movies recorded on plastic discs.

 **Lesson Checkpoint**

1. Why was the invention of the arch important technology in ancient Rome?

2. Explain the need for systems in order for technology to work in the home.

3. **Social Studies in Science** How is a modern kitchen different from a kitchen in the early 1800s?

No more getting lost! Signals from satellites track the exact location of this car.

Satellites with special cameras provide images with many kinds of information.

Lesson 2

What are some new technologies?

Modern technology includes tools that allow us to go far beyond what we can normally see and hear.

Tools for Extending Our Senses

People on ships once had to figure out where they were by looking at stars. Now people can use a Global Positioning System (GPS). This system relies on signals from satellites. A ship's GPS computer uses the signals to figure out the ship's location.

What if you were hiking in a forest? You could use a GPS receiver the size of a cell phone to find your way. Some cars have GPS. Farmers may use GPS on their tractors to locate crops that need their attention.

Cameras in satellites can also make pictures using the infrared light that growing things give off. These satellites track crops, forests, and grasslands over time. Infrared pictures show where plants are too dry or are not growing well. Infrared pictures can also show detailed weather patterns. Forecasters use the pictures to observe and predict the weather.

Tools for Processing Information

A **computer** stores, processes, and sends electronic information incredibly fast! For instance, a computer can rapidly turn countless bits of information about the weather into a weather forecast.

Computer technology is everywhere. A digital watch tells time with a computer chip. Calculators, cameras, and cars all use computer chips.

Optical fibers are making computer networks better. These fibers are thin strands of bendable glass that use light to carry information. The fibers are replacing wires in computer, telephone, and cable television systems. Optical fibers do not get hot like wires. They take up less space. Also, a single fiber can carry more data than hundreds of wires twisted into a fat cable.

Copper wires are being replaced in communication systems by optical fibers.

Small wireless phones are replacing bulky phones fixed in place.

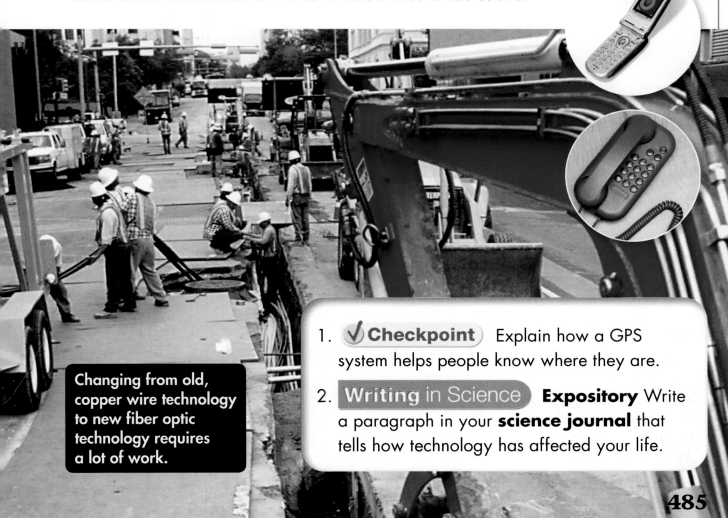

Changing from old, copper wire technology to new fiber optic technology requires a lot of work.

1. ✅ **Checkpoint** Explain how a GPS system helps people know where they are.

2. **Writing in Science** **Expository** Write a paragraph in your **science journal** that tells how technology has affected your life.

Tools for Transporting Materials

Roads are a very important part of our lives. We travel on them to go to work and school. We follow them to pick up and deliver goods. We use them to visit friends and family or just to see the sights.

Fast, safe highways are now in place. Some people call the National Highway System the greatest wonder of the modern world. This system includes all the major highways that go from one state to another. About 80 million trucks carry the nation's supplies on over 260,000 kilometers (160,000 miles) of national highways. About 120 million cars carry passengers from place to place.

The United States began to build the National Highway System so that military vehicles like this one could move quickly over great distances.

Did you ever wonder how complex highway systems are designed? That's the job of highway engineers.

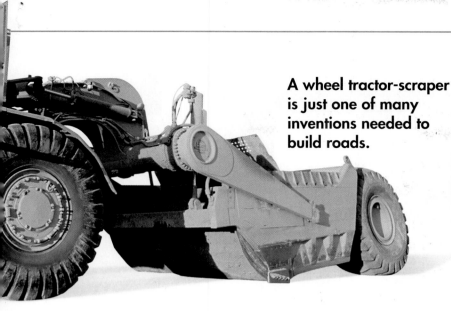

A wheel tractor-scraper is just one of many inventions needed to build roads.

Trains began to transport goods on railroads long before trucks began to transport goods on freeways.

Big tools are needed for building big highways. First, earthmoving machines like the tractor-scraper in the picture lay out the new road. Then workers lay down sand, crushed stone, and concrete or asphalt. Finally, workers paint markings and put up traffic signs.

Roads are not the only pathways over which people and things move. People and freight use railroads and planes such as the ones shown.

The first transportation system in the United States was the nation's rivers. Today, boats push barges loaded with freight over the same rivers. Technology will always help get people and things from place to place.

Planes are now the fastest way to carry cargo. Cargo planes can carry loads that weigh 100,000 kg.

1. **✔ Checkpoint** Why is a modern roadway system important?

2. **Technology** in Science Use the Internet to view maps of the National Highway System. Then plan a trip across the country using the maps.

Using powerful tugboats has improved our nation's river transportation system.

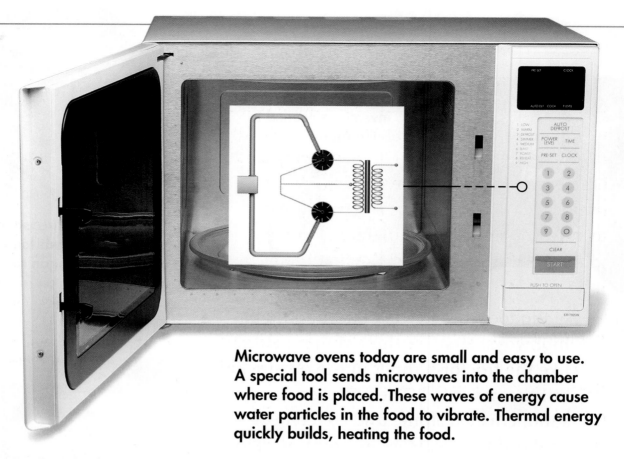

Microwave ovens today are small and easy to use. A special tool sends microwaves into the chamber where food is placed. These waves of energy cause water particles in the food to vibrate. Thermal energy quickly builds, heating the food.

Unexpected Uses

Sometimes technology becomes useful in unplanned ways. For example, back in 1946 Percy Spencer was working to improve radar. He was testing a light bulb that used microwave energy. Microwaves are a form of radiation, like visible light and invisible radio waves.

One day Spencer stood near the tube. He noticed that a candy bar in his pocket melted. Curious, he put popcorn kernels near the microwave energy. They rapidly popped into fluffy pieces.

Spencer realized that if microwaves could quickly cook popcorn, they could quickly cook other foods, too. He made a drawing that led to the first microwave oven. Technology that was first designed for radar is a great help to those who eat in a hurry!

This design by Percy Spencer explains how the first microwave oven would work. The first oven weighed 750 pounds and cost $5,000.

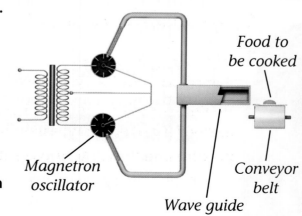

Food to be cooked

Magnetron oscillator

Conveyor belt

Wave guide

Will you watch TV today? Television sets and computers started out using glass tubes to display the picture. But these tubes cannot be made to be very big. Glass is heavy and breaks easily in big screens. Now TV screens are huge. How could this happen? New technology makes the difference. In 1970, James Fergason invented the first modern LCD screen. LCD stands for liquid crystal display. Electricity causes each fluid crystal to act like the shutter in a camera. The crystals either block the light or allow the light to pass through. This causes an image on the screen. Screens using these crystals do not need heavy glass. They are light in weight. They are also flat, as the picture shows.

DVD players that you can carry show movies on tiny LCD screens.

A screen made of glass is shaped like a box. But this LCD screen is flat. Computers using LCD screens do not take up a lot of desk space.

✓ **Lesson Checkpoint**

1. What did Percy Spencer accidentally discover that microwaves could do?

2. What does a computer do?

3. **Writing in Science** Why was it important for Percy Spencer to keep asking questions after his candy bar melted? Answer this question in a paragraph in your **science journal.**

Lesson 3

How does technology help us get energy?

Technology has changed the way we get energy. But most of the energy sources we use today cause problems for the environment. We can use technology to develop cleaner energy sources.

Mills used to grind grain into flour. Others drove machinery that made things.

Using Energy

Plop in a DVD, pop some popcorn in the microwave, and you're set to watch a movie. But be sure everything is plugged in! Today we take our electrical energy for granted. In the past it wasn't so easy.

Before engines and electricity, people relied on wind and water as sources of energy. Water-powered mills like the one shown were built next to rivers. The force of flowing water turned a big wheel. At a sawmill, for instance, the wheel turned a series of rods, gears, and belts. This caused saws to cut wood.

Moving water makes the parts in this lawn sprinkler spray water in different directions.

The force of water runs a modern lawn sprinkler. Study the diagram shown. First, the hose sends water into the sprinkler. The moving water has kinetic energy to do work. Water then turns a waterwheel. Next, the waterwheel turns wheel and axle gears. The gears slowly rock the spray arm back and forth. Finally, water from the spray arm waters the lawn.

Windmills were also used to do work. As you might guess, windmills use the energy of moving air instead of water as a power source. The windmill in the picture is still used today. The turning blades move gears in a small box. The gears move a rod up and down. This pumps water from under the ground.

There are good and bad things connected with using windmills and water mills. They do not pollute the air or water. However, water mills can only work along a river. Both wind and water are renewable energy resources. But they don't supply enough power for all our needs.

1. ✓ **Checkpoint** What renewable sources of energy have people used for centuries to generate power?

2. **Sequence** Use a graphic organizer and describe the steps of how a modern water sprinkler works.

Windmills like this one use wind energy to pump water.

Producing Electricity

We still use waterwheel technology inside hydroelectric power dams. These dams are built on rivers that back up behind the dam to form reservoirs. Study the diagram. The deep water stores potential energy. To release this energy to do work, gates let water rush into the power station. The kinetic energy of the flowing water then spins the blades of waterwheels in turbines. The spinning axle of each turbine drives a generator to make electricity. The electricity is used for power in cities.

Hydroelectric power does not produce much pollution. Since it depends on water, it also is a renewable energy source. But dams can affect fish that travel up the rivers on which the dams are built. The large lake behind the dam floods land, which then changes the environment. There also is a danger of more flooding if a dam breaks.

Generators like this one in a hydroelectric dam change the energy of flowing water into electricity.

Below each generator, the energy of moving water becomes the energy of moving blades in a turbine.

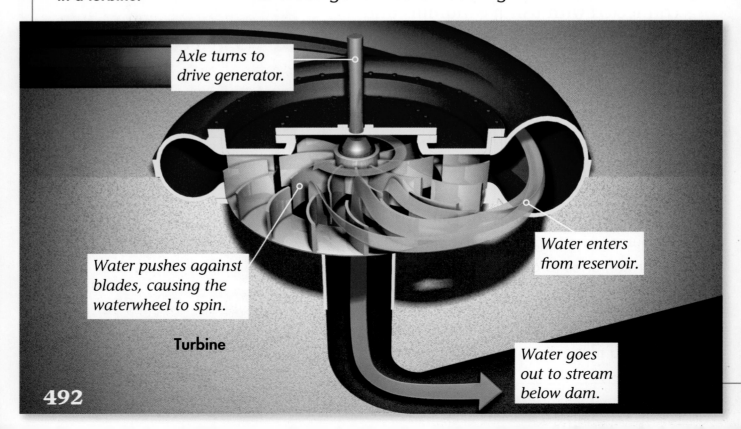

Axle turns to drive generator.

Water enters from reservoir.

Water pushes against blades, causing the waterwheel to spin.

Turbine

Water goes out to stream below dam.

Another way to change energy into electricity is by burning coal, oil, or natural gas. The heat from burning this fuel is used to boil water. Boiling water makes steam. Pressure from steam turns wheels of turbines that drive electricity generators.

This technology is a solution to the problem of producing enough electricity for everyone. But this is an example of how technology can create problems too. Burning fuel for electric generators can pollute the air. Burning fuels to move cars also pollutes the air. People are working on ways to use technology to make cars and generators that pollute less.

Map Fact

Herbert Hoover Dam sits on the Colorado River that divides Arizona and Nevada. It was completed in 1936. Hoover Dam is one of the largest dams in the world.

1. ✔️ **Checkpoint** How are cars a helpful and a harmful example of technology?

2. **Social Studies** in Science Use the library to learn more about how Hoover Dam on the Colorado River was built.

Future Sources of Energy

Our energy needs seem to keep growing. How will we meet these needs in the future? Many people are working to answer that question.

Solar energy is one answer. This energy comes directly from the Sun's rays. Panels, like the ones in the picture, gather the Sun's rays. Each panel has lots of small solar cells spread across it. The cells work together to provide enough power to be useful. Solar energy is a major source of electricity in desert areas where there are many days of sunshine.

Solar panels concentrate the Sun's rays. This energy is changed into electricity.

New technology is making solar energy cheaper to use. Many people put panels on the roofs of their houses. Instead of making electricity, however, they make hot water. First, water runs through small tubes. Next, the energy of the Sun's rays is changed into heat when the panels absorb the rays. Then the heat warms the water in the tubes. Finally, the heated water flows into a container that stores the hot water until it's time to take a shower.

Solar energy warms water in this household appliance.

494

Wind rotates the arms of these windmills to generate electricity.

Wind energy also holds promise. Thousands of windmills like the ones above have already been set up in areas where the wind blows strong and often. To change enough kinetic energy of wind into electrical energy, the blades must be huge. Some blade wheels are wider than a football field is long! Computer technology can sense changing wind conditions. Motors then make shifts in the direction and angle of the blades. Doing this makes the most use of the wind for making the most electricity. These wind farms produce a lot of electricity for the surrounding community.

1. ✓**Checkpoint** What two renewable energy resources might meet more of our energy needs in the future?

2. **Sequence** List the steps that lead from the energy of sunshine in solar panels to the energy of hot water in a water tank. Use a graphic organizer.

Technology Time Line

Throughout human history, people have made discoveries and inventions to improve their lives.

312 B.C.
Rome completes the first aqueducts. Aqueducts brought water to Roman cities.

3500 B.C.
People connect wooden planks with other pieces of wood to make wheels.

1608
Dutch eyeglass maker Hans Leppershey places lenses in a tube and makes the first telescope. The famous scientist Galileo soon improves this tool and makes important discoveries about space.

1957
The Soviet Union launches the first artificial satellite, called *Sputnik 1*. It is only about the size of a basketball but this new piece of technology starts an international race for space.

1948
Opening of the Mount Palomar Observatory in California. It allows scientists to collect new data about our galaxy and beyond. Until 1976 it is the world's largest single-mirror telescope.

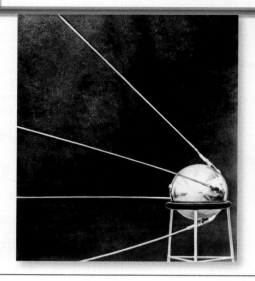

1903
Orville and Wilbur Wright invent the powered airplane. The first flight lasts only 12 seconds but it sparks a whole new wave of inventions that build the airline industry.

1876
Alexander Graham Bell invents the telephone. Imagine what life would be like without telephones.

2004
Spirit, the Mars expedition rover, prepares to drill into a rock. Will manned expeditions to Mars be soon to come?

1969
Astronauts Neil Armstrong and Edwin Aldrin land on the surface of the Moon. The *Apollo 11* astronauts bring moon rocks back to Earth for further study.

✔ **Lesson Checkpoint**

1. What changes in technology have changed the way we get energy?

2. What must we do in order to continue to use non-renewable fuel resources for energy?

3. **Math** in Science   Figure the time in years between the Wright's flight, the launch of *Sputnik 1*, and the first Moon landing. How does this show how fast technology is changing?

Investigate How does a GPS device find your location?

GPS, the Global Positioning System, can tell you your location anywhere on the globe—if you have a GPS device. The Global Positioning System uses GPS satellites to help find your location. In this activity, you solve a problem: How does a GPS device find a location?

Materials

Location of GPS Satellites over North America

metric ruler

3 circle patterns

What to Do

1 **Make a model** of how a GPS device finds your location. The GPS device learns you are 2,500 km from satellite A. On this map 5 cm stands for 2,500 km. So, use a circle pattern to draw a circle around satellite A with a 5 cm radius.

Satellite	Actual Distance from Your Location (km)	Distance on Map from Your Location (cm)
A	2,500 km	5 cm
B	1,500 km	3 cm
C	2,000 km	4 cm

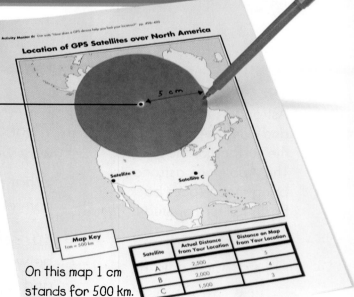

Satellite A

The 5 cm circle shows all the places that are 2,500 km from satellite A. Because you are 2,500 km from satellite A, you must be somewhere on this 5 cm circle.

On this map 1 cm stands for 500 km.

Process Skills

An accurate scale is often important in **making and using a model**.

2 Repeat step 1 for satellites B and C. Use the distances shown in the chart to make 2 more circles. Your location must be on each of these circles too.

3 Your location is the spot where all the circles meet. Mark an **X** on the map to record your location.

The map scale shows that 1 cm on the map equals 500 km on Earth. When you mark the distances in cm, you are using the scale to help measure distance. An accurate scale is important in producing and using a model of how a GPS device works. If the scale is not accurate, you can not find the correct location.

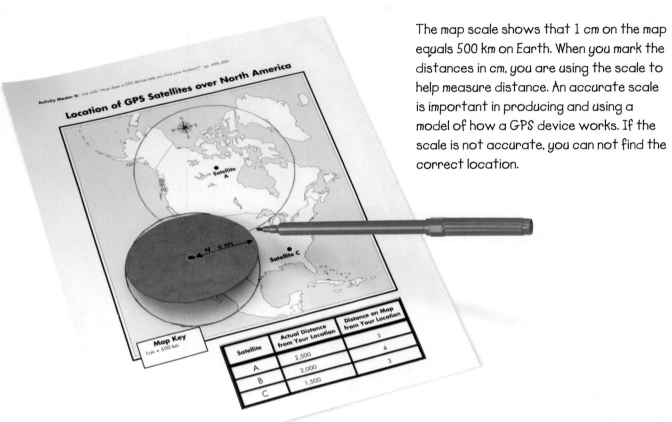

Satellite	Actual Distance from Your Location	Distance on Map from Your Location
A	2,500	5
B	2,000	4
C	1,500	3

The data for this activity includes the satellite locations, your distance from each satellite, the circles you made, and the **X** you made to show your position.

Explain Your Results

1. You needed to know your distance from more than 2 satellites in order to find your location. **Infer** why at least 3 satellites were needed.

2. Describe the scale on this map and tell how you used it to **measure** distance. Why was the scale important in this **model** of how a GPS device finds a location?

Go Further

What would happen if the three satellites were in different places? Use a map to find a new GPS location, or investigate other questions you may have.

Math in Science

Technology
Through the Years

Using a time line is a good way to show the progress of technology through the years. As you have seen, a time line is a number line showing events that took place during a certain span of time.

Any number can be represented as a position on a number line. The position of a number on a number line is important. Since 0.5 is halfway between 0 and 1, the point for 0.5 (or 1/2) should be halfway between the points for 0 and 1. Notice where 0.25 and 0.75 are placed.

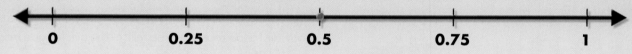

| 0 | 0.25 | 0.5 | 0.75 | 1 |

Since 25 is one fourth of 100, the point for 25 should be one fourth of the distance from 0 to 100.

| 0 | 25 | 50 | 75 | 100 |

In the same way, on a time line, the point for the year 1950 should be halfway between the points for the years 1900 and 2000. 1925 would be one fourth of that distance. 1975 would be three fourths of the distance from 1900 to 2000.

| 1900 | 1925 | 1950 | 1975 | 2000 |

On grid paper copy the time line above. Count grid squares to place the given points correctly. For each event in the table below, mark a point on your time line. Label each point with the year and the event above the line. The first event is already on the line you copied.

Transportation Technology

	Year	Event		Year	Event
1	1804	First steam locomotive	6	1956	Beginning of National Highway system
2	1869	First railroad tracks laid across the U.S.	7	1969	First moon-landing by astronauts
3	1885	First gasoline-powered automobile	8	1981	First space shuttle flight
4	1903	First gasoline-powered airplane	9	1999	First hot-air balloon flight around the world
5	1934	First diesel train in the U.S.	10	2004	First privately-funded space flight

Lab zone Take-Home Activity

Make a time line that shows how technology has changed over the years. You might choose computers, space travel, or buildings. Use library resources to find important dates and events. Choose what events you want to show.

Use Vocabulary

computer (page 485)	**technology** (page 479)
invention (page 479)	**tool** (page 479)

Use the term from the list above that best completes each sentence.

1. An object used to do work is a(n) _____.

2. The use of science knowledge to invent tools and new ways of doing things is called _____.

3. Something that has been made for the first time is called a(n) _____.

4. A(n) _____ stores, processes, and sends information.

Explain Concepts

5. Explain how science and technology are related.

6. Describe one of the technology systems found in your school.

7. Give two examples of ways technology can be helpful and harmful.

8. Compare the good and bad points of windmills and water mills.

9. What are some ways you use a computer every day, even if you don't use a desktop computer?

10. How is an LCD screen an improvement over glass picture tubes in televisions?

11. How has Percy Spencer's discovery changed part of our daily lives?

Process Skills

12. **Infer** Why are electricity-generating wind engines found only in wide-open areas?

13. **Predict** what could help solve our energy problems in the future.

14. **Sequence** Make a graphic organizer like the one shown. Fill it in to show how water can be used to make electricity.

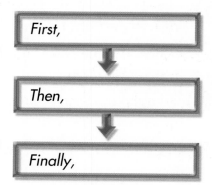

First,

Then,

Finally,

Test Prep

15. Science and technology can

- Ⓐ help people solve problems.
- Ⓑ sometimes create new problems.
- Ⓒ help people experience new things.
- Ⓓ all of the above

16. The heating system in a house connects to the plumbing system when

- Ⓕ the toilet is flushed.
- Ⓖ the microwave oven heats soup.
- Ⓗ the water heater makes some water hot.
- Ⓘ the air conditioning units cool the house.

17. What invention do both DVD and CD players use to make images or sound?

- Ⓐ a camera that takes pictures of infrared light
- Ⓑ a tool that shines a light beam on plastic discs
- Ⓒ wheels that water pressure turn
- Ⓓ a generator that makes microwaves

18. Which of the following is a nonrenewable resource?

- Ⓕ sun
- Ⓖ coal
- Ⓗ wind
- Ⓘ water

19. Explain why the answer you chose for Question 15 is best. Explain why you did not choose one of the other answers.

20. **Writing** in Science

Descriptive Suppose you are living in your town 50 years from now. Brainstorm with a classmate what that would be like. List kinds of technology you might have in your home. Write a paragraph describing some of this technology.

Science Teacher

Dr. Michelle Thaller

Ms. Doris Daou

Are you excited about science? How would you like to get students, teachers, and the public excited about science too? Michelle Thaller and Doris Daou, for instance, are Astronomers and Teachers for NASA. They promote the exciting work NASA is doing to help people study space.

Dr. Thaller and Ms. Daou help schoolteachers use NASA materials in their lessons. They appear on television shows. They speak to thousands of students every year. One area of study they teach audiences about is the use of special telescopes. For instance, following Earth in its orbit around the Sun is the Spitzer Space Telescope. Using infrared technology, it takes pictures of stars and solar systems that hide behind vast clouds of gas and dust.

Science teachers go to college and learn about life, earth, physical, and space science. They train in schools like yours to gain experience in teaching students like you.

Spitzer Space Telescope

Lab zone Take-Home Activity

Find out more about how infrared telescopes work. Describe the difference between pictures taken with visible light and with infrared rays.

Unit D Test Talk

Write Your Answer

To answer the following test questions, you need to write your answer. Read the passage and then answer the questions.

The Sun and other stars appear to move across the sky because Earth is moving. Earth rotates, or spins, on its axis. One complete spin, or rotation, takes 24 hours. This rotation and light from the Sun cause the patterns of day, night, and shadows.

Earth also revolves or moves in an orbit around the Sun. One complete trip around the Sun is one revolution. One revolution takes one year. Earth's axis always points in the same direction. As a result, sometimes the northern half of Earth is tilted toward the Sun and receives the most direct sunlight. Sometimes the southern half of Earth is tilted toward the Sun. Earth's tilt and movement around the Sun causes the patterns of seasons.

The Sun is the star at the center of our solar system. Mercury, Venus, Mars, Jupiter, Saturn, Uranus, and Neptune are other planets besides Earth that orbit the Sun. These and other objects that revolve around the Sun make up the solar system.

Use What You Know

To write your answer to each question, you need to read the passage and the test question carefully. Write your answers in complete sentences. Then read your answer to make sure it is complete, correct, and focused.

1. What causes the patterns of day, night, and shadows?

2. What are two ways that Earth moves?

3. Explain how Earth's tilt and revolution cause seasons.

4. What are the names of the planets in our solar system?

Unit D Wrap-Up

Chapter 15

What patterns do the Earth, Sun, Moon, and stars show?

- Earth's revolution around the Sun and rotation on a tilted axis cause the patterns of day, night, shadows, seasons, and the movement of stars across the sky.

- Light from the Sun and the revolution of the Moon around Earth cause the patterns of the phases of the Moon and eclipses.

Chapter 16

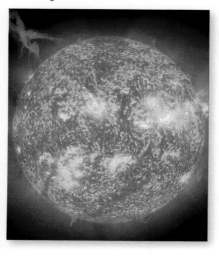

How are the planets in the solar system alike and different?

- The planets in the solar system all rotate on an axis and revolve around the Sun in orbits. The planets are different sizes, different distances from the Sun, and take different amounts of time to rotate and revolve.

- Each planet in the solar system has special features that make it different from the other planets.

Chapter 17

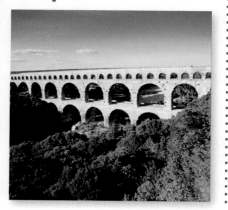

How does technology affect our lives?

- Technology applies the knowledge gained from science to solve problems and improve our lives.

- Technology helps us to get energy to do work and to develop cleaner energy sources.

Performance Assessment

Model a Solar System

Use a large sheet of paper and colored markers to make a model of a solar system that has a star, three planets, and one moon. Describe the parts of the solar system and the patterns your model shows. What is at the center of your model? How are the planets alike and different?

Read More About Space and Technology!

Look for books like these in the library.

Experiment How does the speed of a meteorite affect the crater it makes?

Materials

safety goggles

copier paper box lid

spoon, marble, cup with flour

metric ruler and meterstick

calculator or computer (optional)

Process Skills

In an **experiment**, you **identify** the independent and dependent **variables**. You **control** other variables.

Ask a question.

How does the speed of a meteorite affect the size of the crater it makes?

State a hypothesis.

If a meteorite is moving faster, then will it make a crater with a width that is smaller than, larger than, or about the same size as a crater made by a slower meteorite? Write your **hypothesis**.

Identify and control variables.

The marble is a **model** of a meteorite. The flour is a model of the surface the meteorite hits. Use the same marble and the same amount of flour in all tests. These are **controlled variables**.

Controlled variables are things you need to keep the same if you want a fair test.

The variable you change is the height from which you drop the marble. A marble dropped from a greater height will be moving faster when it hits the flour pile.

The variable you change is the independent variable.

The variable you will measure is the width of the crater.

The variable you measure is the dependent variable.

What are the controlled, independent, and dependent variables?

Test your hypothesis.

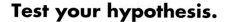

1 In the center of the box lid, make a flat pile of flour.

Be careful!

Follow safety rules. Wear safety goggles. If you cannot safely drop a marble from 1.5 meters, explore ways to solve this problem with your teacher.

2 Place the empty flour cup on the floor. Stand above the cup. Close one eye. Aim down at the cup. Drop a marble into the cup. Practice until the marble lands in the cup every time. Then try dropping the marble from 1.5 m above the cup.

3 Now it is time to make your crater. Drop the marble from a height of 0.5 m (50 cm). Hit the center of the flour pile. Measure the width of the crater.

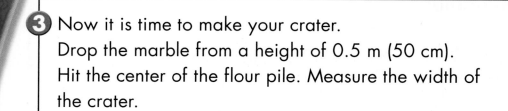

Select a tool to measure the width of the crater in millimeters.

4 Remove the marble. Push the pile back together. Repeat steps 3 and 4 twice.

5 Repeat steps 4 and 5, but drop the marble from 1 m and 1.5 m.

When you repeat your observations and measurements, you can improve their accuracy. Record accurately. Do not change your results because others have different results. Similar investigations seldom turn out exactly the same. However, similar results are expected. Accurate records help scientists learn why there are differences in repeated experiments.

More **Lab** Activities **Take It to the Net**
zone
pearsonsuccessnet.com

Collect and record your data.

	Crater Width (mm)		
	Marble dropped from a height of 0.5 m	Marble dropped from a height of 1 m	Marble dropped from a height of 1.5 m
Trial 1			
Trial 2			
Trial 3			
Average			

Your teacher may ask you to use a calculator or a computer with the right software. These tools can help you find the averages and help you graph your data.

Interpret your data.

Make a bar graph. Study your chart and graph.
What patterns do you see in your data?

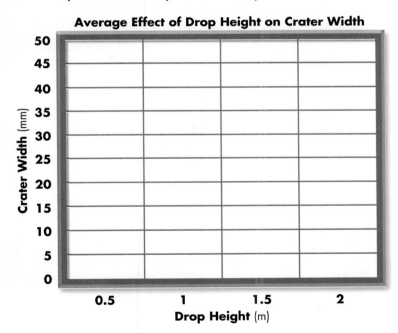

Average Effect of Drop Height on Crater Width

Discuss your observations with others.

State your conclusion.

Describe your results. Compare your hypothesis with your results. **Communicate** your conclusion. Explain the effect of drop height on crater width.

Go Further

Interpret your data to predict the effect of dropping the marble from other heights. Use your model system to check your prediction.

511

Science Fair Projects

Using Scientific Methods

1. Ask a question.
2. State your hypothesis.
3. Identify/control variables.
4. Test your hypothesis.
5. Collect and record your data.
6. Interpret your data.
7. State your conclusion.
8. Go further.

Observing Patterns of Daylight

The Sun appears to rise in the east and set in the west.

Idea: Use a calendar and a watch with a second hand to observe and record the time the Sun rises and sets every day for two months.

Planet-Size Models

One way that planets in the solar system are different is their size.

Idea: Use a metric ruler and posterboard to make models that demonstrate the size of the Sun and each of the planets.

Inventing

People use their knowledge to design new tools and new ways to do things that solve problems and improve their lives.

Idea: Use your knowledge to invent a tool or a way to do something to make a job easier.

EC CRU 10 9 8 7 6 5 4 3 2 1

Metric and Customary Measurement

The metric system is the measurement system most commonly used in science. Metric units are sometimes called SI units. SI stands for International System because these units are used around the world.

These prefixes are used in the metric system:

kilo- means *thousand*
1 kilometer equals 1,000 meters
centi- means *hundredths*
100 centimeters equals 1 meter
milli- means one-*thousandth*
1,000 millimeters equals 1 meter

Length and Distance
One meter is longer than 1 yard.

Area
square centimeter

square inch

Mass
One kilogram is greater than 1 pound.

Volume
One liter is greater than 4 cups.

Temperature
Water freezes at 0°C or 32°F.
Water boils at 100°C or 212°F.

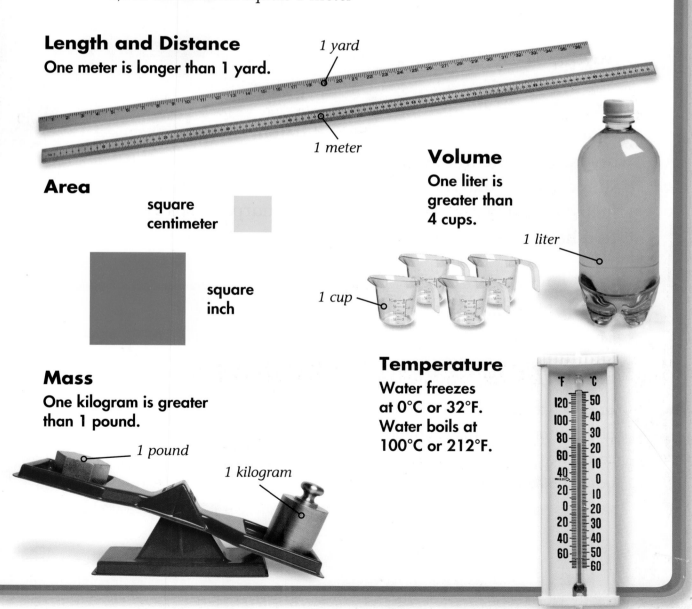

1 yard

1 meter

1 liter

1 cup

1 pound

1 kilogram

LIFE SCIENCE

Design a Toy Bird's Beak

How do birds use their beaks?

A bird's beak is one of many adaptations that help it survive. Birds use their beaks to defend themselves, build nests, and feed their young. They even use their beaks to groom their feathers. But one of the most important ways birds use their beaks is to gather food.

How do bird beaks vary?

You know that bird beaks have different shapes and sizes. Sometimes you can tell what a bird eats by the shape of its beak. The long, thin beak of a hummingbird helps it drink nectar from flowers. The sharp beak of a tern helps it catch small fish.

Take It Home!

Find pictures of birds and their beaks in books or on the Internet. Draw each beak on a separate index card, and label the card with the bird's name. Predict what the bird eats and add that information to your card. Then classify the birds into groups based on their beaks.

eagle, eats fish

Try It!

A toy company has hired your class to help design a new line of toys. Each toy will be a bird that can gather a different kind of food. The first toy will be a bird that gathers small animals buried in sand. Your job is to design a beak for the toy.

What to Do

1. Use the materials to design a bird beak that can gather small animals buried in sand. Sketch your design.
2. Build your beak.
3. Take your beak to the testing station. Have your partner time 30 seconds while you use the beak to gather as many "animals" as possible.
4. Count and record the number of "animals" you gathered.
5. Make changes to your beak and test it again.
6. Compare designs and results with the other groups.

Think About It

1. Which beak design would you recommend to the toy company?
2. How did you change your beak after testing it the first time?
3. What human tools could you use to gather the food at the testing station?

Build a Thermometer!

How are thermometers used?

You know that scientists use thermometers to measure the temperature of the air. Temperature is one way to describe the weather. But thermometers can measure the temperature of many other things as well. Doctors use thermometers to measure the temperature of the human body. In the kitchen, thermometers are used to measure the temperature of food. They can tell you when your dinner is ready to eat! Many machines and electrical devices also use thermometers. For example, a furnace uses a thermometer to tell when more heat is needed to keep a house warm.

How do simple thermometers work?

There are many designs for thermometers. A simple thermometer is a tube that holds a liquid. Heat makes the liquid expand, or take up more space. When the thermometer is put in a warm place, the liquid gets warmer. It expands and moves up the tube. When the thermometer is put in a cool place, the liquid cools and moves down the tube. Numbers on the tube show what the temperature is.

Try It!

You can build a thermometer using simple materials. Then experiment with your thermometer to see how it works.

What to Do

1. Fill the jar 2 cm full with water at room temperature.
2. Add a few drops of food coloring to make the water easy to see.
3. Put the straw in the water. Do not let the straw touch the bottom of the jar.
4. Use clay to seal the mouth of the jar and to hold the straw in place.
5. Put your thermometer in a bowl of very warm water. Observe what happens.
6. Predict what will happen when you put your thermometer in a bowl of very cold water.
7. Test your prediction and observe what happens.

Think About It

1. What did you observe when you put your thermometer in warm water?
2. What causes the liquid to move up and down the straw?
3. How is your thermometer similar to and different from a real thermometer?

Take It Home!

You can make simple tools at home that will measure other properties of weather. Try designing a tool to measure the wind direction or the amount of rain that falls. Draw your design, then build your tool and test it. Use your tool to gather data over a week.

PHYSICAL SCIENCE

Design a Wedge

What are wedges?

Wedges are simple machines made up of two slanted sides that end in an edge. Wedges are used to split or cut objects. They can also be used to fasten objects or fix them in place. The sharp edge of a knife is a wedge that can cut food. The sharp edge of an axe can split wood. The dull edge of a doorstop is used to keep a door open.

How do wedges vary?

Wedges are made of different materials. They also vary in size, angle, and weight. Think of a wedge as a triangle. A wedge with a narrow angle comes to a sharp point or edge. A sharp point or edge can make it easier to cut or split an object. A wedge with a wider angle will have a dull point or edge. A wide wedge can be used to keep a car from rolling backwards. For each job, the right wedge must be used.

Take It Home!

Design a wedge as a doorstop for a door in your home. Sketch your design and choose the type of material you would use. If possible, ask an adult to help you build the doorstop. Then test it on the door.

Try It!

In this activity, you will compare four wedges. Then you will use what you learn to design a wedge for a specific job.

What to Do

1. Trace each of the four wedges on a piece of paper.
2. Compare the sharpness of the wedges and their shapes and sizes.
3. Record your observations on the paper.
4. Weigh each wedge and record your measurements.
5. Use each wedge to try to cut the soap. Record your results.
6. Review your observations and results with your group.
7. Based on the information you collected, design a wedge that would be best for cutting a large pan of soap into bars.
8. Sketch your design and write a short description of it.

Think About It

1. How were the wedges you tested different from each other?
2. Based on your tests, what are the properties of a wedge that cuts soap well?
3. What other tool could you use with a wedge to cut soap? Explain how you would use it.

FOCUS: TEST AND REDESIGN

Design and Build a Kite

Why do people build kites?

People have been building kites for thousands of years. Kites can be beautiful and fun to fly. They also can be useful. Scientists have used kites to study Earth's atmosphere. More than 100 years ago, Wilbur and Orville Wright used kites to test their ideas about flight. What they learned helped them to design and build an airplane.

What is the design process?

The Wright brothers wanted to solve a problem. How do you build an airplane that is safe to fly? They solved this problem using a design process that is still used today. First, they made drawings of the airplane they wanted to build. Then they built models of the airplane and tested them. Some models didn't work. But even if a model failed to fly, they still learned something. They used what they learned to improve their design and build a better airplane. In this activity, you will use the same design process to build a kite!

Try It!

Kites can be different sizes and shapes. They can be made of different materials and have different parts. Not all kites fly well. If your kite does not work at first, think of ways to improve it!

What to Do

1. Use the materials to design a kite that will fly in the wind.
2. Draw your design on a piece of paper.
3. Use the materials to build your kite.
4. Take your kite outside on a windy day. Experiment with your kite to see how well it flies.
5. Observe as other students test their kites. Which fly best?
6. Compare kites and discuss which designs work best.
7. Make changes to your kite and test it again.

Think About It

1. What problem were you trying to solve in this activity?
2. What steps in the design process did you do in this activity?
3. What problems with your design need to be solved?

Take It Home!

Try building a miniature kite using materials such as tissue paper, napkins, wooden skewers, and plastic stir sticks. Use glue to put your kite together, and use sewing thread to fly it. Make sure you add a tail! Fly the kite indoors by pulling it behind you as you walk.

Glossary/Glosario

The glossary uses letters and signs to show how words are pronounced. The mark ′ is placed after a syllable with a primary or heavy accent. The mark ′ is placed after a syllable with a secondary or lighter accent.

To hear the English words pronounced, listen to the AudioText CD.

Pronunciation Key (English)

a	in hat	ō	in open	sh	in she
ā	in age	ȯ	in all	th	in thin
â	in care	ô	in order	₸H	in then
ä	in far	oi	in oil	zh	in measure
e	in let	ou	in out	ə	= a in about
ē	in equal	u	in cup	ə	= e in taken
ėr	in term	ů	in put	ə	= i in pencil
i	in it	ü	in rule	ə	= o in lemon
ī	in ice	ch	in child	ə	= u in circus
o	in hot	ng	in long		

A

absorb (ab sôrb′) to take in (p. 373)

absorber retener (p. 373)

adaptation (ad′ap tā′shən) trait that helps a living thing survive in its environment (p. 48)

adaptación rasgo que ayuda a los seres vivos a sobrevivir en su ambiente (p. 48)

asteroid (as′tə roid′) a small chunk of rock that orbits around the Sun (p. 457)

asteroide pedazo pequeño de roca que orbita alrededor del Sol (p. 457)

atmosphere (at′mə sfir) the blanket of air and gases that surround the Earth (p. 176)

atmósfera capa de aire y gases que rodea la Tierra (p. 176)

atom (at′əm) one of the tiny particles that make up all of matter (p. 282)

átomo una de las pequeñísimas partes que componen toda la materia (p. 282)

axis (ak′sis) an imaginary line around which Earth spins (p. 424)

eje línea imaginaria sobre la cual gira la Tierra (p. 424)

B

blizzard (bliz′ərd) a winter storm with very low temperatures, strong winds, heavy snowfall, and blowing snow (p. 183)

nevasca tormenta de invierno con temperaturas muy bajas, vientos veloces y fuertes caídas de nieve en ráfagas (p. 183)

buoyancy (boi′ən sē) force exerted on an object that is immersed in a gas or liquid that tends to make it float (p. 286)

flotabilidad fuerza que se ejerce sobre un objeto sumergido en un líquido o un gas y que tiende a hacerlo flotar (p. 286)

C

carnivore (kär′nə vôr) a living thing that hunts other animals for food (p. 106)

carnívoro ser vivo que caza a otros animales para alimentarse (p. 106)

cause (ȯz) why something happens (pp. 277, 301)

causa la razón por la cual sucede algo (pp. 277, 301)

change of state (chānj uv stāt) physical change that takes place when matter changes from one state to another (p. 304)

cambio de estado cambio físico que sucede cuando la materia pasa de un estado a otro (p. 304)

chemical change (kem′ə kəl chānj) a change that causes one kind of matter to become a different kind of matter (p. 310)

cambio químico cambio que hace que un tipo de materia se convierta en otro tipo de materia (p. 310)

classifying (klas′ə fī′ing) to arrange or sort objects, events, or living things according to their properties (p. 244)

clasificar organizar o agrupar objetos, sucesos o seres vivos de acuerdo a sus propiedades (p. 244)

collecting data (kə lek′ting dā′tə) to gather observations and measurements into graphs, tables, or charts (p. 26)

reunir datos recoger observaciones y mediciones, y colocarlas en gráficas, cuadros o tablas (p. 26)

communicating (kə myü′nə kāt′ing) using words, pictures, charts, graphs, and diagrams to share information (p. 324)

comunicar usar palabras, ilustraciones, tablas, gráficos y diagramas para compartir información (p. 324)

community (kəm myü′nə tē) all the populations that live together in the same place (p. 74)

comunidad todas las poblaciones que conviven en el mismo lugar (p. 74)

compare (kəm pâr′) to show how things are alike (pp. 5, 245, 389, 453)

comparar decir en qué se parecen las cosas (pp. 5, 245, 389, 453)

competition (kom′pə tish′ən) struggle that happens when two or more living things need the same resource (p. 110)

competencia lucha entre dos o más seres vivos que necesitan el mismo recurso (p. 110)

compression wave (kəm presh′ən wāv) wave that has spaces where particles are squeezed together and spaces where particles are spread apart (p. 396)

onda de compresión onda que tiene zonas donde las partículas están muy juntas y zonas donde las partículas están separadas (p. 396)

computer (kəm pyü′tər) tool which stores, processes, and gets electronic information (p. 485)

computadora aparato que almacena, procesa y obtiene información electrónica (p. 485)

conclusion (kən klü′zhən) decision reached after considering facts and details (p. 101)

conclusión determinación que se alcanza luego de tomar en cuenta los hechos y detalles (p. 101)

condensation (kon′den sā′shən) the changing of a gas into a liquid (p. 157)

condensación cambio de un gas a líquido (p. 157)

coniferous tree (kō nif′ər əs trē) a tree that produces seeds in cones (p. 16)

conífera árbol que produce sus semillas en conos (p. 16)

conservation (kon′sər vā′shən) wise use of natural resources (p. 250)

conservación el ahorro y buen uso de los recursos naturales (p. 250)

constellation (kon′stə lā′shən) a group of stars that make a pattern (p. 438)

constelación grupo de estrellas que forman un patrón o figura (p. 438)

consumer (kən sü′mər) living things that eat food (p. 106)

consumidor ser vivo que come alimentos (p. 106)

contrast (kən trast′) to show how things are different (pp. 5, 245, 389, 453)

contrastar decir en qué se diferencian las cosas (pp. 5, 245, 389, 453)

core (kôr) the innermost layer of Earth (p. 223)

núcleo la capa más profunda de la Tierra (p. 223)

crust (krust) the outermost layer of Earth (p. 223)

corteza terrestre la capa externa de la Tierra (p. 223)

decay (di kā′) to break down, or rot (pp. 118, 206)

descomposición dañarse o pudrirse (pp. 118, 206)

deciduous (di sij′ü əs) loses leaves in fall and grows new ones in spring (p. 14)

deciduo que pierde sus hojas en el otoño y le crecen nuevas en la primavera (p. 14)

decomposer (dē′kəm pō′zər) a living thing that breaks down waste and things that have died (p. 118)

descomponedor ser vivo que descompone desechos y otros seres que han muerto (p. 118)

density (den′sə tē) measure of the amount of matter in a certain amount of space (p. 286)

densidad medida de la cantidad de materia en cierto espacio (p. 286)

desert (dez′ərt) an ecosystem that gets less than 25 cm of rainfall a year (p. 78)

desierto ecosistema que recibe menos de 25 cm de lluvia al año (p. 78)

details (di tālz′) individual pieces of information that support a main idea (pp. 69, 357)

detalles partes de la información que sirven de apoyo a la idea principal (pp. 69, 357)

disease (də zēz′) the name we give an illness (p. 126)

enfermedad el nombre que damos a una alteración de la salud (p. 126)

dwarf planet (dwôrf plan′it) small, ball-shaped object that revolves around the Sun (p. 465)

planeta enano objeto pequeño en forma de bola, que gira alrededor del Sol (p. 465)

earthquake (ėrth′kwāk′) a shaking of Earth's crust caused by sudden, shifting movements in the crust (p. 228)

terremoto estremecimiento de la corteza terrestre causado por movimientos repentinos y ondulantes de ésta (p. 228)

ecosystem (ē′kō sis′təm) all the living and nonliving things that interact with each other in a given area (p. 72)

ecosistema todos los seres vivos y las cosas sin vida que interactúan en un área determinada (p. 72)

effect (ə fekt′) what happens as the result of a cause (pp. 149, 277)

efecto lo que sucede como resultado de una causa (pp. 149, 277)

electric charge (i lek′trik chärj) tiny amount of energy in the particles of matter (p. 374)

carga eléctrica pequeñísima cantidad de energía que hay en las partículas de materia (p. 374)

electric circuit (i lek′trik sėr′kit) the path that a controlled electric current flows through (p. 376)

circuito eléctrico el camino por el que fluye una corriente eléctrica controlada (p. 376)

electric current (i lek′trik kėr′ənt) the movement of an electric charge from one place to another (p. 376)

corriente eléctrica el movimiento de una carga eléctrica de un lugar a otro (p. 376)

element (el′ə mənt) matter that has only one kind of atom (p. 282)

elemento materia que contiene sólo un tipo de átomo (p. 282)

energy (en′ər jē) the ability to do work or to cause a change (p. 359)

energía capacidad de hacer trabajo o causar cambios (p. 359)

environment (en vī′rən mənt) everything that surrounds a living thing (p. 71)

ambiente todo lo que rodea a un ser vivo (p. 71)

equator (i kwā′tər) the imaginary line that separates the north and south halves of Earth (p. 429)

ecuador línea imaginaria que separa la mitad norte y la mitad sur de la Tierra (p. 429)

erosion (i rō′zhən) the movement of weathered materials (p. 232)

erosión el movimiento de materiales meteorizados (p. 232)

estimating and measuring (es′tə māt ing and mezh′ər ing) to tell what you think an object's measurements are and then to measure it in units (p. 210)

estimar y medir decir cuáles crees que son las medidas de un objeto y luego medirlo en unidades (p. 210)

evaporation (i vap′ə rā′shən) the changing of a liquid into a gas (p. 157)

evaporación cambio por el cual un líquido se convierte en gas (p. 157)

experiment (ek sper′ə ment) to formulate and test a hypothesis using a scientific method (p. 140)

experimentar formular y poner a prueba una hipótesis usando un método científico (p. 140)

explore (ek splôr′) to study a scientific idea in a hands-on manner (p. 36)

explorar estudiar una idea científica de manera práctica (p. 36)

extinct (ek stingkt′) no longer lives on Earth (p. 23)

extinto que ya no existe en la Tierra (p. 23)

food chain (füd chān) the movement of energy from one type of living thing to another (p. 108)

cadena alimentaria movimiento de energía de un ser vivo a otro (p. 108)

food web (füd web) the flow of energy between food chains which ties a community together (p. 108)

red alimentaria el flujo de energía entre cadenas alimentarias que une a una comunidad (p. 108)

force (fôrs) a push or a pull (p. 332)

fuerza empujón o jalón (p. 332)

forming questions and hypotheses (fôrm′ing kwes′chənz and hī poth′ə sēz′) to think of how you can solve a problem or answer a question (p. 140)

formular preguntas e hipótesis pensar cómo puedes resolver un problema o responder a una pregunta (p. 140)

fossil (fos′əl) remains or mark of a living thing from long ago (p. 22)

fósil restos o marca de un ser vivo que existió hace mucho tiempo (p. 22)

friction (frik′shən) a contact force that opposes the motion of an object (p. 333)

fricción la fuerza de contacto que dificulta el movimiento de un objeto (p. 333)

gas (gas) the form of matter which has no shape, has particles that are not connected to each other, and takes up whatever space is available (p. 281)

gaseoso estado de la materia en el cual ésta no tiene forma, sus partículas no están conectadas entre sí y ocupa cualquier espacio que esté disponible (p. 281)

germinate (jėr′mə nāt) begins to grow (p. 20)

germinar empezar a crecer (p. 20)

germs (jėrmz) small living things that include bacteria and viruses, many of which can cause illness (p. 126)

gérmenes pequeñísimos seres vivos, como las bacterias y los virus, muchos de los cuales causan enfermedades (p. 126)

grassland (gras′land′) land ecosystem that has many grasses and few trees (p. 76)

pastizal ecosistema terrestre donde hay mucho pasto y pocos árboles (p. 76)

gravity (grav′ə tē) a non-contact force that pulls objects toward each other (p. 336)

gravedad fuerza sin contacto que hace que los objetos se atraigan unos a otros (p. 336)

groundwater (ground′wȯ′tər) water that has slowly made its way through soil and then collects in spaces between underground rock; it is brought to the surface by digging wells (p. 155)

agua subterránea agua que lentamente se filtra por el suelo y luego se acumula entre los espacios de las rocas subterráneas; se cavan pozos para traerla a la superficie (p. 155)

habitat (hab′ə tat) the place where a living thing makes its home (p. 72)

hábitat el lugar donde un ser vivo hace su hogar (p. 72)

heat (hēt) the transfer of thermal energy from one piece of matter to another (p. 366)

calor transferencia de energía térmica de una porción de materia a otra (p. 366)

herbivore (ėr′bə vôr) living things that eat only plants (p. 106)

herbívoro ser vivo que se alimenta sólo de plantas (p. 106)

hibernate (hī′bər nāt) to spend winter resting; body systems slow down in order to save energy (p. 52)

hibernar pasar el invierno descansando; los sistemas del cuerpo funcionan más despacio para ahorrar energía (p. 52)

hurricane (hėr′ə kān) a huge, strong storm that forms over the ocean (p. 182)

huracán una tempestad enorme y muy fuerte que se forma sobre el océano (p. 182)

identifying and controlling variables
(ī den′tə fī ing and kən trōl′ing vâr′ē ə
bəlz) to change one thing, but keep all the
other factors the same (p. 140)

identificar y controlar variables
cambiar una cosa, pero sin cambiar los
demás factores (p. 140)

igneous rock (ig′nē əs rok′) rock that
forms when melted earth materials cool
and harden (p. 200)

roca ígnea roca que se forma cuando
materiales derretidos de la Tierra se
enfrían y endurecen (p. 200)

inclined plane (in klīnd′plān) a slanting
surface that connects a lower level to a
higher level (p. 340)

plano inclinado superficie inclinada que
conecta un nivel bajo con un nivel más
alto (p. 340)

inference (in′fər əns) a conclusion based
on facts, experiences, observations, or
knowledge (p. 173)

inferencia conclusión que se basa en
hechos, experiencias, observaciones o
conocimientos (p. 173)

inferring (in fèr′ing) to draw a conclusion
or make a reasonable guess based on
what you have learned or what you know
(p. 100)

inferir sacar una conclusión o hacer una
predicción razonable con base en lo que
has aprendido o en lo que ya sabes
(p. 100)

inherited (in her′it əd) passed on from
parent to offspring (p. 48)

heredado que ha pasado de padres a
hijos (p. 48)

interpreting data (in tèr′prit ing dā′tə) to
use the information you have collected to
solve problems or answer questions
(p. 26)

interpretar datos usar la información que
has reunido para resolver problemas o
responder a preguntas (p. 26)

invention (in ven′shən) something that has
been made for the first time (p. 479)

invento algo que se hace por primera vez
(p. 479)

investigate (in ves′tə gāt) to solve
a problem or answer a question by
following an existing procedure or an
original one (p. 26)

investigar resolver un problema o
responder a una pregunta siguiendo un
procedimiento existente o uno original
(p. 26)

investigating and experimenting (in
ves′tə gāt ing and ek sper′ə ment ing)
to plan and do an investigation to test a
hypothesis or solve a problem (p. 508)

investigar y experimentar planear
y llevar a cabo una investigación para
poner a prueba una hipótesis o resolver
un problema (p. 508)

kinetic energy (ki net′ik en′ər jē) energy
of motion (p. 361)

energía cinética energía del movimiento
(p. 361)

landform (land′fôrm) a natural feature on
the surface of Earth's crust (p. 224)

accidente geográfico formación natural
sobre la superficie de la corteza terrestre
(p. 224)

larva (lär′və) stage in an insect's life after it hatches from the egg (p. 45)

larva etapa en la vida de un insecto después de que sale del huevo (p. 45)

lava (lä′və) hot, molten rock on Earth's surface (p. 226)

lava roca muy caliente y derretida sobre la superficie de la Tierra (p. 226)

lever (lev′ər) a simple machine used to lift and move things (p. 341)

palanca máquina simple que se usa para levantar y mover cosas (p. 341)

life cycle (līf sī′kəl) the stages through which an organism passes between birth and death (p. 44)

ciclo de vida estados por los que pasa un organismo desde que nace hasta que muere (p. 44)

light (līt) a form of energy that can be seen (p. 370)

luz forma de energía que podemos ver (p. 370)

liquid (lik′wid) matter that does not have a definite shape but takes up a definite amount of space (p. 280)

líquido materia que no tiene una forma definida pero ocupa una cantidad de espacio definida (p. 280)

loam (lōm) soil that contains a mixture of humus and mineral materials of sand, silt, and clay (p. 209)

tierra negra tierra que contiene una mezcla de humus y minerales de la arena, limo y arcilla (p. 209)

lunar eclipse (lü′nər i klips′) Earth's shadow moving across the Moon (p. 434)

eclipse lunar sombra de la Tierra que se mueve sobre la Luna (p. 434)

magma (mag′mə) hot, molten rock that forms deep underground (p. 226)

magma roca derretida y muy caliente que se forma bajo tierra, a gran profundidad (p. 226)

magnetic (mag net′ik) having the property to pull on, or attract, metals that have iron in them (p. 337)

magnético que tiene la propiedad de traer hacia sí, o atraer, metales que contienen hierro (p. 337)

magnetism (mag′nə tiz′əm) a non-contact force that pulls objects containing iron (p. 337)

magnetismo fuerza sin contacto por la cual se atrae a objetos que contienen hierro (p. 337)

main idea (mān ī dē′ə) what a paragraph is about; the most important idea (pp. 69, 357)

idea principal de lo que trata un párrafo; la idea más importante (pp. 69, 357)

making operational definitions (māk′ing op′ə rā′shən əl def′ə nish′ənz) to define or describe an object or event based on your own experience (p. 68)

plantear definiciones operativas definir o describir un objeto o un suceso con base en tu experiencia acerca de él (p. 68)

making and using models (māk′ing and yüz′ing mod′lz) to make a model from materials or to make a sketch or a diagram (p. 36)

hacer y usar modelos hacer un modelo usando materiales, o hacer un dibujo sencillo o un diagrama (p. 36)

mantle (man′tl) the middle layer of Earth (p. 223)

manto terrestre capa intermedia de la Tierra (p. 223)

mass (mas) amount of matter (p. 284)

masa cantidad de materia (p. 284)

matter (mat′ər) anything that takes up space and has mass (p. 279)

materia todo lo que ocupa espacio y tiene masa (p. 279)

metamorphic rock (met′ə môr′fik rok′) rock that forms when existing rock is changed by heat and pressure (p. 201)

roca metamórfica roca que se forma cuando las rocas existentes cambian debido al calor y la presión (p. 201)

microscopic (mī′krə skop′ik) not able to be seen without a microscope (p. 126)

microscópico que no puede verse sin la ayuda de un microscopio (p. 126)

migrate (mī′grāt) to move to another place to find better climate, food, or a mate (p. 52)

migrar mudarse a otro lugar en busca de mejor clima, alimento o pareja (p. 52)

mineral (min′ər əl) natural material that forms from nonliving matter (p. 199)

mineral material natural que se forma a partir de materia sin vida (p. 199)

mixture (miks′chər) two or more kinds of matter that are placed together but can be easily separated (p. 306)

mezcla dos o más tipos de materia que se juntan, pero que se pueden separar fácilmente (p. 306)

Moon (mün) the natural satellite that orbits around Earth (p. 432)

Luna satélite natural que gira alrededor de la Tierra (p. 432)

Moon phase (mün fāz) the different shapes of the Moon between the time a full Moon is visible and the time when no part of the Moon is visible (p. 434)

fase de la Luna la apariencia que tiene la Luna vista desde la Tierra, dependiendo del área iluminada de la Luna en un momento dado (p. 434)

motion (mō′shən) a change in the position of an object (p. 327)

movimiento cambio en la posición de un objeto (p. 327)

natural resources (nach′ər əl ri sôrs′əz) natural materials, such as soil, wood, water, air, oil, or minerals, that living things need (p. 247)

recursos naturales materiales naturales, tales como suelo, madera, agua, aire, petróleo o minerales, que los seres vivos necesitan (p. 247)

nonrenewable resources (non ri nü′ə bəl ri sôrs′əz) resource that cannot be replaced once it is used up (p. 248)

recurso no renovable recurso que no se puede reemplazar una vez que se ha usado todo (p. 248)

nutrient (nü′trē ənt) thing plants need in order to grow (p. 206)

nutriente cosa que las plantas necesitan para crecer (p. 206)

observing (əb zėrv′ing) using your senses to find out about objects, events, or living things (p. 4)

observar usar tus sentidos para aprender acerca de objetos, sucesos o seres vivos (p. 4)

omnivore (om′nə vôr′) living things that eat plants and other animals for food (p. 106)

omnívoro ser vivo que se alimenta de plantas y de otros animales (p. 106)

orbit (ôr′bit) the path of any object in space that revolves around another object in space (p. 456)

órbita el camino que sigue un objeto en el espacio al girar alrededor de otro (p. 456)

organ (ôr′gən) a structure containing different tissues that are organized to carry out a specific function of the body, such as a stomach or intestine (p. 123)

órgano estructura que contiene diferentes tejidos que están organizados para realizar una función específica del cuerpo; ejemplos: el estómago, los intestinos (p. 123)

periodic table (pir′ē od′ik tā′bəl) an arrangement of elements based on their properties (p. 283)

tabla periódica manera de ordenar los elementos con base en sus propiedades (p. 283)

physical change (fiz′ə kəl chānj) a change that makes matter look different without becoming a new substance (p. 303)

cambio físico cambio que hace que la materia se vea diferente, pero sin convertirse en una nueva sustancia (p. 303)

pitch (pich) how high or low a sound is (p. 392)

tono qué tan agudo o tan grave es un sonido (p. 392)

planet (plan′it) a large, ball-shaped body of matter that revolves, or travels, around any star (p. 456)

planeta cuerpo enorme de materia que gira, o viaja, alrededor de cualquier estrella (p. 456)

pollinate (pol′ə nāt) move pollen from the part of a flower that makes pollen to the part of a flower that makes seeds (p. 15)

polinizar mover polen de la parte de la flor que lo produce a la parte de la flor que produce las semillas (p. 15)

pollution (pə lü′shən) waste materials that make the environment dirty (p. 179)

contaminación ocurre cuando materiales de desecho ensucian el ambiente (p. 179)

population (pop′yə lā′shən) all the living things of the same kind that live in the same place at the same time (p. 74)

población todos los seres vivos de la misma especie que viven en el mismo lugar al mismo tiempo (p. 74)

position (pə zish′ən) the location of an object (p. 327)

posición la ubicación de un objeto (p. 327)

potential energy (pə ten′shəl en′ər jē) the energy something has because of its position (p. 360)

energía potencial energía que posee un objeto a causa de su posición (p. 360)

precipitation (pri sip′ə tā′shən) water that falls to Earth as rain, hail, sleet, or snow (p. 159)

precipitación agua que cae al suelo en forma de lluvia, granizo, aguanieve o nieve (p. 159)

predator (pred′ə tər) a consumer that hunts other animals for food (p. 107)

predador consumidor que caza a otros animales para alimentarse (p. 107)

predicting (pri dikt′ing) to tell what you think will happen (p. 162)

predecir decir lo que crees que pasará (p. 162)

pressure (presh′ər) force per unit area that is applied to a substance (p. 281)

presión fuerza por unidad de superficie que se aplica a una sustancia (p. 281)

prey (prā) any animal that is hunted by others for food (p. 107)

presa todo animal al que otros cazan como alimento (p. 107)

producer (prə dü′sər) living things that make their own food (p. 106)

productor ser vivo que produce su propio alimento (p. 106)

property (prop′ər tē) something about matter that you can observe with one or more of your senses (p. 279)

propiedad algo en la materia que puedes observar con uno o más de tus sentidos (p. 279)

pulley (půl′ē) a machine that changes the direction of motion of an object to which a force is applied (p. 343)

polea máquina que hace que cambie la dirección en que se mueve un objeto al que se ha aplicado fuerza (p. 343)

pupa (pyü′pə) stage in an insect's life between larva and adult (p. 45)

pupa etapa en la vida de un insecto entre larva y adulto (p. 45)

recycle (rē sī′kəl) treat or process something so it can be used again (p. 254)

reciclar tratar o procesar algo para poder usarlo otra vez (p. 254)

reflect (ri flekt′) to bounce off of (p. 372)

reflejar hacer rebotar algo (p. 372)

refract (ri frakt′) to bend (p. 372)

refractar desviar o inclinar (p. 372)

relative position (rel′ə tiv pə zish′ən) a change in an object's position compared to another object (p. 329)

posición relativa posición de un objeto en comparación con la de otros objetos (p. 329)

renewable resource (ri nü′ə bəl ri sôrs′) resource that is endless like sunlight, or that is naturally replaced in a fairly short time, such as trees (p. 247)

recurso renovable recurso que no se acaba, como la luz del Sol, o que puede ser reemplazado por la naturaleza en un tiempo relativamente corto, como los árboles (p. 247)

resource (ri sôrs′) *See* Natural Resources, Renewable Resources, Nonrenewable Resources

recurso *Ver* Recursos naturales, Recurso renovable, Recurso no renovable

revolution (rev′ə lü′shən) one complete trip around the Sun (p. 428)

revolución una vuelta completa alrededor del Sol (p. 428)

rock (rok) natural, solid, nonliving material made of one or more minerals (p. 199)

roca material natural sin vida, sólido, compuesto por uno o más minerales (p. 199)

rotation (rō tā′shən) one complete spin on an axis (p. 425)

rotación un giro completo sobre un eje (p. 425)

scientific method (sī′ən tif′ik meth′əd) organized ways of finding answers and solving problems (p. xxvi)

método científico manera organizada de encontrar respuestas o resolver problemas (p. xxvi)

sedimentary rock (sed′ə men′tər ē rok′) rock that forms when small pieces of earth materials collect and become bound together (p. 200)

roca sedimentaria roca que se forma cuando se juntan pequeños pedazos de materiales terrestres (p. 200)

seed leaf (sēd lēf) part of a seed that has stored food (p. 20)

cotiledón parte de la semilla que almacena alimento (p. 20)

seedling (sēd′ling) a new, small plant that grows from a seed (p. 20)

plántula una nueva planta, muy pequeña, que se forma a partir de una semilla (p. 20)

sequence (sē′kwəns) the order in which events take place (pp. 37, 221, 421, 477)

secuencia el orden en que suceden los eventos (pp. 37, 221, 421, 477)

soil (soil) the part of Earth's surface consisting of humus and weathered rock in which plants grow (p. 206)

suelo la parte de la superficie de la Tierra compuesta por humus y rocas meteorizadas en la cual crecen las plantas (p. 206)

solar system (sō′lər sis′təm) the Sun, eight planets and their moons, dwarf planets, and other objects that revolve around the Sun (p. 456)

sistema solar el Sol, los ocho planetas y sus lunas, planetas enanos y todos los demás astros que giran alrededor del Sol (p. 456)

solid (sol′id) matter that has a definite shape and takes up a definite amount of space (p. 280)

sólido materia que tiene una forma definida y ocupa una cantidad definida de espacio (p. 280)

solution (sə lü′shən) a mixture in which one or more substances dissolves in another (p. 308)

solución mezcla en la cual una o más sustancias se disuelven en otra (p. 308)

speed (spēd) the rate at which an object changes position (p. 330)

rapidez tasa a la cual un objeto cambia de posición (p. 330)

star (stär) a massive ball of hot gases that produces its own light (p. 423)

estrella bola enorme de gases muy calientes que produce su propia luz (p. 423)

states of matter (stāts uv mat′ər) the forms of matter — solid, liquid, and gas (p. 304)

estados de la materia las tres formas de la materia: sólida, líquida y gaseosa (p. 304)

summarize (sum′ə rīz′) to cover the main ideas or details in a sentence or two (p. 325)

resumir decir las ideas principales o los detalles en una o dos oraciones (p. 325)

Sun (sun) our star; a huge ball of hot, glowing gases (p. 423)

Sol nuestra estrella; bola enorme de gases muy calientes y luminosos (p. 423)

system (sis′təm) a set of parts that interact with one another (p. 8)

sistema un grupo de partes que interactúan entre sí (p. 8)

technology (tek nol′ə jē) the use of science knowledge to invent tools and new ways of doing things (p. 479)

tecnología el uso del conocimiento científico para inventar herramientas y maneras nuevas de hacer las cosas (p. 479)

telescope (tel′ə skōp) a tool that gathers lots of light and magnifies objects that are far away and makes faint stars easier to see (p. 436)

telescopio instrumento que concentra grandes cantidades de luz. Hace que objetos muy lejanos se vean más grandes y facilita ver astros de luz débil (p. 436)

thermal energy (thėr′məl en′ər jē) the total kinetic energy of all the particles that make up matter (p. 366)

energía térmica el total de la energía cinética de todas las partículas que constituyen la materia (p. 366)

tool (tül) an object used to do work (p. 479)

herramienta objeto que se usa para hacer algún trabajo (p. 479)

tornado (tôr nā′dō) a rotating column of air that touches the ground and causes damage with its high winds (p. 182)

tornado columna de aire que gira y que al tocar tierra causa graves daños con sus fuertes vientos (p. 182)

trait (trāt) a feature passed on to a living thing from its parents (p. 40)

rasgo característica que pasa de padres a hijos entre los seres vivos (p. 40)

tundra (tun′drə) land ecosystem that is cold and dry (p. 80)

tundra ecosistema terrestre que es frío y seco (p. 80)

vertebrate (vėr′tə brit) animal with a backbone (p. 40)

vertebrado animal que tiene columna vertebral (p. 40)

vibration (vī brā′shən) a very quick back-and-forth movement (p. 392)

vibración movimiento muy rápido hacia adelante y hacia atrás (p. 392)

volcano (vol kā′nō) an opening in the Earth's crust from which hot, melted material erupts (p. 226)

volcán abertura en la corteza terrestre por la cual hacen erupción materiales derretidos muy calientes (p. 226)

volume (vol′yəm) amount of space matter takes up (p. 285)

volumen cantidad de espacio que ocupa la materia (p. 285)

water cycle (wȯ′tər sī′kəl) the movement of water from Earth's surface into the air and back again (p. 158)

ciclo del agua el movimiento del agua desde la superficie de la Tierra hacia el aire y nuevamente de regreso (p. 158)

water vapor (wȯ′tər vā′pər) water in the form of an invisible gas in the air (p. 154)

vapor de agua agua en forma de gas invisible en el aire (p. 154)

weather (weŦH′ər) what it is like outside including temperature, wind, clouds, and precipitation (p. 175)

tiempo (atmosférico) las condiciones al aire libre teniendo en cuenta temperatura, vientos, nubosidad y precipitación (p. 175)

weathering (weŦH′ər ing) any process that changes rocks by breaking them into smaller pieces (p. 230)

meteorización todo proceso por el cual las rocas cambian al romperse en pedazos más pequeños (p. 230)

wetland (wet′land′) low land ecosystem that is covered by water at least part of the time during the year; marshes and swamps are wetlands (p. 86)

humedal ecosistema terrestre bajo que permanece cubierto de agua al menos parte del año; las marismas y los pantanos son humedales (p. 86)

wheel and axle (wēl and ak′səl) a simple machine made of a wheel and a rod joined to the center of the wheel (p. 342)

eje y rueda máquina simple que consiste en una rueda y una varilla que atraviesa el centro de la rueda (p. 342)

work (wėrk) what happens when a force moves an object over a distance (p. 338)

trabajo lo que sucede cuando una fuerza mueve un objeto cierta distancia (p. 338)

Index

This index lists the pages on which topics appear in this book. Page numbers after a *p* refer to a photograph or drawing. Page numbers after a *c* refer to a chart, graph, or diagram.

Credits

Photographs

Photo locators denoted as follows: Top (T), Center (C), Bottom (B), Left (L), Right (R), Background (Bkgd).

Cover: ©Flip Nicklin/Minden Pictures, ©David Nardini/Getty Images.

Front Matter: iii Daniel J. Cox/Natural Exposures, (T) Getty Images; v ©Frans Lanting/Minden Pictures; vi ©DK Images; vii (R) ©Randy M. Ury/Corbis, (L) ©Breck P. Kent/Animals Animals/Earth Scenes; viii ©Jack Dykinga/Getty Images; xi ©Douglas Peebles/Corbis; xii ©Lloyd Cluff/Corbis; xv ©RNT Productions/Corbis; xxii ©Timothy O'Keefe/Index Stock Imagery; xxiii Getty Images; xxiv (Bkgd) ©Steve Bloom/Getty Images, (C) ©Robert Sullivan/AFP/Getty Images; xxix Getty Images; xxv ©Frank Greenaway/DK Images; xxviii (BL) Getty Images, (CL) ©Dave King/DK Images; xxx ©Comstock Inc.

Unit Dividers: Unit A (Bkgd) Getty Images, (CC) Digital Vision; Unit B (Bkgd) ©Kim Heacox/Getty Images, (BC) Getty Images; Unit C (Bkgd) ©Lester Lefkowitz/Getty Images; Unit D (Bkgd) Corbis

Chapter 1: 1 (B) ©Wolfgang Kaehler/Corbis, (T, C) Getty Images; 2 (T) ©John Warden/Index Stock Imagery, (BL) ©DK Images, (BL) Getty Images, (BR) ©Nigel Cattlin/Photo Researchers, Inc.; 3 (BL) ©Nigel Cattlin/Holt Studios, (BC) Neg./Transparency no. K13073. Courtesy Dept. of Library Services/American Museum of Natural History; 5 (CR) ©Stone/Getty Images, (Bkgd) ©John Warden/Index Stock Imagery; 6 ©John Warden/Index Stock Imagery; 7 (BR) ©Jim Steinberg/Photo Researchers, Inc., (TR) ©Photographer's Choice/Getty Images; 8 ©DK Images; 9 (CR, TR, BR) ©DK Images, (TC) Getty Images; 10 (R) Silver Burdett Ginn, (TL) Getty Images; 11 ©DK Images; 12 ©Lou Jacobs Jr./Grant Heilman Photography; 13 (TR) ©George Bernard/NHPA Limited, (TR) ©DK Images, (CR) ©TH Foto-Werbung/Photo Researchers, Inc., (BL) ©Niall Benvie/Corbis, (BR) ©The Garden Picture Library/Alamy Images; 14 (BL) ©Stone/Getty Images, (BR) ©Jeff Lepore/Photo Researchers, Inc., (TL) ©Peter Smithers/Corbis; 15 ©DK Images, (TL) Getty Images; 16 ©Carolina Biological/Visuals Unlimited, (TL) Getty Images; 17 (CL) ©M & C Photography/Peter Arnold, Inc., (TR) ©Brad Mogen/Visuals Unlimited, (TC) ©Pat O'Hara/Corbis, (CR) ©Wally Eberhart/Visuals Unlimited, (BR) ©DK Images; 18 (BC) ©Darryl Torckler/Getty Images, (CC) ©Brian Gordon Green/NGS Image Collection, (BC) ©John Poutier/Maxx Images, Inc., (BC) ©Jorg & Petra Wegner/Animals Animals/Earth Scenes, (TL) ©DK Images; 19 ©DK Images, (CR) ©Steve Bloom Images/Alamy Images; 21 (CL) ©DK Images, (CR) Nigel Cattlin/Holt Studios, (BC) ©Kenneth W. Fink/Photo Researchers, Inc., (BC) ©Nigel Cattlin/Photo Researchers, Inc.; 23 (TR) ©Dr. E. R. Degginger/Color-Pic, Inc., (CL) ©John Cancalosi/Peter Arnold, Inc., (TL) Neg./Transparency no. K13073. Courtesy Dept. of Library Services/American Museum of Natural History, (BR) ©David Muench/Muench Photography, Inc, (CR) ©James L. Amos/Corbis; 24 (BL) ©The Natural History Museum, London, (BR, TL) ©DK Images; 26 ©Ed Young/Corbis; 28 (TR) ©Dennis MacDonald/PhotoEdit, (CR) ©Inga Spence/Visuals Unlimited, (CR) ©Steven Emery/Index Stock Imagery, (BR) ©Comstock Inc.; 31 (TL) ©DK Images, (TR) ©Kenneth W. Fink/Photo Researchers, Inc.; 32 (Bkgd) ©MSFC/NASA, (TL, BR) NASA; **Chapter 2:** 33 (B) ©Barbara Von Hoffmann/Animals Animals/Earth Scenes, (Bkgd) ©David Harrison/Index Stock Imagery; 34 (BL) ©David L. Shirk/Animals Animals/Earth Scenes, (T) ©Tom Brakefield/Corbis, (BR) ©Jeff L. Lepore/Photo Researchers, Inc.; 35 (BL, BR) ©Brad Mogen/Visuals Unlimited; 37 (C) ©David Stover/ImageState, (Bkgd) ©Tom Brakefield/Corbis; 38 ©Tom Brakefield/Corbis; 39 (BR) ©Tom Vezo/Nature Picture Library, (BC) ©Zefa/Masterfile Corporation, (BL) ©Taxi/Getty Images, (BC) ©Natural Visions/Alamy Images, (TR) ©Frans Lanting/Minden Pictures; 40 (B) ©Tom Brakefield/Bruce Coleman Inc., (TL) ©Randy M. Ury/Corbis; 41 (CR) ©DK Images, (BC) ©Jim Brandenburg/Minden Pictures, (BR) ©Frans Lanting/Minden Pictures, (CR) Getty Images, (TR) ©Ken Lucas/Visuals Unlimited; 42 (BL) Jupiter Images, (TL) ©David Aubrey/Corbis, (TR) ©Danny Lehman/Corbis, (TR) ©Robert Pickett/Corbis, (CR) ©The Image Bank/Getty Images, (BR) ©Brian Rogers/Visuals Unlimited, (TL, TR) ©DK Images, (BR) ©Charles Melton/Visuals Unlimited; 45 (B) ©Brad Mogen/Visuals Unlimited, (T) ©Dick Scott/Visuals Unlimited; 46 (CL) ©Bettmann/Corbis, (BL) ©Keren Su/China Span/Alamy Images, (TL) ©Zefa/Masterfile Corporation; 47 (TR) ©Carolina Biological Supply Company/Phototake, (CL, BL) ©DK Images, (TL) ©Breck P. Kent/Animals Animals/Earth Scenes, (BR) ©Randy M. Ury/Corbis; 48 (BR) ©DK Images, (TR) ©Ken Lucas/Visuals Unlimited, (TL) ©Tony Evans/Timelapse Library/Getty Images; 49 (CL) ©Frans Lanting/Minden Pictures, (TR) ©Kevin Schafer/Corbis, (CR) ©Gary W. Carter/Corbis, (BR) ©DK Images; 50 ©Vittoriano Rastelli/Corbis, (TL) ©Photodisc Green/Getty Images; 51 (TC) ©Rod Planck/Photo Researchers, Inc., (CC) ©James Robinson/Animals Animals/Earth Scenes, (TL) ©Michael Quinton/Minden Pictures, (TR) ©Chris Newbert/Minden Pictures, (CL) ©The Image Bank/Getty Images, (BL) ©Rolf Kopfle/Bruce Coleman Inc., (TR) ©Tim Laman/NGS Image Collection, (BC) ©Suzanne L. & Joseph T. Collins/Photo Researchers, Inc., (CC) ©Steve E. Ross/Photo Researchers, Inc., (TC) ©Ken Wilson/Papilio/Corbis, (CR) ©David Aubrey/Corbis, (BR) ©E. R. Degginger/Bruce Coleman, Inc., (BL) ©Rick & Nora Bowers/Visuals Unlimited; 52 (TR) ©DK Images, (CR) ©George Grall/NGS Image Collection, (BR) ©Jeff L. Lepore/Photo Researchers, Inc., (TL) ©Eric and David Hosking/Corbis, (TL) ©Photodisc Blue/Getty Images; 53 (T) ©Gerry Ellis/Minden Pictures, (B) ©Terry W. Eggers/Corbis; 54 (TL) ©James L. Amos/Photo Researchers, Inc., (B) ©DK Images, (CL) ©Layne Kennedy/Corbis; 55 (TL) ©DK Images, (TR) ©Breck P. Kent/Animals Animals/Earth Scenes; 56 (R) ©Breck P. Kent/Animals Animals/Earth Scenes; 56 (B) Senekenberg Nature Museum/©DK Images, (TL) Colin Keates/Courtesy of the Natural History Museum, London/©DK Images; 57 ©Ross M. Horowitz/Getty Images; 58 ©Larry L. Miller/Photo Researchers, Inc.; 60 Digital Vision; 61 ©Masa Ushioda/Visual & Written/Bruce Coleman, Inc.; 63 ©DK Images; 64 (TL) ©Dutheil Didier/SYGMA/Corbis, (BL) ©Reuters/Corbis; **Chapter 3:** 65 (Bkgd) Getty Images, (T) ©Photodisc Green/Getty Images; 66 (T) ©Mark E. Gibson Stock Photography, (BL) ©J. Eastcott/Y. Eastcott Film/NGS Image Collection, (BR) ©Enzo & Paolo Ragazzini/Corbis; 67 (BL) ©Andy Binns/Ecoscene, (BR) ©Jim Zipp/Photo Researchers, Inc., (CR) ©Alan Carey/Photo Researchers, Inc., (TR) ©Steve Kaufman/Corbis; 69 ©Mark E. Gibson Stock Photography; 70 ©Mark E. Gibson Stock Photography; 71 ©Siede Preis/Getty Images; 72 Getty Images; 73 (Bkgd) ©Melissa Farlow/Aurora & Quanta Productions, (TC) ©DK Images, (B) ©Kurt Stier/Corbis; 74 (CL) ©Royalty-Free/Corbis, (BL) ©Alan Carey/Photo Researchers, Inc.; 75 (CR) ©Joseph Van Os/Getty Images, (L) ©Kennan Ward/Corbis, (BR) Darren Bennett/Animals Animals/Earth Scenes; 76 ©OSF/Animals Animals/Earth Scenes; 77 (T) ©Enzo & Paolo Ragazzini/Corbis, (BL) ©Jason Edwards/NGS Image Collection, (BR) ©Steve Kaufman/Corbis; 78 (TL) ©Jack Dykinga/Getty Images, (BR) Jerry Young/©DK Images, (TL) ©DK Images; 79 (Bkgd) ©J. Eastcott/Y. Eastcott Film/NGS Image Collection, (TL) Daniel J. Cox/Natural Exposures; 80 (BL) Daniel J. Cox/Natural Exposures, (TL) ©Ed Reschke/Peter Arnold, Inc.; 81 (TL) ©Andy Binns/Ecoscene, (TR, CL, BL) Daniel J. Cox/Natural Exposures; 82 ©Tim Laman/NGS Image Collection; 83 (TR) ©Michio Hoshino/Minden Pictures, (TL, BR) ©Jim Brandenburg/Minden Pictures, (BL) ©Jay Dickman/Corbis, (BR) ©David Ulmer/Stock Boston; 84 (CR) ©Roy Toft/NGS Image Collection, (TR) ©Claus Meyer/Minden Pictures, (BR) ©Ken Preston-Mafham/Animals Animals/Earth Scenes, (TL) Alamy; 85 (BL) ©Michael & Patricia Fogden/Minden Pictures, (T) ©Tui De Roy/Minden Pictures; 86 (B) Daniel J. Cox/Natural Exposures, (TR) ©Jim Zipp/Photo Researchers, Inc., (TL) ©Roy Toft/NGS Image Collection; 87 (Bkgd) Daniel J. Cox/Natural Exposures, (TR) ©Joseph H. Bailey/NGS Image Collection; 88 (TL) ©Medford Taylor/NGS Image Collection, (BR) ©Fred Bavendam/Peter Arnold, Inc.; 89 (TR) ©Mick Turner/PhotoLibrary, (Bkgd) ©Royalty-Free/Corbis; 90 Getty Images; 95 ©Ken Preston-Mafham/Animals Animals/Earth Scenes; 96 ©Bettmann/Corbis; **Chapter 4:** 97 ©M. Colbeck/OSF/Animals Animals/Earth Scenes; 98 (T) ©Stephen Frink/Corbis, (BL) ©Carol Havens/Corbis, (BR) ©K. H. Haenel/Zefa/Masterfile Corporation; 99 (BL) ©D. Robert and Lorri Franz/Corbis, (TR) ©Jim Brandenburg/Minden Pictures, (CR) ©Dr. Gopal Murti/Photo Researchers, Inc., (BR) ©Gerald Hinde/ABPL/Animals Animals/Earth Scenes; 101 (CR) ©Richard Walters/Visuals Unlimited, (Bkgd) ©Stephen Frink/Corbis, (BR) ©Bob Marsh/Papilio/Corbis, (CC) ©David Boag/Alamy Images; 102 ©Stephen Frink/Corbis; 103 (CR) Brand X Pictures, (BR) ©Patti Murray/Earth Scenes/Maxx Images, Inc., (CR) ©Laura Sivell/Papilio/Corbis, (TR) Getty Images; 104 (B) ©Richard Kolar/Animals Animals/Earth Scenes, (T) ©Rick Raymond/Index Stock Imagery; 105 (T) ©Michael & Patricia Fogden/Corbis, (B) ©B. Jones/M. Shimlock/Photo Researchers, Inc.; 106 (BL) ©Chase Swift/Corbis, (BC) ©Carol Havens/Corbis, (BR) ©Frank Blackburn/Ecoscene/Corbis, (TL) ©Hope Ryden/NGS Image Collection; 107 (B) ©D. Robert and Lorri Franz/Corbis, (TR) ©K. H. Haenel/Zefa/Masterfile Corporation, (CL) ©Randy Wells/Corbis, (BL) ©Danny Lehman/Corbis; 108 (TL, BL) Getty Images, (BR) ©Yva Momatiuk/John Eastcott/Minden Pictures, (BR) ©Naturfoto Honal/Corbis, (CC) ©Kevin R. Morris/Corbis; 109 (C) Minden Pictures, (R) ©Claudia Adams/Alamy Images, (BL) ©Tom Brakefield/Corbis; 110 (TL) ©Gerry Ellis/Minden Pictures, (CL) ©Michael & Patricia Fogden/Corbis, (BL) ©Martin Harvey/Photo Researchers, Inc., (TL) ©Photodisc Green/Getty Images; 111 ©Gerald Hinde/ABPL/Animals Animals/Earth Scenes; 112 (T) ©DK Images, (CL) ©Raymond Gehman/Corbis, (BL) ©Scott Camazine/Photo